The Poem's Two Bodies

he Poem's Two Bodies: The Poetics of the 1590 *Faerie Queene* DAVID LEE MILLER

Princeton University Press, Princeton, New Jersey

Published by Princeton University Press, 41 William Street,
Princeton, New Jersey 08540
In the United Kingdom: Princeton University Press,
Guildford, Surrey

Library of Congress Cataloging in Publication Data will
be found on the last printed page of this book

ISBN 0-691-06744-9

This book has been composed in Linotron Caslon Old Face

Clothbound editions of Princeton University Press books are
printed on acid-free paper, and binding materials are chosen
for strength and durability. Paperbacks, although
satisfactory for personal collections, are not usually suitable
for library rebinding

Printed in the United States of America by Princeton
University Press, Princeton, New Jersey

For Lynn
You frame my thoughts, and fashion me within . . .

The ultimate image afforded by the discourse (by the 'portrait') is that of a natural form, pregnant with meaning, as though meaning were merely the ulterior predicate of a primal body.—Barthes, *S/Z*

Contents

Acknowledgments

I HAVE REWORKED some material from previous essays into the first two chapters of this book, and would like to thank the editors of *MLQ*, *ELH*, and *PMLA* for permission to do so. A section of chapter 1 was delivered at the 1987 Southeastern Renaissance Conference and published in *Renaissance Papers 1987*. For the chance to try out ideas in conference papers I am grateful to the Southeastern Renaissance Conference; the Spenser Society; the Modern Language Association; the South Atlantic M.L.A.; the Renaissance Society of America, North Central Division; and the organizers of "Spenser at Kalamazoo," sponsored by the International Congress of Medieval Studies. Thanks are also due to the Folger Shakespeare Library for a month's sponsored research in the summer of 1985, to the University of Alabama for a sabbatical leave in the spring of 1985, to the University of Alabama Research Grants Committee for two summers' support in 1984 and 1985 (projects 1216 and 1287), and finally to Northwestern University for a stimulating summer of reading and debate at the School of Criticism and Theory in 1982.

For their indispensable help I would like to thank Nati Krivatsky and the staff at the Folger Shakespeare Library, the Reference and Inter-Library Loan staffs at Alabama's Gorgas Library, and two outstanding research assistants, Jill Onega and Anne Turner.

I feel a distinct continuity between the impulse to write this book and the inspiration of two former teachers, A. B. Giamatti and Leslie Brisman. I am equally grateful to many of the graduate faculty at the University of California, Irvine, for the time, interest, and energy they invested in me. At the University of Alabama I must first thank Claudia D. Johnson (with a very full heart) for her administrative ability to create release time *ex nihilo*; if I am indebted to others for the beginnings of this project, I owe her the chance to finish it. Elizabeth Meese contributed to my conception of the argument in ways she does not know about, and therefore cannot be held responsible for. William A. Ulmer carefully worked over the whole manuscript, some chapters more than once. For consultation on matters respectively legal, medieval, and Greco-Latin, I am indebted to Joseph Hornsby, John P. Hermann, and Richard Baldes. Other colleagues have read and commented on parts of the manuscript, or have lent their support: Harold Toliver, John D. Kilgore, Donald Cheney, A. Leigh DeNeef, S. Clark Hulse, Leonard Barkan, Judith Anderson, Jerome Dees, Jonathan Goldberg, and Elizabeth J. Bellamy. I'm particularly grateful to Richard Helgerson and Stephen Orgel for their early encouragement. Finally, it is a special pleasure to acknowledge my longstanding debt of intellectual friendship to Gregory S. Jay, whose habits of thought and phrase are part of this book's texture. I only wish there had been time to learn more from him.

As every writer with a family knows, the heaviest debts are run up at home. Doris Stinson has been a staunch combination of friend, housekeeper, and baby sitter while this book was taking shape. John Pruett Miller isn't old enough, yet, to read these words, but his mere imminence concentrated my mind wonderfully (as Dr. Johnson remarks), and his presence has been a daily inspiration. Meanwhile my wife Lynn's encouragement, sense of humor, and extra time with John made the daily work of writing not only worthwhile, but possible. "Hart need not wish none other happinesse. . . ."

Tuscaloosa
July 1987

Abbreviations

ELH   *ELH: A Journal of English Literary History*
ELR   *English Literary Renaissance*
HLQ   *Huntington Library Quarterly*
JEGP   *Journal of English and Germanic Philology*
JWCI   *Journal of the Warburg and Courtauld Institutes*
MLN   *Modern Language Notes*
MLQ   *Modern Language Quarterly*
MP   *Modern Philology*
PMLA   *Publications of the Modern Language Association*
PQ   *Philological Quarterly*
SpN   *Spenser Newsletter*
SpStud *Spenser Studies: A Renaissance Poetry Annual*
TSLL   *Texas Studies in Language and Literature*
UTQ   *University of Toronto Quarterly*

The Poem's Two Bodies

Whatever may be their use in civilised societies, mirrors are essential to all violent and heroic action.—*Virginia Woolf*

Introduction

he title of this study is meant to suggest the particular constellation of interests I bring to a reading of Spenser's *Faerie Queene*, Books I–III. Most obvious is the allusion to Kantorowicz,[1] whose influential account of Tudor "political theology" started me thinking more seriously about Spenser's poem as a historical and political act. I speak of the *poem's* two bodies in deference to the specific form of Spenser's discourse, and as a way of insisting on both halves of the venerable and pointless debate between historicism and formalism. It is necessary for historical criticism to acknowledge the textual force and value specific to poetry, both as verse and as fiction; it is equally necessary for formalist criticism to reflect on the historical force and value of the category of the "aesthetic," especially in the study of texts for which this post-Enlightenment term is something of an anachronism. I have therefore tried to bear in mind that while Spenser offers *The Faerie Queene* as a literary and not a literal portrait of Elizabeth, she herself was already, as monarch, a kind of historical fiction, an allegorical figure invested with the visionary body of the state.[2] The resulting critical argument neither privileges literature as a pure textuality that demystifies the fictions of history, nor posits history as a preliterary domain of empirical data that can ground the otherwise errant play of literary interpretation. Instead the argument combines an effort to assess the

[1] Ernst Kantorowicz, *The King's Two Bodies: A Study of Medieval Political Theology* (Princeton: Princeton Univ. Press, 1957).

[2] Louis Adrian Montrose, "The Elizabethan Subject and the Spenserian Text," in *Literary Theory/Renaissance Texts*, ed. Patricia Parker and David Quint (Baltimore: Johns Hopkins Univ. Press, 1986), pp. 303–40.

3

ideological force of literary form with an effort to register the force of ideology *on* literary form.

HISTORY, IDENTITY, AND THE PROBLEM OF CLOSURE

I take the allegory of *The Faerie Queene* to be organized with reference to the anticipated-but-deferred wholeness of an ideal body, which serves to structure the reading of the text in a manner comparable to the use of a vanishing point to organize spatial perspective in drawing. This "body" is an ideological formation derived from the religious myth of the *corpus mysticum* and its imperial counterpart, the notion of the monarch as incarnating an ideal and unchanging political body. Spenser's allegory defers the closure that would perfect this body, but does not in this way cleanse the notion of extraliterary force; rather, in opening a textual space where the production of a corporal mirage coincides with the work of reading, Spenser seeks to "fashion" his readers as the *figurae* of a millennial imperium.

The ground on which these concerns meet is the human body itself as a figure of identity, and for this reason I have drawn on psychoanalytic theory. Psychoanalysis studies the zones and members of the body as a kind of preverbal symbolic vocabulary in which infants begin to speculate about their experience of parental nurturance, protection, and punitive authority. Freud suggested that the adult ego derives from an intuition of the body surface as the threshold between self and world, a notion Lacan has extended in his essay "The Mirror Stage as Formative of the Function of the I."[3] It is no accident

---

[3] Jacques Lacan, "The Mirror Stage as Formative of the Function of the I," in *Ecrits: A Selection*, trans. Alan Sheridan (New York: Norton, 1977), pp. 1–7. See also Fredric Jameson, "Imaginary and Symbolic in Lacan: Marxism, Psychoanalytic Criticism, and the Problem of the Subject," in *Yale French Studies* 55/56 (1977): 338–95.

that we conceive abstract unities of all kinds in the image of the body: each of us is born into chaos, and the world we share is a cosmos whose gradual composition at once depends on and contributes to the development of a stable body image. Even the constants of perception, such as visual clues that register depth in space or the outlines and textures of things, are learned. We learn that material objects subsist beneath the discontinuous succession of their appearances. Eventually, in what is called the "mirror stage," we learn to identify with the reflected image of our bodies. As we grow in mastery of the motor functions, our intuition of the self as an immanent force, coordinating our complex physical whole from within, grows also. This intuition of the self emerges from a sort of primal metaphor, an instinctual carrying over of body values like wholeness and coordination into psychological and cognitive registers.

In the course of this development each of us also takes on and internalizes a special word, a proper name that serves as the sign of personhood, implicitly attributing to us as social and psychological creatures the unity and continuity of a physical body. In this way our names call us to the ceaseless personal labor that produces us as metaphors of our bodies. And once this carrying over of values has begun, it is essentially open-ended. Our quest for the body's wholeness informs every realm of social and cultural experience. As both the medium through which we know ourselves individually and the name we give to those mirages of collective wholeness that inform the symbolic realms of art, politics, and religion,[4] the body is at once the most intimate and unapproachable of metaphors.

These aspects of psychoanalytic thought seem pertinent to a discussion of Spenser's allegory for several reasons. To begin with, Spenser's declared moral purpose is to invest his vision

---

[4] See Leonard Barkan, *Nature's Work of Art: The Human Body as Image of the World* (New Haven: Yale Univ. Press, 1975).

of glory in the body of "a gentleman or noble person."⁵ He undertakes this project within and on behalf of a manifestly patriarchal order of secular power. Elizabeth's female sex complicated the psychodynamics as well as the politics of secular authority during Spenser's lifetime, but the nature and extent of royal power, though always in flux and contested on all sides, nevertheless remained relatively constant: it was sacred, hierarchical, and central. If it was more so in theory than in practice, this meant among other things that the crown relied heavily on the deep emotional resonance of parental archetypes to generate loyalty.⁶ Spenser's portrayal of Elizabeth is sometimes obliquely critical, as recent criticism has argued,⁷ but it remains on balance a work of glorification, specifically glorification of the body politic in the person of Elizabeth.

Kenneth Burke in *Attitudes Toward History* suggested the

⁵ "A Letter of the Authors to Sir Walter Raleigh," in *Spenser: "The Faerie Queene,"* ed. A. C. Hamilton (New York: Longman, 1977; reprint with corrections, 1980), p. 737. All citations of *The Faerie Queene* and "A Letter of the Authors" are to this edition.

⁶ On the practical limits of royal power (and the consequent importance of patronage as an instrument of political control) see Wallace T. MacCaffrey, "Place and Patronage in Elizabethan Politics," in *Elizabethan Government and Society: Essays Presented to Sir John Neale*, ed. S. T. Bindoff, J. Hurstfield, and C. A. Williams (London: Athlone Press, 1961), pp. 96–97. Maureen Quilligan, *Milton's Spenser: The Politics of Reading* (Ithaca: Cornell Univ. Press, 1983), pp. 176–85, comments usefully on the ideological function of court poetry in "accommodating the disturbing fact of Elizabeth's gender."

⁷ See Quilligan, *Milton's Spenser*, pp. 67–70, 189–90; Judith Anderson, " 'In liuing colours and right hew': The Queen of Spenser's Central Books," in *Poetic Traditions of the English Renaissance*, ed. Maynard Mack and George deForest Lord (New Haven: Yale Univ. Press, 1982), pp. 47–66; David Norbrook, *Poetry and Politics in the English Renaissance* (London: Routledge, 1984), chaps. 3 and 5; Michael O'Connell, *The Historical Dimension of Spenser's "Faerie Queene"* (Chapel Hill: Univ. of North Carolina Press, 1977), pp. 52–54, 105–7; Thomas H. Cain, *Praise in "The Faerie Queene"* (Lincoln: Univ. of Nebraska Press, 1978), chaps. 6 and 7; and William A. Oram, "Elizabethan Fact and Spenserian Fiction," *SpStud* 4 (1984): 38.

relevance of psychoanalytic categories to a study of the artist's affirmation of authority symbols.[8] A primary social function of the artist is to mediate the investment of adult authority symbols with "the deepest responses" of our experience—namely those "found in the 'pre-political' period of childhood" (p. 209). The affirmation of authority symbols must therefore work its way through incest awe and the attendant threat of castration to a "ritual of 'transcendence' " (p. 210), an adjustment of the (implicitly male) subject's erotic disposition to his vision of adult responsibility. Because it involves a dramatic change of identity, this adjustment must pass through a symbolic regression and rebirth like those the Redcrosse knight undergoes in the House of Holiness. A dramatic change in identity, however, tends also to be represented as a change of sex. When socialization is projected as rebirth, then, the "ritual" follows a recognizable plot in which the subject, neutered by incest awe and the threat of castration, returns to the womb and is reborn into androgyny, symbolizing wholeness and reconciliation with authority. I argue that this plot underlies and organizes the body symbolism of *The Faerie Queene*.

I use Lacan's well-known essay on ego formation because it articulates the dynamics of castration and socialization with a theory of mirroring. As far as I know, the only sustained application of Freudian theory to the poem is James Nohrnberg's Ericksonian discussion of "psychological archetypes."[9] Lacan's

---

[8] Kenneth Burke, *Attitudes Toward History* (1937; reprint Berkeley: Univ. of California Press, 1984).

[9] James Nohrnberg, *The Analogy of "The Faerie Queene"* (Princeton: Princeton Univ. Press, 1976). In addition to the essay by Jameson cited in note 3, I have profited from the discussions of psychoanalysis in Angus Fletcher, *Allegory: The Theory of a Symbolic Mode* (Ithaca: Cornell Univ. Press, 1962), chap. 6; and William Kerrigan, "The Articulation of the Ego in the English Renaissance," in *The Literary Freud: Mechanisms of Defense and the Poetic Will*, ed. Joseph H. Smith (New Haven: Yale Univ. Press, 1980), (pp. 261–308). Kenneth Gross, *Spenserian Poetics: Idolatry, Icono-*

7

hostility to American ego psychology is notorious, and the general absence of castration symbolism from Nohrnberg's account offers a minor illustration of the reason for that hostility. I admire *The Analogy of "The Faerie Queene"* enormously and rely on it extensively, but the commitment to a sympathetic accommodation of the poem's concordances—which I think explains Nohrnberg's preference for a developmental psychology—is one I cannot share. Lacan's refusal to mitigate the castration of the human subject seems truer to the tragic dignity Trilling admired in Freud; more important, the Lacanian reinvention of Freud by way of Saussure, Lévi-Strauss, and Kojève's reading of Hegel realigns the Freudian terms *phallus* and *castration* with what we have learned from structuralism about language and meaning. In this way Lacan gives us a Freud whose pertinence to cultural interpretation of all sorts seems greatly amplified.

One reason the structural hypothesis about human culture has proved influential is that it explains why closure must be deferred, or why the body image can never finally subsume the symbolic registers into which we carry it. Once we have posited "a system of differences without positive terms," it is immediately apparent that any effort to circumscribe this system simply adds to it; try to gather difference into the embrace of a synthetic term and you will only introduce one more gesture of differentiation with no intrinsic power to enforce closure. "Intrinsic" is an important qualification, since closure (or the appearance of closure) is a fact of daily experience. Saussure confronts this dilemma in linguistic terms when he tries to delimit his proper "object" of study. "If we could embrace the sum of word-images stored in the minds of all individuals," Saussure argues, "we could identify the social bond that constitutes language. It is a storehouse filled by the members of a

clasm, and Magic (Ithaca: Cornell Univ. Press, 1985), pp. 148–49, comments in passing on the aptness of Lacan's essay for a theory of romance.

given community through their active use of speaking."[10] If this "storehouse" really had the properties of an object, it would have no history; it does have a history because acts of speaking react upon the language spoken, modifying it through usage.

The structural hypothesis has important consequences for our understanding of power and authority in historical terms. How are closures enforced in practice if they are impossible in principle? We can see this problem more clearly, perhaps, by taking up a specific example, the *Retractionum Libri Duo* of St. Augustine. In this unfinished work of bibliography and self-censorship, written near the end of his career, Augustine sought to consolidate his diverse writings into an "authorized" corpus, purged of heterodoxy and chronologically ordered to reveal a continuous progress toward perfect apprehension of the body of Christian truth. Augustine finished only two books of *The Retractations*, as they have come to be known, but for our purposes it will be sufficient to examine the prologue in which he seeks to justify the project.[11] The discursive situation of this prologue is complex: the *Retractations* already exemplifies Paul de Man's notion of "crisis"—it "puts the act of writing into question by relating it to its specific intent"[12]—and the prologue undertakes to state the "specific intent" of the *Retractations* in turn. In this brief presentation of himself as Christian writer-teacher, Augustine precipitates the crisis latent in such a role, at once revealing and resisting the infinite regress that opens under the ground of his authority.

[10] Ferdinand de Saussure, *Course in General Linguistics*, ed. Charles Bally et al., trans. Wade Baskin (New York: McGraw-Hill, 1966), p. 13.

[11] *Saint Augustine: The Retractations*, trans. Sister Mary Inez Bogan, vol. 60 of *The Fathers of the Church: A New Translation* (Washington, D.C.: Catholic Univ. of America Press, 1968), pp. 3–5.

[12] Paul de Man, *Blindness and Insight: Essays in the Rhetoric of Contemporary Criticism*, 2d ed., rev. (Minneapolis: Univ. of Minnesota Press, 1983), p. 8.

The evangelical *auctor* finds himself caught between two necessities. First there is the necessity of error in human discourse, succinctly stated in a passage Augustine quotes from Proverbs: "In a multitude of words, you shall not avoid sin" (10:19).[13] Then there is the necessity of judgment by God, and the terrifying prospect of a divine memory that forgets nothing: for "of every idle word men speak, they shall give account on the day of judgment" (Matt. 12:36). These mark off between them the untenable ground of authority from which Augustine speaks. Discourse is inherently perilous: Augustine also cites the admonition of James, "Let every man be swift to hear, but slow to speak" (1:19). Yet the human community, even the community of Christian worship, cannot sustain itself without discursive authority. "Early in manhood," Augustine recalls, "I had begun to write or speak to the people, and so much authority was attributed to me that, whenever it was necessary for someone to speak to the people and I was present, I was seldom allowed to be silent and to listen to others and to be 'swift to hear but slow to speak.' " Authority here is a burden, a communal demand for discourse: "It was necessary for someone to speak to the people" (p. 4). Human authority in this form is a power but also a compulsion to speak; the power to remain silent is God's alone.[14]

The Christian community thus forces its teachers to err by forcing them to speak from a position only the Logos is competent to occupy. Another passage Augustine cites, again from

---

[13] For Augustine's citations of scripture, I follow Bogan's translations in the edition cited in note 11.

[14] On possibilities for approaching divine silence, see Jerome A. Mazzeo, "St. Augustine's Rhetoric of Silence: Truth vs. Eloquence and Things vs. Signs," in *Renaissance and Seventeenth-Century Studies* (New York: Columbia Univ. Press, 1964), pp. 1–28. Mazzeo concludes that "for St. Augustine all dialectic, true rhetoric, and thought itself were but attempts to reascend to that silence from which the world fell into the perpetual clamour of life" (p. 23).

James, admonishes, "Let not many of you become teachers, my brethren, knowing that you will receive a greater judgment. For in many things we all offend. If anyone does not offend in word, he is a perfect man" (3:1–2). Here is the essential contradiction of evangelical authority, a statement that acknowledges the need for authoritative discourse even as it denies the possibility of discourse without error and promises judgment for errors when they infallibly occur. Recalling Paul's warning that "if we judged ourselves, we should not be judged by the Lord" (1 Cor. 11:31),[15] Augustine seeks in the *Retractations* "to judge myself before the sole Teacher whose judgment of my offenses I desire to avoid" (p. 4). Prompted by anxiety in the face of an overwhelming power, he seeks to disarm God's judgment with a sort of preemptive strike against himself: "With a kind of judicial severity," he writes, "I am reviewing my works . . . and, as it were, with the pen of a censor, I am indicating what dissatisfies me" (p. 3). And so once again he takes up the untenable ground of human authority, this time to judge his previous exercises of the same authority. Augustine can correct the errata of his teaching only by repeating the gesture that produced them.

The two books of retractations Augustine lived to finish were first printed in a rare edition of 1486, and then in the comprehensive edition of his works published around the turn of the sixteenth century. The *OED* cites numerous references to the *Retractations* during the sixteenth century in England, among them passages from familiar works by More, Sir Thomas Norton, and Ralegh. It seems likely then that in

---

[15] Verse 29 of the same chapter in 1 Corinthians elucidates what is at stake in such judgments: the Geneva text reads, "For he that eateth and drinketh vnworthily, eateth and drinketh his owne damnation, because he discerneth not the Lords bodie." Augustine's citation shifts the context from perversion of the communion ritual, through failure to perceive and acknowledge the *corpus mysticum*, to a comparable perversion of his own written corpus, through failure to perceive and enunciate correctly the unity of doctrine.

1595, when Spenser published his hymns to earthly love and beauty together with a heavenly pair written "to amend, and by way of retractation to reform" the earthly ones,[16] he was relying specifically on Augustinian precedent. Certainly he repeats the contradictions Augustine struggled with, contradictions reflected in Elizabethan usage of the word "retractations" itself, which could mean a repetition as well as a correction or cancellation. Like Augustine before him, Spenser can retract youthful error only by repeating it, producing "in stead" of the offending hymns a second pair that offers to supplant the others but can only be added to them.

This seemingly erratic and peripheral moment in Spenser's canon leads to a central feature of his allegorical poetics, a sort of internalized iconoclasm that makes the poetry a perpetually self-displacing mode of discourse. Critics as diverse as Alpers, Kaske, and Murrin have argued in different ways that *The Faerie Queene* is an extended rhetorical performance but not a coherent fictional heterocosm.[17] The terms of this argument

[16] *Spenser: Poetical Works*, ed. J. C. Smith and E. de Selincourt (1912; reprint, New York: Oxford University Press, 1979), p. 586. Citations of Spenser's poetry (except for *The Faerie Queene* and "A Letter of the Authors") are taken from this edition. Hereafter, verse citations will be identified parenthetically by line number, and prose citations (from dedications) by the title *Works* plus page number.

[17] Paul J. Alpers, *The Poetry of "The Faerie Queene"* (Princeton: Princeton Univ. Press, 1967); Carol V. Kaske, "Spenser's Pluralistic Universe: The View from the Mount of Contemplation (F.Q. I.x)," in *Contemporary Thought on Edmund Spenser*, ed. Richard C. Frushell and Bernard J. Vondersmith (Carbondale: Southern Illinois Univ. Press, 1975), (pp. 121–49). Michael Murrin, in "Review Article: The Varieties of Criticism," *MP* 70 (1973): 350–56, combines a critique of Berger's "second world" thesis with an argument for rhetorical approaches to the poem. See also Murrin's "The Rhetoric of Faeryland," in *The Rhetoric of Renaissance Poetry from Wyatt to Milton*, ed. Thomas O. Sloan and Raymond B. Waddington (Berkeley: Univ. of California Press, 1974); reprinted in Murrin, *The Allegorical Epic: Essays in its Rise and Decline* (Chicago: Univ. of Chicago Press, 1980). pp. 73–95.

must be revised, however, if we assume that the poem, the world in the poem, and the world that the poem is in share a common ontology that is itself allegorical. It follows from this assumption that a certain formal reciprocity among poet, protagonist, and reader, or between the represented action and the act of representation, must be a constant and integral dimension of the allegory, part of its mirroring system.[18] Thus (for example) the commonest misreadings one encounters among students coming to the poem for the first time tend to be prefigured within the text. So does an affirmative protocol for right readings, as DeNeef has recently argued.[19] It is as if the text contained an implicit self-censoring principle, or were doubly written as itself and its own simultaneous retractation.

This makes it possible to argue, as Goldberg has, that the text endlessly reinscribes "the place of loss."[20] But if the text also contains an affirmative protocol, then we should recognize this loss as something the intentional structure of the discourse seeks to recuperate. It does this by subsuming loss dialectically as a negative moment that forever promises to call forth *veritas filia* out of the womb of time. In this specific sense Spenserian allegory is always implicitly typological. The deferral built into this structure never finally recuperates the ontological

[18] Isabel MacCaffrey, *Spenser's Allegory: The Anatomy of Imagination* (Princeton: Princeton Univ. Press, 1976), offers a sustained analysis of the poem in these terms. Nohrnberg, in the preface to *Analogy*, remarks that "Everyone will be able to supply examples of 'the poem about the poem within the poem,' but an insistent reading of the text in this way will also yield a more general perception: the equation of the poem's more prominent internal agents with the various mental operators implied by the mere existence of the text" (p. xiii). I would broaden Nohrnberg's formulation to include places, objects, and actions as well as agents, and would substitute "rhetorical" for "mental."

[19] A. Leigh DeNeef, *Spenser and the Motives of Metaphor* (Durham: Duke Univ. Press, 1982).

[20] Jonathan Goldberg, *Endlesse Worke: Spenser and the Structures of Discourse* (Baltimore: Johns Hopkins Univ. Press, 1981), p. 11.

emptiness of the text, but it does articulate that emptiness against the promise of its recuperation: the poem's most earnest trope is precisely its effort to recalculate the traces of its loss and errancy according to a table of symbolic reappropriation. The form of this trope is dialectical in that it reinscribes ontological vacancy as a privation intrinsic to the body alone, which is refigured as a scene of emergence for the spirit. The text itself is also a body, the poetic "body natural"; its groundlessness is reappropriated as a controlled iconoclasm toward fleshly or graven images.[21] This internalized iconoclasm rationalizes the deferral of presence, the text's deferral of its own essential form, as a sustained refusal of premature closure, reflected thematically in a refusal to hasten the apocalypse: the delusion of too literal and impatient a millennial expectancy is exposed in the poem's opening episode, the Redcrosse knight's encounter with Errour. Thus Spenser does not, like Hegel, stage his own writing as the end of history, the final reappropriation of itself by Spirit; rather he identifies his text with history, with the work of clarifying and embodying Spirit in human form. As a result Spenser structures his poetics in the way he understood history to be structured, as a strange loop in the path of Being, ultimately lost to itself and indefinitely in quest of the mysterious divine body without which it can neither be nor become anything.

THE HISTORICAL MOMENT AND THE FORCE OF FORM

During the sixteenth century the public order of Church and State underwent profound and far-reaching transformations of which our own world is a distant consequence. The

---

[21] In *Spenserian Poetics* Kenneth Gross offers a subtle and extended discussion of idolatry and iconoclasm as mutually demystifying imaginative tendencies.

infinite legal and political complexity of the socioeconomic or-
ders we inhabit need not prevent us from seeing that they are
structured into overlapping "units" that range from prisons to
churches, condominiums, government agencies, private
clubs, professional organizations, universities, multinational
corporations—all group entities whose legal status and practi-
cal self-definition rest on the fiction that they are metaphysical
bodies. In very broad terms, then, one way of constructing a
historical context for *The Faerie Queene* is to place the poem
within the long emergence of corporate logic from the eccle-
siastical into the secular domain, particularly the confused and
often violent emergence of the sovereign state as a consolida-
tion of medieval legal and political institutions powerful
enough to rival the Church.

At the same time, it is necessary to recognize that the meth-
odological problems raised by any such "placing" of the poem
are themselves infinitely complicated. At the most general level
this is true because the texts in question—whether Elizabethan
poems, Tudor statutes and polemical tracts, or modern literary
criticism and theory—all function as the agents and the media
of historical change, not merely as its passive registers. Der-
rida's analysis of the double logic of signification provides an
exemplary formulation of this problem: signifiers "refer" to
preexistent signifieds which they also work to constitute, or re-
constitute, through the strategic force of reinscription at play
within the form of referential logic. To summon any referent
into representation is therefore an overdetermined action in
which the multiple ratios of force and form remain incalcula-
ble—except by means of further representations that only
"solve" the dilemma by displacing it.[22] The fact that there is

---

[22] Here and in my subsequent remarks on continuity, I touch on
matters treated by Thomas M. Greene in the essay on "Historical Solitude"
that opens *The Light in Troy: Imitation and Discovery in Renaissance Poetry*
(New Haven: Yale Univ. Press, 1982) pp. 4–27; see especially his percep-

no escape from this infinite regression does not seem to me a good reason for ignoring it, or for dismissing it as a merely "formal" problem. If early readings of Derrida mistook the notion of *différance* as antihistorical, it seems clear now that it is, on the contrary, profoundly historical, perhaps the most powerful formulation in our own time of the irreducible problem of temporality. To deny or persistently misrecognize this problem is itself a deeply antihistorical gesture.

One way of responding to this problem—it cannot be solved—is to say with Oscar Wilde that what matters is not whether one lies, but how well. That we live by necessary fictions means in practice that we live by doublethink, or ideology. Customs, habits, contracts, innuendos, popular songs, television news, jokes, white lies, necessary lies, and beautiful lies all provide ad hoc channels for the ongoing production of a doublethink that will sustain—while we daily transgress them—the fictions we use to stay organized and control the world (or try to). Renaissance defenses of poetry like Sidney's that seek to affirm both the illusion and the truth value of what is at once fictive and didactic are engaged in a deeply conflicted effort to finesse this problem.[23] In practice this defense sanctions a kind of hieratic doubletalk, or allegory, in which the fictiveness of truth may be discerned as readily as the truth of fiction. Thus Spenser's poem assumes the enormous responsibility of intending what Foster Provost summarizes as "a grand self- and national culture,"[24] but as "literature" (to use

---

tive discussion of etiological constructs as the basis for "emergence" into the present. Greene, like Nohrnberg, prefers an Ericksonian psychoanalytic model; my other principal departure from his emphases lies in my insistence on the ideological elements in, and functions of, what Greene calls the Elizabethan *mundus significans*.

[23] See Jacqueline T. Miller, *Poetic License: Authority and Authorship in Medieval and Renaissance Contexts* (New York: Oxford Univ. Press, 1986), chap. 3.

[24] In "Treatments of Theme and Allegory in Twentieth-Century Criti-

the modern word) it embodies that orthodox intention in a form that is structurally and essentially, not just circumstantially, incomplete.

Spenser's willingness to entrust his best wisdom and eloquence to a self-displacing mode of discourse—to gamble on the interested work of his readers—is what opens his writing to the disruptive force of history; it is also what makes his text still productive, and therefore critically interesting. Yet it would be no less reductive to ignore the historical context of this wager than it is problematic to specify that context. My own effort to situate both the ideological investments and the radical productiveness of Spenser's text begins with the following assumption: *The Faerie Queene* reflects a poetics of incorporation that could have been formulated only *after* the Reformation in England had hastened the long-term process through which the national state assumed the role of preeminent corporate entity in political life, and *before* the idea of the state had detached itself from the person of the monarch.[25] The poem's cultural heritage is vast, various, and ancient, but its national-imperial impetus and its particular allegorical form

---

cism of *The Faerie Queene*," Foster Provost offers the following statement of the poem's comprehensive theme: "A grand self- and national culture, forming the complete human being, the complete monarch, and the complete nation for the uses of earth and the uses of heaven, spurred by the force of love, which moves Arthur and Britomart, and with them Tudor England, ambitiously toward an ideal of personal and civic perfection within the Christian world view, in defiance of mutability, vice, and Satan" in *Contemporary Thought on Edmund Spenser*, ed. Richard C. Frushell and Bernard J. Vondersmith (Carbondale: Southern Illinois Univ. Press, 1975), p. 12.

[25] In "The Land Speaks: Cartography, Chorography, and Subversion in Renaissance England," *Representations* 16 (Fall, 1986): 51–85, Richard Helgerson traces the emergence of the *land* as an alternative and potentially competing image of the sovereign state. His discussion is especially interesting for the way he sees the authorial function and the cartographic counter-inscription of national identity strengthening one another in their growing independence from the crown.

are intimately tied to the disruptions whereby a secular, juri-dico-political corporation vested in the person of the monarch came to supplant the supranational spiritual corporation vested in the person of the Pope.

Rosemond Tuve observes that Gloriana "holds that role of shadowy but great importance, the Sovereignty itself, in a sense 'the realm.' "[26] We may begin to sense the force of this conceit by recalling that national sovereignty in sixteenth-century Europe was by no means a clearly established or unproblematic political fact. Royal absolutism in England never achieved the degree of development it did in France and Spain, so Bodin's formulation of the doctrine of sovereignty does not apply as well to the political institutions of England. Bodin locates the sovereignty of the state specifically in the crown, a significant revision of the medieval conception of the state as made up of a head together with its members. In England, however, the medieval conception never was entirely superseded, and if in the early seventeenth century James I tried to impose a version of the metaphor closer to Bodin's, that may be less a sign of the nature of royal power in England than evidence, as Marie Axton suggests, that "James did not really understand the complexity of the role he was asked to play."[27] The investment of patriotic feeling in a specifically royal iconography during Elizabeth's regime was a fragile triumph, one that she herself had begun to outlive by the turn of the century.

In the fourth volume of his massive *History of English Law*, W. S. Holdsworth concludes an analysis of the differences be-tween England and the continental states as follows:

[26] Rosemond Tuve, *Allegorical Imagery: Some Medieval Books and Their Posterity* (Princeton: Princeton Univ. Press, 1966), p. 347.

[27] Marie Axton, *The Queen's Two Bodies: Drama and the Elizabethan Succession* (London: Royal Historical Society, 1977), p. 146.

The English king therefore was far from being the sovereign power in the state. Nor do I think that any lawyer or statesman of the Tudor period could have given an answer to the question as to the whereabouts of the sovereign power in the English state. The doctrine of sovereignty was a new doctrine in the sixteenth century; nor is it readily grasped until the existence of a conflict between several competitors for political power makes it necessary to decide which of these various competitors for political power can in the last resort enforce its will.[28]

In this context, Elizabeth's crucial role in *The Faerie Queene*—where she is not just the poet's principal addressee, but his principal mimetic object as well—takes on a special significance: it enters into that far-reaching (if imperfectly grasped) invention and reinscription of English sovereignty that was well underway during the sixteenth century. Like Bodin, Spenser tends to invest state sovereignty in the crown, a conception that may be seen as reflecting both his historical moment and his class interests as an Irish bureaucrat. Renwick discerns three cultural-political factions in the Ireland Spenser "occupied" on behalf of England: the native Irish, the Anglo-Irish, and the English officials. It is the last of these in particular that may be seen as comprising a distinct social and economic, as well as ethnic and political, "class." They were, as Renwick says, "the servants of the new monarchic and national state of England created by the Tudors, little enough, perhaps, in origin and person, but representing the royal supremacy and holding [both lands and offices] by the royal prerogative."[29] The *View*, which is certainly critical of Elizabeth's policies, is

[28] W. S. Holdsworth, *History of English Law*, 3d ed., rev. (London: Methuen, 1924), 4: 208.
[29] Edmund Spenser, *A View of the Present State of Ireland*, ed. W. L. Renwick (Oxford: Clarendon, 1970), p. 173 (hereafter cited parenthetically as *View*).

nonetheless fundamentally committed to the doctrine of royal sovereignty, which was "the necessary presupposition of the official world of the new monarchy, in and by which [Spenser] lived" (p. 188).

Taking his cue from the queen's political transformation of chivalric and Petrarchan rhetorics, Spenser draws on the resources of Neoplatonism to infuse the monarch's body politic with an erotically compelling visionary glory: the transcendental beauty that the Platonic lover beholds in the personal soul of his Beatrice or Laura is assimilated to Elizabeth's political power in the vision of a "lover" who seeks her favor as ardently as Arthur seeks Gloriana, and whose historical gestalt is as profoundly constituted by the fiction and figure of royal sovereignty as Fairyland itself is. Spenser may criticize his queen and may express ambivalence about the consequences of this "erotic idealization of a power relationship,"[30] but he does not break the frame of his foreconceit, which is both a forceful ideological synthesis and a deeply interested mystification.

There is something implicitly Nietzschean in Holdsworth's recognition that the historical delimitation of a concept like sovereignty emerges from a contest of individual and institutional wills. The "last resort" of political power in any age is violence, and I do not mean to ignore the kinds and degrees of violence through which the effects of power are registered in the production of truth.[31] At one extreme there is the violence Spenser saw in Ireland, and defended as necessary, and advocated as policy: asked by what means he would pacify the land,

[30] Louis A. Montrose, " 'The Perfecte Paterne of a Poete': The Poetics of Courtship in *The Shepheardes Calender,*" *TSLL* 21 (1979): 42.

[31] The modern Nietzschean who has done most to develop this line of argument is of course Michel Foucault. For his methodological debt to Nietzsche, see "Nietzsche, Genealogy, History," in *Language, Counter-Memory, Practice: Selected Essays and Interviews by Michel Foucault,* ed. Donald F. Bouchard, trans. Bouchard and Sherry Simon (Ithaca: Cornell Univ. Press, 1977), pp. 139–64.

Eudoxus in *A View* replies, "even by the sword" (p. 95). This too is a figure of sovereignty: "By the sword," he explains, "I mean the royal power of the prince, which ought to stretch itself forth in her chief strength." The sword is all too literal as well, however. Eudoxus protests to the contrary: "By the sword which I named I do not mean the cutting off of all that nation with the sword, which far be it from me that I ever should think so desperately or wish so uncharitably, but . . . the redressing and cutting off of those evils which I before named, and not of the people which are evil" (p. 95). But metaphysical evils must be excised with real swords, and the protestation rings hollowly against the detailed military plans that follow.

Yet another form of violence attending the emergence of state sovereignty was the cessation in England, during the reign of Henry VIII, of all teaching and study of canon law, a direct consequence of the fact that the break with Rome emerged from a divorce case tried and appealed in the ecclesiastical courts. A new truth was required, and so was a new academic machinery for its ex post facto production and defense. The purpose of this truth or fiction was precisely to disguise the violence with which a new distribution of power was wrenching itself loose from the status quo; and so it suddenly became necessary to realize that an authoritative precedent for the relation of ecclesia to imperium lay in the fourth-century reign of the Roman Emperor Constantine. As Holdsworth observes, "The violence of the change was skillfully disguised by the fiction of the restoration of an old independence" (*History of English Law*, 4: 47).

It may be useful to consider the broader cultural imperatives that require the creation of authoritative precedents where they do not exist. Perhaps the most powerful critique of this culture and its imperatives comes from Nietzsche, whose *Genealogy of Morals* treats the implicitly contractual nature of social existence as the problem, first and foremost, of creating "man" as a remembering animal, "an animal *with the right to make promises*."[32] The basis of Christian ethics is that unbroken span of conscious volition which extends into the past as memory and into the future as intention: this continuum of self-conscious existence is the phenomenal ground of all "responsibility."

Opposed to continuous conscious identity, resistant to the renunciations and investments it requires, is the force of forgetfulness, "an active and in the strictest sense positive faculty of repression" (*Genealogy*, p. 57). It is active and positive because, as a power of erasure, it voids the tabula on which memory's records are inscribed "so as to make room again for new things, above all for the nobler functions and functionaries, for regulation, foresight, premeditation (for our organism is an oligarchy)" (p. 58). In this sense oblivion is not only opposed to consciousness, it is paradoxically also the ground of consciousness; without forgetting, Nietzsche argues, there could strictly speaking be no "present." Forgetting provides what we might call the space of representation within which memory can appear. Nietzsche's argument stresses that this space is not just passively available, but must be cleared by force, and that such force is no conscious agency of the will, but the expression of a deeper will to oblivion which is, in effect, the background out of which and against which consciousness emerges.

Consciousness, however—like the modern state—erects its sovereignty at considerable cost. The savage history of the state's punitive apparatus appears in this view as essentially a "*mnemotechnics*": castration, flaying, breaking on the wheel, drawing and quartering, and the like were the counterforce

---

[32] Friedrich Nietzsche, *On the Genealogy of Morals*, trans. Walter Kaufmann and R. J. Hollingdale, and *Ecce Homo*, trans. Kaufmann (New York: Vintage, 1969), p. 57 (hereafter cited parenthetically as Nietzsche, *Genealogy*).

employed by civilization to create memory and conscience in the human animal (*Genealogy*, pp. 61–62). In effect this argument rewrites both Platonic amnesis and Christian original sin: where these doctrines define forgetting as essentially privative, a bodily inertia, Nietzsche sees forgetting as positive and derives memory from violence against the body. He displays such fine contempt for the "slave morality" this violence produces because he anticipates Freud's insight into the mechanism of internalization that converts aggression into guilt: for Nietzsche, conscience is the result of an abject identification with the punitive machinery of the Masters. Anger toward them is sublimated into "bad conscience" through a self-deceiving capitulation that rationalizes passivity as a virtue.

Underlying the cultural imperative to link present actions to justifying precedents, then, is the deeper need for continuity itself as the phenomenal basis of social existence. Obliviousness appears as the genealogical ground of memory in that punitive violence arose as a mnemonic counterforce to its active power; it appears as the structural ground of memory in that its erasures provide the very space of representation within which memory operates—the "mystic writing pad" on which mnemonic notations are inscribed, or the force against which memory's counterforce must prevail to create an *impression*.[33]

This argument traces a connection between violence as a physical and historical event, violence as a subject for representation, and violence as part of the dynamics of representation. Eugene Vance, citing Frances Yates on the special mnemonic value of violent or grotesque imagery, suggests that "violence may be understood as being not only the 'subject' of oral epic narrative but also as an *aide-mémoire* or as a 'generative' force in the production of its discourse. By extension, it is interesting to ask if the semiological prominence given to

[33] See Jacques Derrida, *Writing and Difference*, trans. Alan Bass (Chicago: Univ. of Chicago Press, 1978), pp. 196–231.

23

violence in classical and post-classical culture—the sacrifices, the circumcisions, the tortures, the beheadings, the crucifixions, the quarterings, the burnings—was not primarily mnemonic in function."[34] Such speculations suggest the special relevance of these ideas to the poet, who is among the earliest cultural figures for the triumph of memory over oblivion. The poet and his heroic protagonist reciprocally motivate one another, for if the violence of the hero's exploits helps to produce the *energeia*[35] that makes poetic discourse memorable, "it is the commemorative posterity of the singer that inspires the epic blows of the hero" (Vance, "Poetics of Memory," p. 380).

Compared to the measured tones in which Vance observes that "our daily cultural life is constituted as a balance of the dialectical forces of repression and recollection" (p. 378), the Zarathustran pitch of Nietzsche's rhetoric may sound shrill. Yet a moment's reflection on the burden of Vance's essay should make clear that Nietzsche's prophetic bluster is a kind of a stylistic corollary to the argument it so vividly conveys. The mnemonic value of such vividness is a standard topic of Renaissance rhetoric and poetics, and forms a basic strategy of Spenser's gothic extravagance in *The Faerie Queene*. Arthur, for example, after his rescue of Redcrosse, warns against reviewing the knight's errors too fully, too soon, since "the things, that grievous were to do, or beare, / Them to renew, I wote, breeds no delight." He continues:

[34] Eugene Vance, "Roland and the Poetics of Memory," in *Textual Strategies: Perspectives in Post-Structuralist Criticism*, ed. Josué V. Harari (Ithaca: Cornell Univ. Press, 1979), p. 383 (hereafter cited parenthetically as Vance, "Poetics of Memory").

[35] On Renaissance usage of the terms *energeia* and *enargeia*, see Alpers, *Poetry of "The Faerie Queene*," pp. 102–6; and Robert L. Montgomery, *The Reader's Eye: Studies in Didactic Literary Theory from Dante to Tasso* (Berkeley: Univ. of California Press, 1979), p. 210 n. 12. Further sources are cited by Montgomery.

. . . th'onely good, that growes of passed feare,
Is to be wise, and ware of like agein.
This dayes ensample hath this lesson deare
Deepe written in my heart with yron pen,
That blisse may not abide in state of mortall men.[36]

Alluding to the Biblical trope of memory as a writing on the fleshy tables of the heart, Arthur complicates the value of commemoration by reinscribing it within a scriptural thematics of law and grace. Augustine fears the infinite precision of a divine memory that will call every syllable of human discourse to account; Arthur foreshadows the divine compassion that will lay aside the iron pen of the law. Una, however, insists on stripping Duessa before the knights' eyes, no doubt comforting Redcrosse immeasurably with the sight of her bald scalp, rotten gums, dried and suppurating dugs, scabby skin, bear's claw, eagle's talon, and fox's tail streaked with dung.

This blazon of disgust composes what Sidney would call a "notable image of vice"; it draws commemorative power from the stylistic and imagistic violence with which it *strikes, pierces,* and *possesses* "the sight of the soul." Judith Anderson has remarked that in redescribing Spenser's poetics under the sign of catachresis, or *abusio,* I tend to confuse Spenser with Busirane.[37] It is a shrewd perception: Spenser often recurs to the scriptural trope of writing on the heart as an implicit model for his own poetics, notably in lines 204–59 of "An Hymne of Heavenly Love"; the injunction to "read through loue" (line 224) is a comprehensive rubric for students of *The Faerie Queene,* and Busirane is a profoundly unsettling image of the

---

[36] *The Faerie Queene* I.viii.44.5–9, emphasis added. Subsequent citations from *The Faerie Queene* will be given parenthetically with book, canto, stanza, and line numbers indicated as above.

[37] Judith Anderson, "Spenser at Kalamazoo (1985)," *SpN* 16, no. 2 (Spring-Summer 1985): 48.

perversions such a poetics must seek to ward off. In the chapters that follow I try to acknowledge a number of Spenser's strategies for healing the wounded heart, or "recuperating" human desire (including his own genuine desire not to be Busirane) through a program of sublimation. But I argue too that this program has from the start already inflicted the wound it offers to heal. It is no accident that Sidney's phrasing resonates so perilously in the sanctum of Busirane's palace, nor that the "figure" of abuse who inhabits that chamber of illusions is found inscribing his desires in the fleshy tables of the heart.

A BRIEF ITINERARY

The argument of the following chapters is developed primarily through commentary on Spenser's poetry. This reflects a conscious decision as well as an intellectual habit on my part. What is unfortunately called the "New Historicism" in Renaissance studies has sometimes been marked by reluctance to sustain close readings of literary texts. The work of its most gifted advocates is so consistently engaging that this tendency hardly seems a drawback; yet I think there is something to be gained from a demonstration of just how intimately literary and nonliterary texts may be read against one another. This procedure has its own drawbacks, for it is hard to reconcile the demands of argumentation with those of commentary. I hope it has compensatory advantages in showing the sustained power of a historicist thesis to read, intensively and inventively, a text as complex as *The Faerie Queene*.

An important aspect of the ideological synthesis informing Spenser's poetry is the poetic vocation it underwrites: the poet who envisions a resurgence of empire in Elizabeth is himself cast in the Virgilian role of imperial laureate. My first chapter concentrates on the emergence in Spenser's early work of two related motifs: the sense of vernacular poetry as an autonomous

domain with its own history and permanence, a literary coun-
terpart to national sovereignty; and the demand for recognition
commensurate with a laureate's dignity. These motifs are re-
lated according to the "specular" logic that characterizes all
rhetorically constructed relations, and each of the chapters that
follow explores this logic in some fashion. Chapter 2 focuses
on the allegory of *The Faerie Queene*, especially Book I, to
demonstrate how the poem may be read both ideologically and
formally, at once as romance allegory and a reinscription of
national sovereignty. Here it will already be apparent that my
notion of reading the historical force of the poem is inseparable
from an insistence on reading the tropical forces at work in
legal and political texts. The second half of chapter 2 develops
this argument explicitly, using rhetorical terms to describe
what Spenser's poem has in common with the historical texts
in and through which the early modern state was, so to speak,
troped into being in sixteenth-century England.

Chapter 3 develops the Lacanian allegory mentioned earlier,
focusing on Arthur's interventions in the first two books and
on his projected marriage with Gloriana. This psychogenetic
account of the poem's "second" body is interwoven with a his-
torical speculation about that body's textual genesis in Eliza-
beth's coronation progress. Through close readings of related
passages in Books I and II, I argue that Arthur's history, his
dream, and his quest for Gloriana fuse political, erotic, and
economic motives in a strategy that identifies the projective
form of the poem with the vision of a Protestant imperium.

No study concerned with ideological constructions of the
human body can avoid the question of gender. I argue that the
aesthetic body of Spenser's poem mirrors the sociopolitical
body of Tudor ideology, and proceed in chapters 4 and 5 to
attempt a detailed reading of the resulting sexual allegory.
Chapter 4 treats Alma's castle and the chronicles read there,
showing how far both are organized by the interplay between

symbolic castration and the mirage of phallic completion.
Spenser himself appears caught up in this play: in different
ways, the passages in question all advance a covert allegory of
his historically contingent political desire as the self-authoriz-
ing origin of that visionary body which forms the obscure telos
of British history.

As we approach its midsection, *The Faerie Queene* passes
through an allegorically feminine phase in its quest for her-
maphroditic completeness. Chapter 5 focuses on Spenser's con-
struction of the feminine; it culminates in a reading of the Gar-
den of Adonis passage, where I find Spenser's allegory
appropriating feminine procreativity on behalf of a patriarchal
symbolic order. I approach the Garden, however, by way of
the episodes that precede it in cantos 5 and 6, to show how this
appropriation informs both the "entrelacement" of narrative
and the political problem of dynastic succession. Spenser's "na-
ture" departs from and returns to the Logos in her production
of species, in this way mastering the discontinuities of Time's
destructive force. Discontinuities in the narrative and the dy-
nastic succession are likewise overcome by the power of the
masculine universal, which guarantees its own perpetuity
through the controlled assimilation of feminine procreativity.

Clearly there are more than two bodies for the reader of this
book to keep track of. What my title names is not an interpre-
tive paradigm that simplifies the work of reading Spenser, but
a structural duality, a specularity that complicates the work of
reading both Spenser and his historical context. In turning this
book over to such readers as it may find, I hope it complicates
their work in ways that prove fruitful.

Thy gracious Souerains praises to compile
And her imperiall Maiestie to frame . . .
—*Spenser, To Buckhurst*[1]

1. "her imperiall Maiestie to frame"

y subject in this chapter is the way Spenser's early publications consolidate an image of their author as "Englands Arch-Poet"—the title that adorns the first folio edition of his collected works in 1611. Like the personal self, this public identity emerges within a system of specular relations. The identification that informs all others is stressed in the phrase *"Englands Arch-Poet"*: Spenser as mirror to the nation incorporate. This mirroring informs every aspect of his relation to Elizabeth, including his position in the ranks of a bureaucracy constituted by the doctrine of royal sovereignty, his participation in creating Elizabeth as a living icon of imperial sovereignty, and his desire for an image of poetic vocation scaled to imperial precedent. Spenser's relation to the literary tradition must also be understood in these terms—not only because the myth of Virgil's imperial status grounds the vocational ideal for poetry in what was for centuries Western history's most imposing image of secular power, but also because, despite its classical roots, Spenser's notion of laureate prestige emerges specifically from the glorification of vernacular literature as an autonomous domain with its own history and permanence: a reflection of the national state.[2]

---

[1] The dedicatory sonnets to *The Faerie Queene* appear in *Works*, pp. 410–13. I cite individual sonnets by abbreviated titles: To Hatton, To Lady Carey, and so on.

[2] Paul Alpers, "Pastoral and the Domain of Lyric in Spenser's *Shepheardes Calender*," *Representations* 12 (1985): 94–95, argues that the *Calender* asserts a "qualified but nonetheless genuine independence" from the court which amounts to "a kind of *literary* authority." Alpers suggests the term "domain" to characterize this qualified independence or " 'aesthetic space' in terms of

Spenser therefore invents himself as poet in relation to literary history—and reinvents literary history in relation to himself as poet—under pressure of a mixed literary *and* political need to glorify the emergent Tudor dynasty. In *The Shepheardes Calender* and other texts from the early stages of Spenser's career, we can follow the textual strategies of this project as well as trace the anxieties it produces in a poet who feels at once conspicuous and unrecognized, powerful and defenseless, cautious and yet almost recklessly exposed.

FASHIONING AUTHORIAL STATUS

The public identity Spenser sought to fashion may be designated by the rhetorical term "ornament," a kind of synecdoche. La Primaudaye observes that Pythagoras coined the term *World* (i.e., cosmos) as a way of designating the creation's organization, "for this word *World* signifieth as much as Ornament, or a well disposed order of things."[3] The social and literary senses of the term are related to the cosmic sense in that "ornaments," properly speaking, are insignia that designate status or rank within a cosmic hierarchy. "As in English," writes Angus Fletcher, "the Greek term *kosmos* has a double meaning, since it denotes both a *large-scale order* (macrocosmos) and the small-scale *sign of that order* (microcosmos). It could be used of any decoration or ornament of dress."[4] It may also be used to describe authorial insignia whose rhetorical

---

rule and authority." His reference to the legal definition of *demesne* suggests specifically how the independence of such literary authority is qualified: the term is "applied either to the absolute ownership of the king, or to the tenure of the person who held land to his own use, mediately or immediately from the king." My purpose in the present chapter is to explore some of the ways in which Spenser's poetic domain, however "empowered by . . . the world of learning," derives "mediately" from the figure of incorporated sovereignty.

[3] Quoted by James Carscallen, "The Goodly Frame of Temperance: The Metaphor of Cosmos in *The Faerie Queene*, Book II," *UTQ* 37 (1968): 136.

[4] Fletcher, *Allegory*, pp. 108–20 (hereafter cited parenthetically).

purpose is to situate or resituate the poet in social and cultural hierarchies. The term's double reference will prove especially valuable if it helps us focus on the specularity of the rhetorical relations at work: the poet who "frames" his ideal portrait of Elizabeth within complex allegorical images of the social hierarchy seeks at the same time and in the same gesture—by reflex, as it were—to be himself constituted in the image of sovereignty, or as the 1596 title page would declare, "to live with the eternity of her fame."

The 1590 dedicatory sonnet to Walsingham emphasizes what is at stake in the production of the poet's ornament:

> That Mantuane Poetes incompared spirit,
> Whose girland now is set in highest place,
> Had not Mecaenas for his worthy merit,
> It first aduaunst to great Augustus grace,
> Might long perhaps haue lien in silence bace,
> Ne benc so much admir'd of later age.
> This lowly Muse, that learns like steps to trace,
> Flies for like aide vnto your Patronage;
> That are the great Mcccnas of this age. . . .   (lines 1–9)

In another and considerably more ironic respect, however, this sonnet touches on one of the principal obstacles to Spenser's quest for Virgilian status. Even as Spenser was composing his address to Walsingham, the English economy was headed into a decade of shortages and inflation that devastated the personal fortunes of Elizabeth's great courtiers, through whom patronage had always filtered down from the crown to a mixed crowd of artisans and professionals. Jonson and Camden might moralize the poet's death in 1599 as an exemplum of impoverished genius, but the Mycenas to whom Spenser appeals in this sonnet died in the year of its publication "so overwhelmed by debt that his coffin had to be hidden away from his creditors, and buried at night."[5]

---

[5] For the comments of Jonson and Camden, see R. M. Cummings, ed.,

Spenser's efforts to institute a Virgilian laureateship in Elizabethan England got underway during the final stages of a long decline in royal and court patronage of such arts as poetry, painting, tapestry, and glazing. These were the material means of production of princely "magnificence"—that ambiguous quality Spenser sets forth in the person of Arthur—and for this reason the early Tudors had begun cultivating them late in the fifteenth century in emulation of the Burgundian court under Charles the Bold. In the Household Ordinance of 1478, Edward IV decreed that the royal establishment should be guided by neither prodigality nor avarice, but the "vertue called liberalite." Gordon Kipling remarks:

> We recognize here, of course, a quotation from the *Nichomachean Ethics*, but we would probably also be correct in recognizing it as a quotation from Guillaume Fillastre's *La Toison d'Or* (ca. 1470). Fillastre, the chancellor of the Order of the Golden Fleece, uses Aristotle's famous definition *in setting magnificence for the first time at the head of the princely virtues*, and in his household reorganization Edward IV obviously follows suit. In keeping with this definition, the royal household was divided into two parts. The *Domus Regie Magnificencie* or household "above stairs" consisted of several standing offices . . . charged with impressing the outside world with ostentatious display.[6]

Edmund Spenser: The Critical Heritage, (New York: Barnes and Noble, 1971), p. 136 (hereafter cited parenthetically as Cummings, *Spenser: Critical Heritage*); and William Nelson, *The Poetry of Edmund Spenser: A Study* (New York: Columbia Univ. Press, 1963), p. 11. On Walsingham's death I quote Carolly Erickson, *The First Elizabeth* (New York: Summit, 1983), p. 394 (hereafter cited parenthetically as Erickson, *First Elizabeth*). G. K. Hunter has recounted the marginalization of humanists at court in *John Lyly: The Humanist as Courtier* (Cambridge: Harvard Univ. Press, 1962), chap. 1; reprinted in *Elizabethan Poetry: Modern Essays in Criticism*, ed. Paul J. Alpers (New York: Oxford Univ. Press, 1967), pp. 3–40.

    [6] Gordon Kipling, "Henry VII and the Origins of Tudor Patronage," in *Patronage in the Renaissance*, ed. Guy Fitch Lytle and Stephen Orgel (Prince-

Henry VII extended the production of magnificence in various ways, adding a number of standing offices to the superior household. He appointed a Royal Librarian who built a collection "heavily committed to the Burgundian tradition of 'learned chivalry' " that runs from Caxton through Henry VIII's court to Sidney and Spenser (Kipling, "Henry VIII," pp. 124–25). Still following Burgundian precedent, Henry appointed a Court Chronicler, and supported various belletrists (including Skelton and Hawes) with appointments to the royal household (pp. 131–32). Comparable support was provided for tapsters, glaziers, and the drama. In short, Henry's reign "transformed the royal household into a major influence upon the development of the fine arts in England"; it "set a standard of courtly patronage and established a distinctive royal style for his descendants" (p. 164).

The political unrest of the mid-sixteenth century devastated the Burgundian tradition created by the early Tudors. Roy Strong opens *The English Icon* by describing "the total collapse of a settled court culture and, with it, that of active royal patronage. . . . Edward, Mary, Elizabeth, James . . . all failed to engage in active artistic patronage."[7] In seeking to reinstate some form of laureateship, then, Spenser had to confront the overburdened and highly competitive network of court patronage as an outsider, lacking not only a vigorous national literary tradition but also an established place at court. For this reason his *Shepheardes Calender*, clearly a laureate debut, had to create the space it sought to occupy as the "classic" of a new golden age.[8] Beyond merely fabricating a literary-historical genealogy

---

ton: Princeton Univ. Press, 1981), p. 119 (emphasis added; hereafter cited parenthetically as Kipling, *Henry VIII*).

[7] Roy Strong, *The English Icon* (New York: Pantheon, 1969), p. 1.

[8] See Richard Helgerson, *Self-Crowned Laureates: Spenser, Jonson, Milton, and the Literary System* (Berkeley: Univ. of California Press, 1983), pp. 55–82.

for itself, the *Calender* had to reclaim a serious public role for poetry as such. Spenser's poetic canon therefore opens with an address "To His Booke" in which the unknown father of a bastard text sends it out to find sponsorship before venturing into polite circles. In "Teares of the Muses" Terpsichore will expand this implicit scenario, portraying the Muses' children as dispossessed heirs in the kingdom of modern letters, forced to appear as outsiders whose birth secures no special place. They have lost what was—in the early Tudor tradition of Burgundian "magnificence" as well as the idealized antiquity of Renaissance humanism—their birthright.

In setting out to recover this patrimony, the orphan Muse can only have recourse to the means at hand, suing for preferment like any other *arriviste*. (The fiction of royal usurpation implies that the poet's efforts to create countenance are really efforts to recover his "natiue heritage" ["Teares," line 341], but the rhetorical design of such a fiction is transparent.) The similar pretensions of the *Calender* are reflected in its most obvious formal features. Its conspectus of pastoral "forms and attitudes"; its range in imitating and alluding to the chief models of English, Continental, and classical pastoral; the variety of its metrical forms and the special complexity of the forms chosen for Colin's displays of technical virtuosity; its annotated format, and even to some extent its archaic diction— all work (in the phrase of E. K.) to "bring great . . . auctoritie to the verse" (*Works*, p. 417).[9]

These implicit pretensions are seconded by E. K. at every

[9] Harold Toliver in *Pastoral Forms and Attitudes* (Berkeley: Univ. of California Press, 1971), pp. 64–70, comments on the prevalence in the *Calender* (and its textual apparatus) of "the ambition-humility complex and its mixed style" (p. 64). More recently Louis Adrian Montrose has offered an influential revaluation of pastoral as a symbolic discourse used to negotiate power relations: see, for example, " 'The Perfecte Paterne' "; " 'Eliza, Queene of Shepheardes,' and the Pastoral of Power," *ELR* 10 (1980): 153–82; "Gifts and Reasons: The Contexts of Peele's *Araygnement of Paris*," *ELH* 47 (1980): 433–61.

turn, beginning with his advertisement of great expectations in the epistle to Harvey: the New Poet "shall be not onely kiste, but also beloued of all, embraced of the most, and wondred at of the best. No lesse I thinke, deserueth his wittinesse in deuising, his pithinesse in vttering, his complaints of loue so louely" (*Works*, p. 416) and so forth. Spenser's humility in writing pastoral is easily turned to account through a list of names designed to show how illustrious the tradition of humility really is. The list ends with Immerito, who follows tradition as a sign of deference but also of skill, "so as few, but they be wel sented can trace him out" (p. 418). Well scented, that is, or happily endowed with a glossator. Fearing that "many excellent and proper deuices . . . would passe in the speedy course of reading, either as vnknowen, or as not marked" (p. 418), E. K. has gone before to point them out, his glosses literally "marks" of respect. "Vncouthe vnkiste" is the line he borrows from Chaucer's Pandarus, and the glosses are little scholarly pandars, soliciting hugs and kisses for the paranomasias and pretty epanorthoses.

The idea of poetic vocation these devices seek to revive is a distinctly Renaissance inheritance, inseparable from the emergence of vernacular texts that dignify literature as a reflection of the secular state. We see these notions entering English poetry initially in the work of Chaucer, whose authorial persona represents an ironic and highly self-conscious development of the humility conventional among medieval writers in the vernacular. A. C. Spearing traces the influence of Dante, Petrarch, and Boccaccio in specific passages where a characteristically "Renaissance" sense of literary history begins to emerge from Chaucer's comically ostentatious gestures of self-deprecation.[10] Prominent among these is the envoy to *Troilus and Criseyde*:

[10] A. C. Spearing, "Renaissance Chaucer and Father Chaucer," *English*

> Go, litel bok, go, litel myn tragedye,
> Ther God thi makere yet, er that he dye,
> So sende myght to make in som comedye!
> But litel book, no makyng thow n'envie,
> But subgit be to alle poesye;
> And kis the steppes, where as thow seest pace
> Virgile, Ovide, Omer, Lucan, and Stace.

Spearing remarks of these lines that

> Probably no earlier writer in English had referred to his
> own work by either of the grand titles of *tragedye* or *comedye*:
> and I suppose too that no earlier writer in English had re-
> lated his work to *poesye* as Chaucer does here—*poesye*, by
> contrast to the native word *makyng*, evidently meaning all
> that is represented by the catalogue "Virgile, Ovide, Omer,
> Lucan, and Stace": classical literature, together with those
> vernacular works that begin to emulate its dignity and per-
> manence. . . . Chaucer is doing something quite new in
> English in this stanza: he is introducing the conception of
> what we now call "literature," and with it that of a history
> of literature in which a work in English may have a place,
> however modest, alongside the great writers of antiquity.
> ("Renaissance Chaucer," p. 19)

Spearing suggests that the following stanza, with its recogni-
tion of "so gret dyversite / In Englyssh and in wrytyng of oure
tonge" and its concern for accurate transmission and rendition
of the text, constitutes "an astonishing act of imagination for a
fourteenth-century English writer. In this stanza, Chaucer
virtually invents the possibility of a history of English poetry"
(p. 20).

Spearing traces the beginnings of a self-conscious vernacu-
lar tradition in the relations between Chaucer and his fifteenth-
century imitators. By the time Skelton writes his brash envoys

---

34 (1985): 1–38 (hereafter cited parenthetically as Spearing, "Renaissance
Chaucer").

(one in Latin and one in English) to "The Crowne of Laurell," the conventional humility of the medieval craftsman has given way to a jocular presumption of rivalry with the classics: "Barbara cum Latio pariter jam currite versu," he writes— "Though foreign you now run an equal race with Latin verse" (line 1525).[11] Deriving less from Chaucer, perhaps, than from the Burgundian traditions that influenced courtly styles in various media under Henry VII, this new sense of the status and authority to which vernacular poetry might aspire generates a combative anxiety about the risks of prominence:

> Your fame may sprede
> In length and brede.
> But then I drede
> Ye shall have nede
> You for to spede
> To harnness bryght,
> By force of myght,
> Ageyne envy
> And obloquy.   (lines 1551–59)

Or as the Latin verses have it, "Nor should you be sorry to endure the attacks of mad dogs; for great Virgil bore the brunt of similar threats and Ovid's muse was not exempt" (lines 1530–32).

Mad dog Envy barks again in the preface to Spenser's *Shepheardes Calender*, but the implicit scene of combat is no longer chivalric, as it was when Skelton buckled his verses into harness:

11 "The Crowne of Laurell" is the title given by "I. S." (John Stowe?) in *Pithy, Plesaunt and Profitable Workes of Maister Skelton, Poete Laureate, Nowe Collected and Newly Published*, STC 22608 (1568). For convenience I quote Skelton's poems from the text of *John Skelton: The Complete English Poems*, ed. John Scattergood (New York: Penguin, 1983). Translations of the Latin verse are from *The Complete Poems of John Skelton, Laureate*, ed. Philip Henderson, 3d ed. (London: Dent, 1959).

Goe little booke: thy selfe present,
As child whose parent is vnkent:
To him that is the president
Of noblesse and of cheualree,
And if that Enuie barke at thee,
As sure it will, for succoure flee
Vnder the shadow of his wing,
And asked, who thee forth did bring,
A shepheards swaine saye did thee sing,
All as his straying flocke he fedde:
And when his honor has thee redde,
Craue pardon for my hardyhedde.
But if that any aske thy name,
Say thou wert base begot with blame:
For thy thereof thou takest shame.
And when thou art past ieopardee,
Come tell me, what was sayd of mee,
And I will send more after thee.

Spenser has neither Chaucer's relaxed humility nor Skelton's comic bluster. Where Chaucer cautions his little book against envy, Spenser warns his against being envied. Where Skelton trumpets his authorship—"Dicite, Skeltonis vester Adonis erat; / Dicite, Skeltonis vester Homerus erat" (lines 1523–24)—Spenser advises the *Calender* to conceal its "name," or parentage, and in fact signs the verses "Immerito."

The force of Spenser's originality is considerable. He has already begun to modify the convention when he salutes his book on the first page instead of the last, recreating the envoy as a framing device. He then literalizes the formulaic "Goe little booke," extending it into a sustained metaphor of the poem as orphan or illegitimate child, forced to make its own way in the world. This too was a conventional figure, as Sidney's use of it in the preface to *Arcadia* might suggest, but for Spenser it means something different. Sidney had both a name and a place (however unsatisfactory) at court; his literary toys were the illegitimate offspring of a mind and a talent dedicated to greater expectations, "entitled" by rank as well as by nature to wield kingdoms' causes. The *Calender*'s "parent is vnkent" because he lacks precisely the rank and eminence of "his honor" Sir Philip; the ambitions to which Sidney was born and bred are "hardyhedde" indeed in a man who owes his education to charity. It is more than just literary obscurity, then, that Spenser acknowledges in the signature "Immerito."

In the series of envoys before us, each poet implicitly addresses his text as an authorial alter ego. Chaucer's genial self-mockery eases his deference to both an aristocratic audience and a classical heritage; his defense is to disarm envy. Skelton projects a more broadly comic defiance of both, allying himself with the classics in the face of contemporary envy even as he challenges the Latin poets to a galloping metrical footrace. Spenser, though, mingles social and literary status in a way that reflects his desire to convert literary achievement into social and professional capital. His address implicitly characterizes the text as an ambitous "new man" in the royal court, seeking to overcome the disadvantage of low birth through patronage and conspicuous ability. Go, he says, seek out the most promising young belletrist at court—the Earl of Leicester's protégé—for in a place of intense rivalry, where envy is endemic and gossip can prove fatal, you will need the protection of someone in power. Deflect questions about your parentage by shifting ambiguously into a pastoral lexicon that seems charmingly "literary" but serves also as an idiom in which to "negotiat by colour of otiation."[12] In this way you may perhaps mask my ambition with a quaint rusticity while seeking countenance for it from one who knows only too well how to read the literary-social code in which my suit is presented. If anyone openly demands your "name," acknowledge the shame of low birth;

[12] The phrase is Puttenham's, quoted by Montrose in "Gifts and Reasons," p. 439.

and if you survive at court, report what you hear of my reputation, for only then will I risk the next step in my bid for public status.

The pronoun shifts in "To His Booke" call attention to this strategy of self-projection more tellingly than anything in the passages from Chaucer or Skelton. The poem's presentation of itself to Sidney refigures the act of dedication, which the poet acknowledges as "*my* hardyhedde," while its reception at court reflects his own, or "what was sayd of mee." Every writer implicitly creates his identity as writer in and through the texts he publishes, but Spenser here twins himself with remarkable strategic self-consciousness. Instead of a self-made man he offers us the fiction of a self-made poem, repudiating its natural origin in an implicit appeal for the patronage, or foster fatherhood, of Sidney, Harvey, and the public audience they so clearly represent. Thus during the 1580s Spenser preserved a strategic anonymity while the identity "Colin," or simply "that . . . Gentleman who wrate the late shepheardes Callender," was created by the text and its reception as a public entity distinct from Edmund Spenser, gentleman.[13] Instead of deriving its authority from him the *Calender* created an authority he could later assume with ease, almost with nonchalance: who knows not Colin Clout?

The envoys seek to promote such a reception by dramatizing it in advance. Immerito awaits his poem's success as we begin but announces it as we conclude, for while the prologue verses project hypothetical dangers and prudent responses to them, suggesting at last that public acceptance is a precondition for the poet's willingness to go on, the epilogue opens on a note of plain triumph: "Loe I have made a Calender for every yeare." Each reading of the *Calender* as a whole thus appears to *enact* the favorable reception E. K. solicits for "our new Poete"

[13] The reference to Spenser as "that . . . Gentleman" is Puttenham's, cited in Cummings, *Spenser: Critical Heritage*, p. 62.

(*Works*, p. 416), transforming the opening signature "Immerito" into the closing tag "Merce non mercede," or "for reward but not for hire."[14] The Latin motto is a complex enigma, playing solicitation off against an edgy assertion of independence or integrity, but underlying these is the clear implication that between "Goe little booke" and "I aske nomore," Immerito has acquired merit. The *Calender* itself is the means through which this merit has been produced, or through which "Immerito" has been rewritten as *merce*; it is also, in this figurative system of exchange, the product offered "for reward." Thus the opening line of the epilogue functions as a dramatic gesture of closure, invoking the text as a fully realized commodity: "Loe I have made a Calender." It subtly identifies the reader with the poetic voice, collapsing the moment of reading into that of writing and so fabricating an imaginary scene in which the speaker, the reader, and posterity join in admiration of the poem they have all just "finished."

This idealized moment of presence is cast in monumental terms by the lines that follow:

Loe I have made a Calender for every yeare,
That steele in strength, and time in durance shall outweare:
And if I marked well the starres reuolution,
It shall continewe till the worlds dissolution
To teach the ruder shepheard how to feede his sheepe,
And from the falsers fraud his folded flocke to keepe.
Goe lyttle Calender, thou hast a free passeporte,
Goe but a lowly gate emongste the meaner sorte.
Dare not to match thy pype with Tityrus hys style,
Nor with the Pilgrim that the Ploughman playde a whyle:
But followe them farre off, and their high steppes adore,

---

[14] This paraphrase of the Latin motto is given by Hugh MacLean in *Edmund Spenser's Poetry*, Norton Critical Edition, 2nd ed. (New York: Norton, 1982), p. 467.

CHAPTER I

The better please, the worse despise, I aske nomore.
Merce non mercede.

The opening bravura with its classical resonance expands to cosmological and millennial-imperial dimensions as the perfect closure of calendric form yields a prophecy of perpetual timeliness. The next lines descend gracefully from the prospect of apocalypse to the homely pastoral labors of a Protestant ministry, yet the downward modulation of tone is carried by a deep associative continuity linking the figure of astrochronology, the sweep of imperial aeviternity, the note of apocalyptic expectancy, and the theme of militant wariness against Catholic machinations. Published in 1579, the *Calender* follows hard on "a sudden resurgence of the Catholic faith in England, as astonishing in its swiftness as in its scope. In the Late 1570s English Catholicism awoke, aroused from within in response to the unaccountable rhythms of popular piety and from without by a new generation of fiery young priests schooled for martyrdom in the seminaries of Douai and Rome" (Erickson, *First Elizabeth*, p. 333). The *Calender*'s publication also rounds out a decade in which Elizabeth lived under the constant threat of rebellion and assassination, having been excommunicated in 1570; it was precisely during this period of heightened vulnerability that Elizabeth began to consolidate the popular ideology that made her an icon of England's divine preservation. It was also during this period that Sidney and others in Leicester's political faction embraced a militant anti-Catholic foreign policy, fed by the mirage of a Protestant League in Europe. These concerns fused in the late 1570s with the controversial and still unresolved issue of calendar reform, for the Old Style calendar was burdened with the cumulative error of a millennium, while the Gregorian reform of 1577 represented Papal authority. The Reformed Church needed its own calendar, something the royal mathematician John Dee

42

was just then attempting to construct. Spenser, whose *Shepheardes Calender* "established a political rhetoric that was to remain popular until the Civil War" and whose April blazon of Elizabeth "was a seminal work in creating the image of the Virgin Queen,"[15] explicitly claims to have brought off a Protestant reformation of the Old Style calendar, converting astronomical precision into a figure for artistic triumph while projecting literary didacticism as an ideological defense of the Protestant imperium.

The final lines of the envoy sustain a downward modulation of tone into Chaucerian humility, but the grandeur of the opening lingers quietly in the unconstrained quality of this condescension: the poet recommends "a lowly gate emongste the meaner sorte" only after declaring the poem's "free passeporte," or authority to travel at will. Spenser defers to a native literary tradition with strong political overtones, for Chaucer and Langland had both been pressed by John Bale "into the company of religious prophets" who "attacked abuses in the Church and thus contributed in the triumph of the true faith" (Norbrook, *Poetry and Politics*, p. 41). The insular and vernacular emphases of this tradition stand out partly through the implied contrast with Chaucer's *Troilus* envoy, which Spenser echoes recognizably in the line "followe them farre off, and their high steppes adore" (compare "kis the steppes, where as thow seest pace"): where Chaucer does reverence to Greek and Latin classics, Spenser adores Chaucer and Langland. In a complex rhetorical maneuver, he designates Chaucer as an elect forebear by declining to "match . . . hys style," but does so in verses that match the lowly gait of "Tityrus hys style" to perfection. A fifteenth-century Chaucerian like Hoccleve joins reverence for "My mayster Chaucer, flour of eloquence" with dismay "that thou thyn excellent prudence / In thy bed mortal

---

[15] Norbrook, *Poetry and Politics*, pp. 89, 94 (hereafter cited parenthetically).

43

mightyst noght byquethe" (Spearing, "Renaissance Chaucer,"
p. 21); but Spenser lays paradoxical claim to the bequest, re-
viving Chaucer's distinctive manner most strikingly in the
moment of his deference to Chaucer. The envoy concludes on
a dignified note, an assertion of sovereign indifference: "The
better please, the worse despise, I aske nomore." Then follows
the tag-phrase *Merce non mercede*, which asks for more, pre-
sumably from "the better." In doing so it advertises the textual
production of value by transforming the poet's ornament from
"Immerito" to *merce*.

THE ERASURE OF JOHN SKELTON, LAUREATE

Another, more celebrated ornament of poetic status fash-
ioned by the *Calender* is the name "Colin Clout," which be-
came Spenser's laureate signature. In his first gloss to *The Shep-
heardes Calender*, E. K. tells us the name was "not greatly vsed,
and yet haue I sene a Poesie of M. Skeltons vnder that title.
But indeede the word Colin is Frenche, and vsed of the French
Poete Marot (if he be worthy of the name of a Poete) in a
certein Aeglogue" (*Works*, p. 422). He goes on to explain that
Spenser "secretly shadoweth himself" under this name after
the example of Virgil, who called himself "Tityrus," adding
that the poet thought Colin "much fitter, then such Latine
names, for the great vnlikelihood of the language." This ex-
planation explains very little, of course, since a French name
"not greatly vsed" hardly seems to answer the requirements of
verisimilitude, while "Tityrus" itself occurs in the very next
eclogue—where it is glossed by E. K. as a reference not to
Virgil but to Chaucer, "that good old man" who kept his sheep
"on the hils of Kent" (*Works*, pp. 424–26).[16] Here as else-

---

[16] E. K. has already explained in the Epistle to Harvey that Colin refers
to Chaucer as "Tityrus the God of shepheards, comparing hym to the wor-
thines of the Roman Tityrus Virgile" (*Works*, p. 416). In the same passage

where in his commentary, it is hard to tell how much of E. K.'s obtuseness is genuine and how much of it may be a poker-faced parody of the glossarial mode, intended less to explain the wandering of names than to draw us into their maze. Did he know that " 'Collyn' derives from Latin *colonus* 'farmer' and was used as early as the reign of Edward II to indicate a person of humble birth"? "Cloute," meaning rag or patch, reemphasizes the notion.[17]

The diffidence with which E. K. recollects "a Poesie of M. Skeltons" does not attach much import to the reference, and critical comment has generally taken the hint. Fish remarked in 1965 that Spenser "takes more than his nom de plume from Skelton," but no extended consideration of what Spenser took has been attempted; from Nelson's comment in 1939 that "Spenser's use of the name Colin Clout . . . suggests the extent to which Skelton's poem had become associated with matters of religious controversy" to Norbrook's echo in 1984 ("Spenser's poetic persona, Colin Clout, carries similar associations with the poetry of social and religious protest"), there is little sense of Skelton as a significant literary precedent for the *Calender*.[18]

---

he coins the phrase "this our new Poete" in apposition to a phrase designating Chaucer as "that good old Poete."

[17] Scattergood, *Skelton: English Poems*, p. 466, citing R. S. Kinsman, "Skelton's 'Colyn Cloute': The Mask of 'Vox Populi,' " in *Essays Critical and Historical Dedicated to Lily B. Campbell*, Univ. of California Publications, English Studies: 1 (Berkeley: Univ. of California Press, 1950), pp. 17–23. E. K. may tacitly acknowledge the etymology when he remarks in the Epistle that Spenser chose "Colin" for "the baseness of the name" (*Works*, p. 418).

[18] Stanley Eugene Fish, *John Skelton's Poetry* (New Haven: Yale Univ. Press, 1965), p. 203; William Nelson, *John Skelton, Laureate* (New York: Columbia Univ. Press, 1939; reprint, New York. Russel and Russel, 1964), p. 233; Norbrook, *Poetry and Politics*, p. 59. On Skelton's notion of the "master poet," see Robin Skelton, "The Master Poet: John Skelton as Conscious Craftsman," *Mosaic* 6 (1973): 67–92; for the view that his work reflects Burgundian influences, see Gordon Kipling, "John Skelton and Burgundian Letters," in *Ten Studies in Anglo-Dutch Relations*, ed. Jan Van Dor-

And yet it was during the 1570s that Skelton's posthumous reputation reached its high point. In 1574 Richard Robinson reported sighting Skelton on Mount Helicon in the company of Homer, Virgil, Ovid, Chaucer, Lydgate, Wager, Heywood, and Barnaby Googe, while in 1579 an anonymous poet returned from Cupid's camp with news of Skelton's presence there in company with Homer, Virgil, Ovid, Hesiod, Euripides, Chaucer, and Gower.[19] Not until *after* the early works of Sidney and Spenser had set wholly new standards for English versification do we find a growing condescension toward the roughness of both style and tone in Skelton's satire; thus Puttenham, whose *Arte of English Poesie* (1589) advances a courtly and aristocratic aesthetic, will denounce Skelton as a "rude rayling rimer" fit for the company of "tavern minstrels" and guilty of "vsurping the name of a Poet Laureat" (Edwards, *Skelton: Critical Heritage*, pp. 61–62). Whether Spenser himself would have included Skelton in Cuddie's strictures against rolling "rymes of rybaudrye" ("October," line 76) is uncertain; Puttenham's view reflects a conservatism at odds with the "poetry of religious and social protest" that Spenser tacitly aligns himself with in the *Calender*. The poet who was soon to write "Mother Hubberds Tale" may well have found in Skelton's satiric attacks on Wolsey a precedent for his own defense of Grindal and assault on Burghley, while in Skelton's public laureateship and appointment as tutor to Henry VIII he may also have seen precedent for his own ambitions at court.

Spenser probably read Skelton in the edition of 1568 published by Thomas Marshe. One way of assessing the earlier

---

sten (London: for the Sir Thomas Browne Institute, 1974), pp. 1–29. A fuller consideration of Spenser's relations to his immediate predecessors is needed.

[19] Anthony S. G. Edwards ed., *Skelton: The Critical Heritage* (London: Routledge, 1981), p. 10 (hereafter cited parenthetically as Edwards, *Skelton: Critical Heritage*).

poet's significance for him would be to reexamine this edition with an eye to what might have interested the New Poet of 1579. Here he would have found Skelton referring to himself not only in a single poem as Colin Clout, but throughout the volume as "Skelton laureate" and "Poeta Skelton," implicitly asserting the idea of a laureate poetic career. The volume begins with "The Crowne of Laurell"— written near the end of Skelton's career—and this in itself is significant, for it suggests the extent to which Skelton was remembered as England's laureate, even though his laureation was little more than an academic ceremony that had since fallen out of use. Since the individual pieces are not chronologically arranged, the volume presents no clear picture of the poet's career, yet a good deal might be inferred from the versified bibliography Skelton gives at the end of "The Crowne of Laurell" (lines 1170 ff.). This passage mentions "of Soveraynte a noble pamphlet" (line 1191) and a "Tratyse of the Triumphis of the Rede Rose" (line 1223); it summarizes the morality interlude *Magnyfycence* (lines 1192–97), and advertises Skelton's place as "creauncer" (tutor) to the future Henry VIII, then Duke of York, for whom he devised a treatise "callid *Speculum Principis*" (lines 1226–32). The same passage dismisses several of the satires as "trifels" (line 1235).

In the same poem Spenser would have seen an expanded version of the conceit that informs tributes like Richard Robinson's: a visionary procession of laureates beginning with Apollo himself, who concludes a long lament for Daphne with the lines,

> But sith I have lost now that I entended,
> And may not atteyne it by no medyacyon,
> Yet, in remembraunce of Daphnes transformacyon,
> All famous poetis ensuynge after me
> Shall were a garlande of the laurell tre.   (lines 318–22)

There follows an international procession of laureates, including (among others) Quintillian, Theocritus, Hesiod, Homer, Cicero, Ovid, Lucan, Statius, Virgil, Juvenal, Livy, Ennius, Aulus Gellius, Horace, Terence, Plautus, Seneca, Boethius, Boccaccio, Macrobius, Plutarch, Petrarch, and Propertius, refreshing themselves at every seventh line with Bacchus's "ruddy flotis" (drops or flowings). The list concludes with Gower, Chaucer, and Lydgate, who are richly attired but "wantid . . . the laurell" (line 397). These three approach Skelton and invite him into their "collage above the sterry sky" (line 403) in a scene clearly modeled on Dante's encounter in the *Inferno* with Homer, Horace, Ovid, and Lucan, "la bella scola / di quel segnor de l'altissimo canto" (IV.94–95). Lydgate closes by declaring Skelton worthy "by all our holl assent" to be "Avaunced by Pallas to laurell preferment" (lines 433–34). The significance this passage would doubtless have had for Spenser is stressed in the prefatory verses Thomas Churchyard contributed to the 1568 edition: "You see howe forrayn realms / Aduance their Poets all; / And ours are drowned in the dust, / Or flong against the wall" (Edwards, *Skelton: Critical Heritage*, p. 57). In the lines that follow, Churchyard plays out a weaker version of the strategy Skelton himself employs in the laureate procession, listing the poets of foreign realms who "Wan prayse and fame, and honor had, / Eche one in their degree," and going on to a roll call of underrated English masters: Piers Plowman, Chaucer, Surrey, Vaux, Phaer, Edwards, and of course Skelton. Richard Robinson and the anonymous poet of Cupid's camp make the third and fourth in this sequence of imitations, following Skelton and Churchyard in their attempts to forge an English literary history.

Spenser would have seen himself foreshadowed in such passages. The *Calender* embodies the same pretensions and the same sense of literary history in more complex and indirect ways, and it initiates a comparable chain of reiterations as writers like Nashe and William Webbe follow the lead of E. K., working out the poem's implicit self-images in the simplified medium of critical prose (Cummings, *Spenser: Critical Heritage*, pp. 56–60). There is a certain irony in this situation, since the very program of secularization for which Skelton so bitterly attacked Wolsey has come full circle in the emergent empire's need to advance its own poets above those of foreign realms: "And should the challenge of deepe conceit, be intruded by any forreiner, to bring our own english wits, to the tutchstone of Arte, I would preferre, diuine Master Spencer, the miracle of wit to bandie line for line for my life, in the honor of England, against Spaine, France, Italie, and all the worlde" (Cummings, p. 60). Thomas Nashe published these words in the same year Puttenham's treatise appeared with its decisive rejection of Skelton's claim to importance, and the coincidence suggests just how successful Spenser was in assuming the role Skelton tried to play. It also suggests a possible reason for F. K.'s diffidence in mentioning the one true laureate among Tudor poets, for if Immerito adoringly follows the "high steppes" of Chaucer and Piers Plowman from "farre off," he treads rather more closely on Skelton's heels. By the end of his career, however, Spenser can ask, "Who knowes not Colin Clout?" without a moment's concern that anyone will think this time of "a Poesie of M. Skeltons vnder that title." Over the years he has fashioned, or perhaps stolen, his own cosmic ornament by teaching a generation of readers *not to know* who wrote

> And yf ye stande in doute
> Who brought this ryme aboute,
> My name is Collyn Cloute.

FIGURING HIERARCHY

The dedicatory sonnets to the 1590 *Faerie Queene* demonstrate the interdependence of the various "identities" the poet seeks to fashion in the course of framing England's imperial majesty. His portrait of Elizabeth is set within an ornamental border depicting a pageant of the body politic, a procession of the essentially "allegorical" personae with which the members of her courtly hierarchy are invested. The queen and her court are specular images of each other, for Elizabeth is constituted *as* queen by the hierarchy that explicates her sovereignty just as surely as the hierarchy itself is constituted by its sovereign point of reference. Yet if Elizabeth is in one sense the radiant center that fixes all else in place, there is another sense in which the poet as "the author of their praise" (To Northumberland, line 10) is her effaced or repressed counterpart, a center for the rhetorical production of sovereignty. In the border of Spenser's allegorical portrait we can therefore read a specular relation between the poem, which internalizes the social hierarchy in its formal organization, and the social order, which appropriates the formal organization of allegory in its display of power relations. The poet's labor in mirroring hierarchy has value precisely *because* this order, like any rhetorical construction, is based on mutually constitutive relations: it is the constructive force of his rhetoric—its power to give life to what "els would soone haue dide" (To Northumberland, line 11)— that he offers in exchange for "countenaunce," the mask of Poet in the social allegory of the court.

The collection of dedicatory sonnets attached to most copies of the 1590 *Faerie Queene* may be thought only marginally "literary." Spenser criticism has certainly ignored them, as though they occupied not just the threshold of Spenser's text but the boundary between literature and the extraliterary realm of court politics and patronage. Yet their threshold status means that these sonnets mediate the poem's relation to the social order around it. In a recent essay Carol Stillman shows in detail how the dedicatory sonnets "are arranged in exact accordance with the heraldic rules for precedence."[20] Spenser

[20] Carol Stillman, "Politics, Precedence, and the Order of the Dedicatory

seems to have intended them as a miniature sequence: address-
ing Hunsdon, Lord High Chamberlain to her Majesty, he
writes,

> Renowmed Lord, that for your worthinesse
> And noble deeds haue your deserued place,
> High in the fauour of that Emperesse,
> The worlds sole glory and her sexes grace,
> Here eke of right haue you a worthie place,
> Both for your nearnes to that Faerie Queene,
> And for your owne high merit. . . .   (lines 1–7)

Hunsdon's noble deeds in quelling the Northern rebellion
have earned him a "deserued place" in Elizabeth's favor—that
of Lord High Chamberlain—and his "place" in the sequence
of dedicatory sonnets reflects the status of his office with pre-
cision. The repeated rhyme word stresses this consonance of
decorums whereby the warrior preserves his sovereign, the
sovereign rewards her warrior with high office, and the poet
rewards both together by assigning them places "of right" in
"the record of enduring memory" (lines 5, 12). What these
lines particularly stress about the organization of the sequence
as a whole is its absent point of reference, for the basis of prec-
edence is "nearnes to that Faerie Queene."[21] Like *The Faerie
Queene* itself, then, the dedicatory sonnets refer to the absent
body of the monarch; they manifest what may be called a struc-
ture of Gloriana's traces. Their "literary" mode of doing so is
well illustrated by this play on notions of place and placement:
the rules of precedence say nothing about where Spenser
should allude to the structure of the sequence, but as so often

Sonnets in *The Faerie Queene*," *SpStud* 5 (1985): 143–48. (I quote from the
abstract on p. ix of this volume.) Predictably, Stillman's discovery comes as
part of the solution to an editorial problem concerning the accidental omis-
sion of seven sonnets from some copies of the 1590 edition, and not from
any critical interest in the sonnets themselves.

[21] In context this phrase also refers to the fact that Hunsdon was the
queen's cousin.

in his poetry we find the self-conscious allusion to placement placed "in the middest," in the ninth sonnet out of seventeen.

In the eighth sonnet Spenser refers to the sequence as "this same Pageaunt" (line 6). Elsewhere he uses the word "pageaunt" for emblematic processions like those in the House of Pride and Busirane's castle, modeled on ceremonies of court life, and for whole books of the poem—so perhaps it should not be surprising to find the dedicatory sonnet sequence taking shape in the same way, as a ceremonial procession in profile, depthless but heavily ornamented. The extent of this analogy may be suggested by analyzing the sequence in terms of Fletcher's theory of allegory. Specifically, the dedicatory sonnets illustrate (1) the authoritarian basis of allegory (pp. 22–23 and 135–40); (2) the function of ornaments, or *kosmoi*, as insignia of hierarchical status, cited earlier; (3) the tendency of allegory to constrict or compartmentalize meaning (pp. 28–33); (4) the corporate protagonist (pp. 35–38); (5) the taboo of the ruler (p. 273); and (6) the emotive nature of ornament (pp. 117–20).

The authoritarian basis of allegory is implicit in its reliance on hierarchies. By the same token the heraldic rules of precedence, as a complex and historically specific instance of such hierarchies, tend to structure life itself "allegorically." The elaborate formulas of address that make the titles of the dedicatory sonnets too long for convenient reference (e.g., "To the right honourable the Lo. Ch. Howard, Lo. high Admiral of England, knight of the noble order of the Garter, and one of her Maiesties priuie Counsel. &c.") are pure instances of *kosmoi*, or "ornaments," in Fletcher's sense: they specify status, and in doing so elaborate the implicit image of hierarchical totality within which stations of rank are distributed. Other, less explicit ornaments of status also mark the diction of the sonnets at various points. For instance, the opening phrase of the very first sonnet ("Those prudent heads") implies a cryptic mimesis of the political body by its conspicuous placement at the "head" of the sequence.

Fletcher observes that the systematic character of allegory tends to preserve the distinctness of its individual agents and so to restrict or compartmentalize the significance of each. He also observes that "this personifying process has a reverse type, in which the poet treats real people in a formulaic way so that they become walking Ideas" (p. 28). Spenser's addresses to his dedicatees are formulaic in this sense as well, casting each in the generic "type" most appropriate to his or her status and interests. The catalogue of types includes the magistrate, the warrior, the noble lord, the aristocratic patron, the epic poet, the love poet, and the virtuous and beautiful lady. Individuation may be achieved by inflecting the type slightly or by crossing types, but several of the sonnets appear to be almost pure apostrophes to the type itself. The first two, addressed to Hatton and Burghley, are nearly indistinguishable appeals to "the magistrate" for leniency. Northumberland receives a paradigmatic address to the nobility:

> The sacred Muses haue made alwaies clame
> To be the Nourses of nobility,
> And Registres of euerlasting fame,
> To all that armes professe and cheualry.
> Then by like right the noble Progeny,
> Which them succeed in fame and worth, are tyde
> T'embrace the seruice of sweete Poetry,
> By whose endeuours they are glorifide,
> And eke from all, of whom it is enuide,
> To patronize the authour of their praise,
> Which giues them life, that els would soone haue dide,
> And crownes their ashes with immortall baies.
> To thee therefore right noble Lord I send
> This present of my paines, it to defend.

The right noble lord himself is not mentioned until the couplet, where he is belatedly recruited to meet the obligations of his type. Walsingham receives a comparably generic address to the aristocratic patron, or Mycenas, while the "Precedent of

all that armes ensue" finds embodiment in Sir John Norris
(line 7). The final sonnet, "To all the gratious and beautifull
Ladies in the Court," registers their lower status partly in the
anonymity of its collective address, but it does so by manifest-
ing a generic mode that has operated implicitly throughout the
sequence.

The same sonnet offers an aesthetic analogue to the body
politic:

> The Chian Peincter, when he was requirde
> To pourtraict Venus in her perfect hew,
> To make his worke more absolute, desird
> Of all the fairest Maides to haue the vew.   (lines 1–4)

The anecdote to which Spenser here alludes was a common-
place of Renaissance mimetic theory. Analogies between Venus
and the personified state were unavoidable in Elizabeth's court,
but as Panofsky notes there were also specific precedents for
the comparison between painting an ideal visual image and de-
scribing an ideal moral one:

> In a most remarkable instance even the "antiartistic" Plato
> compared his paragon for the perfect state, an adequate ex-
> ample of which can never actually exist, to the procedure of
> a painter who in his work presents a paradigm of the most
> beautiful human being; and such a painter, Plato asserts,
> must be considered an excellent artist, not although, but
> precisely because he could not prove the empirical existence
> of so perfect a creature. Aristotle formulated this basic view
> in his characteristically lapidary manner: "Great men are
> distinguished from ordinary men in the same way as beau-
> tiful people from plain ones, or as an artfully painted object
> from a real one, namely, in that that which is dispersed has
> been gathered into one."[22]

[22] Erwin Panofsky, *Idea: A Concept in Art Theory*, trans. Joseph J. S.
Peake (Columbia: Univ. of South Carolina Press, 1968), p. 15. I have
slightly altered the phrasing of the translation.

Fletcher adapts this notion to the theory of allegory when he considers the relatively more complex protagonists of a major work such as *The Faerie Queene* to be assembled like mosaics out of discrete conceptual counters. "Is not the nature of such heroes," he asks, "comparable to the nature of a whole poem like 'The Phoenix and the Turtle,' where the whole was a complex system of interrelated terms, each of which was circumscribed?" (p. 35). He suggests that such "conceptual heroes" tend to generate secondary personalities or subcharacters which represent aspects of themselves. This has become a familiar approach to the protagonists of *The Faerie Queene*, especially Arthur and Gloriana, but it also describes a social and political structure in which the various officers of the government derive their authority from, and function as specialized extensions of, the crown, where the body politic and its sovereignty are concentrated. In this sense the structure of Gloriana's traces is at once political and literary.

Elizabeth's two bodies may both be absent from this structure, yet insofar as the sequence is ordered according to the principle of "nearnes to that Faerie Queene" and ornamented with signatures of the totality she incarnates, her political body is reflected everywhere within it. Much the same thing has been said of the poem itself. In a discussion of thematic ambivalence that powerfully evokes the ideological function of aesthetic form in *The Faerie Queene*, Fletcher associates this feature of the poem's design with the Freudian notion of taboo:

> Social ambivalence is not always easy to show in Spenser . . . because his poem is a largely idealized defense of the Establishment. More readily apparent are the deeper kinds of psychological conflict we have already seen. These might be subsumed under the heading of taboo. . . . Of the three kinds of taboo which Freud treated in *Totem and Taboo*—of enemies, of rulers, of the dead—all can be illustrated by Spenser's poem. Most marked of all is the taboo of the

ruler: Gloriana is the unapproachable yet infinitely desirable object of courtly desire. She is at once the avenging Britomart, the melting Amoret, the chaste, athletic Belphoebe, the transparently beautiful Florimell, the just Mercilla, the truthful Una. . . . The taboo on Gloriana holds the poem together, even unfinished, like a retreating glow of light around the deity, lambent in the distance, deadly when we approach it. While the taboo keeps the courtier from his actual Queen, and the reader from the final vision of the fictive Queen, it ineluctably draws both courtier and reader into her embrace. (p. 272)

Fletcher has earlier discussed the emotive charge carried by insignia of rank, which have, he says, "more than a 'merely' decorative or 'merely' hierarchical function. Nothing could be more likely to arouse intense emotional response than the status symbol" (pp. 117–18). Hierarchical insignia in a monarchy carry a specific emotive charge, then, because they distribute the ambivalent charisma of the royal taboo, just as the bearers of such insignia distribute the duties, powers, and prerogatives of the crown.

This distribution of emotional ambivalence is easiest to observe at the highest and lowest ends of the sociopolitical scale. Thus Spenser's address to the ladies of the court revolves its elaborate compliment from Elizabeth to her "faire Dames" with a patronizing facility that turns mildly flirtatious in the couplet:

Much more me needs to draw the semblant trew,
Of beauties Queene, the worlds sole wonderment,
To sharpe my sence with sundry beauties vew,
And steale from each some part of ornament.
If all the world to seeke I ouerwent,
A fairer crew yet no where could I see,
Then that braue court doth to mine eie present,
That the worlds pride seemes gathered there to bee.

56

Of each a part I stole by cunning thefte:
Forgiue it me faire Dames, sith lesse ye haue not lefte.
(To the Ladies, lines 5–14)

The cosmic and cosmetic meanings of "ornament" are fused in
the phrase "some part of ornament." Having recomposed the
scattered ornaments of feminine beauty into the cosmic body
whose "parts" they are, the poet will address that awful pres-
ence in a rhetoric of abject adoration, but it is clear from the
tone of these lines that such beauty offers no real terror in its
dispersal, where it may only cunningly be said to "tyranyse"
(To Lady Carey, line 9).

By contrast the opening sonnets to "Those prudent heads"
Hatton and Burghley are marked by an anxiety unmatched in
the verses that follow. The reason may have less to do with
personal or factional animosity toward either than with their
"nearnes to that Faerie Queene." Here alone Spenser reverts
to the pose Richard Helgerson has identified with literary am-
ateurism, that of the prodigal poet whose work is not a spur
and "euerlasting monument" to virtue and valorous deeds
(compare To Howard, line 12) but "ydle rymes" presented
"vnfitly," "the labor of lost time, and wit vnstayd" (To Hatton,
line 13; To Burghley, lines 6–7).[23] In *The Shepheardes Calen-
der* Spenser had portrayed this figure in Colin Clout, who
served at once to advertise the author's skill in making and to
draw off onto himself (almost like a lightning rod) the negative
values of passion, immaturity, and self-indulgent excess asso-
ciated with the cultural stereotype of the prodigal. Eleven years
later, in 1590, the type of the wayward boy is revived in the
phrasing of the sonnets to Hatton and Burghley, as though the

---

[23] Helgerson, *Self-Crowned Laureates*, pp. 21–34, 55–67. See also his
The Elizabethan Prodigals (Berkeley: Univ. of California Press, 1976). I
differ somewhat from Helgerson's view of Colin Clout: see David L.
Miller, "Authorship, Anonymity, and *The Shepheardes Calender*," *MLQ* 40
(1979): 233–36.

figure of the sage and sober governor had summoned this apparition as its dialectical complement. Perhaps it has: in analyzing the affirmation of authority symbols, Kenneth Burke suggests, as we have seen, that an approach to the epiphany of authority at the summit of the social hierarchy will be marked by incest awe and the threat of castration—effects of the "taboo of the ruler." From this point of view Spenser's reversion to an adolescent self-image associated with an early phase of his own career would appear as an instance of symbolic regression, a defensive way of "assuming castration" through self-abasement.

The sequence of dedicatory sonnets thus fixes a complex image of social and political hierarchy, ranking the "members" of a political body each in its prescribed station and designating each according to its corporate function. Two crucial figures, however, do not appear within this "pageant": that of the poet and that of the queen. In one sense Elizabeth has already taken her place at the "head" of the procession, on the title page and in the formal dedication that follows, set on its own page entirely in capitals and shaped in an ornamental pattern. In another sense Elizabeth *is* the procession, or rather the procession, as an exposition of the hierarchy she embodies, offers an abstract "pourtraict" (etymologically a "drawing out") of the royal body politic, "her imperiall Maiestie to frame." The poet himself, then, is the only persona whose relation to the hierarchy remains strategically indeterminate.

The poet's lack of a prescribed "place" in this pageant is both an opportunity and a source of anxiety. The anxiety, most pronounced in Spenser's addresses to Hatton and Burghley, can also be traced in economic figures of negotiation and indebtedness. Such rhetoric is a generic feature of dedicatory prose and verse, and at times Spenser can play on the conventions with a witty self-consciousness. For example, a common strategy is for the poet to dispraise the text he is dedicating as far from adequate recompense for the favors he has received, offered merely as a pledge of his good will and earnest of future payment. The sonnet to Lady Carey adopts a version of this strategy, affirming that only "a golden quill, / And siluer leaues" (lines 10–11) could adequately represent her, and offering itself as no more than a

> . . . humble present of good will:
> Which whenas timely meanes it purchase may,
> In ampler wise it selfe will forth display.   (lines 12–14)

Timely means were not long in coming, for Spenser dedicates "Muiopotmos" to Lady Carey within the year.[24] Dispraising the poem yet again as inadequate payment—"for so excellent fauours as I haue received at your sweet handes, to offer these fewe leaues as in recompence, should be as to offer flowers to the Gods for their diuine benefits"—Spenser now resorts to a principle of common law: "Therefore I haue determined to giue my selfe wholly to you, as quite abandoned from my selfe, and absolutely vowed to your seruices: which in all right is euer held for full recompence of debt or damage to haue the person yeelded. My person I wot wel how little worth it is. But the faithfull minde and humble zeale which I beare unto your La: may perhaps be of more price. . ." (*Works*, p. 516).[25]

---

[24] *Complaints* was published in 1591, but "Muiopotmos" bears a separate title page dated 1590 (*Works*, p. 515).

[25] Spenser's wit in this passage skirts the grim realities of imprisonment for debt, enforced by a common law writ known as *capias ad satisfaciendum*. Sir William Blackstone summarizes the law in book 3 of his *Commentaries on the Laws of England*: "Executions in actions where money only is to be recovered, as a debt or damages (and not any specific chattel) are of five sorts," the first being "against the body of the defendant" (3: 414; New York: W. E. Dean, 2:320). Execution against the person of the debtor was a relatively late (and relatively severe) development in the history of common law. In the sixteenth century, imprisoned debtors were responsible for feeding and sustaining themselves; when they were unable to do so, the law (as stated with brutal candor by Plowden) gave them permission to die by the grace of God. See A.W.B. Simpson, *A History of the Common Law of Contract: The*

Spenser's tone of genteel banter may reflect touches of personal affection, but it also reflects a lack of "serious" power and status in Spenser's feminine addressee. The sonnet to the ladies of the court is pitched in a similar tone for much the same reason. It turns most playful in closing accounts on the economic metaphor, an indication of how little is really at stake in the transaction: "Of each a part I stole by cunning thefte: / Forgiue it me faire Dames, sith lesse ye haue not lefte." The anatomical pun in "cunning" rather archly casts the female pudendum as an absent "part" that ironically cannot be "less."

Each of the dedicatory sonnets enacts some figure of transaction, and the sequence as a whole illustrates Burke's notion of culture as a public "symbol exchange." This is true whether the sonnet works out a specifically personal indebtedness, like that to Lord Grey, or sets forth in generic terms the symbolic economy relating poets to noblemen and military heroes. Precisely because of their generic cast, the sonnets to Northumberland, Walsingham, and Norris offer schematic formulations of the exchange system. Northumberland is told that the Muses have traditionally both nursed and "glorifide" the aristocracy, gifts tantamount to secular immortality for those "that els would soone haue dide," and is asked in return to "defend" the poet's gift; Walsingham, "the great Mecenas of this age," is offered "bigger tunes to sound your liuing prayse" in return for "protection" of "this lowly Muse"; and Norris, one of the "Martiall crew" who give "honourable prize / To the sweet Muse," is asked to "Loue him, that hath eternized your name." From sonnet to sonnet throughout the sequence, gifts and favors circulate in an intricate dance of the courtly graces.

The mixed sense of opportunity attended by anxiety that results from the poet's indefinite placement in the courtly hierarchy is clearly reflected in these transactions, which allow us

---

Rise of the Action of Assumpsit (Oxford: Clarendon, 1975), pp. 587–95, for a discussion of the law, including citations from Blackstone and Plowden.

to trace his speculative investments in the symbolic economy. What he trades for is "countenaunce" (To Oxford, line 3; To Essex, line 13), a term whose several senses are all relevant: Spenser wants sanction, he wants a place of honor at court, and he wants, above all, a *face*, a public identity as Elizabeth's laureate. The scope of these ambitions generates anxiety about the envy they will inevitably arouse among competitors for patronage, so Spenser's most often repeated request is for protection against backbiting. In the 1591 dedication to *Colin Clouts come home againe*, Spenser asks Ralegh, "with your good countenance protect [the poem] against the malice of euill mouthes, which are alwaies wide open to carpe at and misconstrue my simple meaning" (*Works*, p. 536). The dedicatory sonnets to the 1590 *Faerie Queene* likewise ask repeatedly "to bee / Defended from foule Enuies poisnous bit" (To Oxford), to be patronized "from all, of whom it is enuide" (To Northumberland), to be maintained "Against vile Zoilus backbitings vaine" (To Buckhurst), and to be granted "protection of her [the Muse's] feebleness" (To Walsingham).

"Vile Zoilus" presents a mortal threat to the poet because their strategies are so similar: envy works through verbal exchanges to fashion a value-laden image of its object, and in doing so seeks indirectly to enhance the status of its own "author." Spenser and Zoilus share the same audience, too, which means finally that the source of protection and the source of danger are also the same: royal power. Hence the ambivalence, the loss of confidence, that marks Spenser's addresses to Hatton and Burghley: instead of offering them life itself he offers mere recreation, and instead of asking for protection he asks merely to be tolerated. The recreative apology Spenser offers in these sonnets mirrors the playfulness of his address to the ladies at the bottom of the courtly hierarchy: the patronizing intimacy with which he indulges them is exactly what he himself craves from "The rugged brow of carefull Policy." In both instances the emphasis on play marks a regression from the didactic and memorial services stressed in his negotiations with the intermediate figures, men who are neither powerless nor too powerful.

SPENSER'S "GNAT"

One text that shows the interplay between this regressive tendency and the ideal reciprocity of the poet's mature transactions with his patron is "Virgils Gnat," published in the 1591 *Complaints* volume but "Long since dedicated To the most noble and excellent Lord, the Earle of Leicester, late deceased" (*Works*, p. 486). The poem translates a piece of psuedo-Virgilian juvenilia known as the *Culex*, which begins with an informal address by the immature Virgil to his imperial patron Caesar. In this address Virgil offers the poem as an interlude of no real consequence in his poetic career, but the progression to epic is repeatedly invoked as the young poet characterizes his present style, subject, and Muse in contrast with their epic counterparts. He asks his imperial patron to "come sliding soft, / And favor my beginnings graciously" *because* they are not yet epic (lines 37–39), implying that well-favored beginnings are a prerequisite to distinguished ends, and he promises worthier verse "when as season more secure / Shall bring forth fruit" (lines 9–10), discreetly assuming his imperial auditor as the source of security. In a poem dedicated to his patron such hints already suggest Spenser's own Virgilian ambitions, for they closely echo the language of the dedicatory sonnets:

> So Maro oft did Caesars cares allay.
> So you great Lord, that with your counsell sway
> The burdeine of this kingdom mightily,
> With like delightes sometimes may eke delay,

The rugged brow of carefull Policy:
And to these ydle rymes lend litle space. . . .
(To Hatton, lines 8–13)

But when my Muse, whose fethers nothing flitt
Doe yet but flagg, and lowly learne to fly
With bolder wing shall dare alofte. . . .
Then shall it make more famous memory
Of thine Heroicke parts. . . .
Till then vouchsafe thy noble countenaunce,
To these first labours needed furtheraunce.
(To Essex, lines 7–14)

Most Noble Lord the pillor of my life
And Patrone of my Muses pupillage,
Through whose large bountie poured on me rife,
In the first season of my feeble age,
I now doe liue. . . .   (To Lord Grey, lines 1–5)

To this list should be added the sonnet to Walsingham ("That Mantuane Poetes incompared spirit"), which sets forth the Virgilian precedent for Spenser's laureate ambitions in terms that stress the crucial role of Mycenas.

When Spenser refers to "these ydle rymes" or "these first labours" in addressing Hatton and Essex, he is lapsing into a juvenile rhetoric just as he seeks to negotiate the passage to epic maturity. "Virgils Gnat" similarly sets the mature poet's quest for public "countenaunce" against a regressive fantasy of retirement into a playful and protective intimacy, a nurturing indulgence that is almost maternal. It does this by way of the dedicatory sonnet to Leicester, which laments the insecurity of Spenser's poetic "season"; the presentation of Virgil's happy intimacy with Augustus then becomes just as loaded as the story of the gnat and the inadvertent shepherd.

The dedicatory sonnet thus reframes the poem itself to create an allegory where there was none:

> Wrong'd, yet not daring to expresse my paine,
> To you (great Lord) the causer of my care,
> In clowdie teares my case I thus complaine
> Vnto your selfe, that onely priuie are.   (lines 1–4)

The allegory behind these "clowdie teares" is a private one: Leicester alone is "privie," and despite Greenlaw's hypothesis relating the poem to "Mother Hubberds Tale,"[26] the reader who tries to crack Spenser's code is himself put in the position of Mother Hubberd's priest:

> . . . he vew'd it nere,
> As if therein some text he studying were,
> But little els (God wote) could thereof skill:
> For reade he could not. . . .   (lines 379–82)

By the time "Virgils Gnat" appeared in *Complaints*, however, Leicester had been dead for three years. The act of publication, then, layers a second allegory over the first. Turning from Leicester to the public audience for whom this second allegory is intended, Spenser asks his readers specifically *not* to worry the biographical background:

> But if that any Oedipus unware
> Shall chaunce, through power of some diuining spright,
> To read the secrete of this riddle rare,
> And know the purporte of my euill plight,
>   Let him rest pleased with his owne insight,
> Ne further seeke to glose upon the text:
> For griefe enough it is to grieued wight
> To feele his fault, and not be further vext.
>   But what so by my selfe may not be showen,
> May by this Gnatts complaint be easily knowen.
>
>   (lines 5–14)

[26] Edwin Greenlaw, *Studies in Spenser's Historical Allegory* (1932; reprint New York: Octagon, 1967), pp. 115–32.

As publication alters the intentional act of the poet, so the act of interpretation is here placed in a social context. The poet is at pains to avoid public discussion of his "fault," which for some reason (it would be tactless to insist on knowing why) "may not be showen" except by appropriating "this Gnatts complaint." The reader who ignores this plea for discretion will only vex the author, making a delicate situation worse and so earning the censure Thomas Nashe brought against Gabriel Harvey: "Who publickely accusde or of late brought *Mother Hubbard* into question, that thou shouldst by rehearsall rekindle against him the sparkes of displeasure that were quenched?"[27] Partly because Nashe thought Spenser "further vext" by public discussion of "Mother Hubberds Tale," the poem is often identified with the "fault" allegorized in "Virgils Gnat," but Nashe's remarks "glose upon the text" in the only really appropriate way when they stress the perils of unguarded public utterance.

In this sense the sonnet to Leicester inverts Spenser's usual tendency to draw the reader toward membership in an ideal commonwealth, instead transforming Virgil's easy familiarity with Augustus into an elaborate secrecy. Like the Sphynx on the road to Thebes, Spenser here shuts us out with a "riddle rare," constituting an ironic "discursive community" of which he is himself the only living member. Of course the most thorough exclusion would have been to deny potential Oedipuses any access to the text at all: published, it flaunts the act of concealment as a sign of what Terpsichore, in "Teares of the Muses," calls "discountenaunce" (line 340). By adjusting the relationship with Leicester so publicly, Spenser calls attention to its public end, the poet's entry into civil conversation; his

[27] *The Works of Edmund Spenser: A Variorum Edition*, ed. Charles Grosvenor Osgood and Henry Gibbons Lotspeich (Baltimore: Johns Hopkins Univ. Press, 1947), 7, pt. 2: 580–81.

impeded speech dramatizes the patron's role in sponsoring poetic voice.

Most of "Virgils Gnat" is taken up with the title character's complaint to the shepherd who swatted him, which under the pressure of Spenser's imposed allegory becomes a fable of patronage. A lengthy description of the classical underworld as a region of completed destinies leads to a contrast with the gnat's own posthumous "career": unburied, he has been turned away at the frontiers of Elysium. The shepherd responds by completing the rituals of memory and praise that will secure an afterlife for the gnat. It is a curiously exact reversal of the roles conventionally assigned to poet and patron, as when Spenser urges the nobility

> To patronize the authour of their praise,
> Which giues them life, that els would soone haue dide,
> And crownes their ashes with immortal baies.
>
> (To Northumberland, lines 10–12)

But under the stress of Spenser's allegoresis, "Virgils Gnat" suggests the reciprocity, or specular reversibility, of this relationship. Poet and patron must in effect eternize one another, for when the poet commemorates his patron's virtues he does so with a voice the patron himself has helped to create. "Teares of the Muses" makes the same point in its closing lines, where the poet falls abruptly silent as the learned sisters break their instruments in despair. "The rest untold no liuing tongue can speake,"[28] says Spenser in the last line of the poem—meaning that the instruments of culture are essential to civil conversation, since without them no private voice can make itself heard.

The poems in *Complaints* were written at different times and then published together in 1591, no doubt to capitalize on in-

---

[28] The 1591 text reads "louing tongue"; I adopt "liuing" from the 1611 folio (*Works*, p. 656).

terest generated by *The Faerie Queene*. Because they are early texts—written by an author who in an important sense was not yet "Spenser"—these poems reflect not only the shape and content of Spenser's literary-political ambitions but also the textual strategies by which he pursued those ambitions and the patterns of anxiety and frustration they generated. The same thing is true of the *Calender* and the dedicatory sonnets to *The Faerie Queene*: in all these texts we can trace the author's efforts to write himself into the social and cultural "text" of Elizabeth's England.

Such motives are more deeply submerged in *The Faerie Queene*, but as later chapters argue, they are powerfully if obscurely at work there. So too is the network of specular relations within which we have traced the production of laureate "ornaments," although its configuration shifts as the poet's vocational concerns lose their relative prominence. Chapter 2 shows how the play of speculation between such pairs as poet and monarch, reader and poem, or protagonist and quest object is subsumed in *The Faerie Queene* by a more comprehensive mirror relation between the aesthetic body of romance allegory and the political body of the Tudor dynasty. The function of ideology in the poem is to mediate that specularity. Chapters 3 through 5 will extend this argument by showing in considerable detail how both the structural armature of the poem and the major allegorical scenes of Books I-III reflect an aesthetic theology of "the poem's two bodies."

How might I that fair wonder know
That mocks desire with endless No?—*John Dowland*

2. The Poem's Two Bodies

n the fifteenth of January 1559, a sacred transformation was wrought in the person of Elizabeth Tudor. The ceremony of royal coronation had not technically been classed as a sacrament since the twelfth century, but in many ways it still bore the stamp of its ecclesiastical original, the ordination of a bishop; each smallest detail of word, gesture, and regalia was understood as "the outward and visible sign of an inward and spiritual grace."[1] At the heart of this inwardness, created and sustained by an impressive array of sacred objects and solemn actions, lay the archmystery that anchored all others, the investiture of a natural body with the *corpus mysticum* of the realm. Drawn by analogy from Western culture's central religious ceremonies, this "political sacrament" tended to deify both Elizabeth and the state she governed, converting what was essentially a species of personification into mystified or doctrinal form as a legal and political incarnation.[2]

This incarnation of empire is the central "figure" of Spenser's *Faerie Queene*, at once its founding trope and its title character.[3] Conceived and designed to abet the glorification of the

[1] Randolph S. Churchill, *The Story of the Coronation* (London: Verschoyle, 1953), p. 20; Percy Ernst Schramm, *A History of the English Coronation*, trans. Leopold G. Wickham Legg (Oxford: Clarendon, 1937), pp. 6–9.

[2] Religious controversy surrounding the coronations of Edward, Mary, and Elizabeth Tudor appears to have hastened the secularizing of the ceremony; work in progress by Richard C. McCoy suggests that Elizabeth in particular relied more on civic pageantry than on the less public rite of coronation to glorify herself as a figure of English sovereignty.

[3] Nearly every critic who writes on *The Faerie Queene* speaks to the role of

body politic in Elizabeth, Spenser's epic reflects a distinctly imperial and theocentric poetics. In his seminal study of early Renaissance "political theology," Kantorowicz observes that "in 16th-century England, by the efforts of jurists to define effectively and accurately the King's Two Bodies, all the christological problems of the early Church concerning the Two Natures once more were actualized and resuscitated in the early absolute monarchy."[4] These same problems reemerge in the aesthetic theology of *The Faerie Queene*, where an implicit doctrine of "the poem's two bodies" shapes the literary self-image of Spenser's epic tribute to early absolute monarchy under Elizabeth.[5]

Elizabeth. Early work by Frances Yates on contemporary images of the queen (see *Astraea: The Imperial Theme in the Sixteenth Century* [London: Routledge, 1975]) opened a rich vein of inquiry, brought to bear on the reading of Spenser's poem most recently by Robin Headlam Wells, *Spenser's "Faerie Queene" and the Cult of Elizabeth* (Totowa: Barnes and Noble, 1983); p. 153 of this study provided the epigraph for the present chapter. The main focus of work since Yates has been on establishing the historical context of Spenser's celebration of his queen or on analyzing specific representations of her in the poem (e.g., Cain, *Praise in "The Faerie Queene"*). My emphasis on the role of sovereignty in the implicit poetics of the poem owes a debt to Goldberg, *Endlesse Worke*, pp. 122–65.

⁴ Kantorowicz, *The King's Two Bodies*, p. 17.

⁵ The traces of Christian empire are everywhere in the text. Andrew Fichter offers a clear account of the dynastic framework for Britomart's quest in *Poets Historical: Dynastic Epic in the Renaissance* (New Haven: Yale Univ. Press, 1982), but it is worth stressing how pervasive imperial symbolism is in the poem. It informs not only the explicitly dynastic narrative patterns and iconic images Fichter analyzes but details and episodes not obviously political. Goldberg's reading of the river marriage as imperial pageantry is a case in point; his argument has been extended by subsequent commentaries on the ocean-river complex as an imperial image of "the source": David Quint, *Origin and Originality in Renaissance Literature: Versions of the Source* (New Haven: Yale Univ. Press, 1983), p. 161; and John Guillory, *Poetic Authority: Spenser, Milton, and Literary History* (New York: Columbia Univ. Press, 1983), chap. 2. The opening lines of Book I are also imprinted with royal-imperial associations. The royal stole used in the coronation ceremony bears the ubiquitous red cross of Saint George, and another piece of coronation regalia, "St. George's Spurs," reminds us why we first see Red-

The complexities of the bold conceit through which Spenser aspired, in Ralegh's phrase, to "write [his] Queene anew" lead us at once toward a formal investigation of the internal dynamics of the poem's two natures and toward a historical estimate of its engagement with the Tudor reinvention of the received "text" of English monarchy. Although these are divergent aspects of a single problem, it will be convenient to approach them separately. We will start with the less difficult of the two issues, a description of the "aesthetic theology" of *The Faerie Queene*. Kantorowicz' remark suggests that the legal problematics of the king's two bodies should be understood as a special case of the body-soul dualism endemic to Christian and Platonic thought. At a similar level of generality the same may be said of key structural features in the broadly Platonized Christianity that informs the long medieval tradition of allegorical and philosophical fiction, so it should not be surprising if the structure of Spenser's allegory is illuminated, initially, by selective comparison between such works as Boethius's *Consolation of Philosophy* or Petrarch's "The Ascent of Mount Ventoux" (*De Rebus Familiaribus* IV.1) and an ambitiously syncretic text like the *Fowre Hymnes*. Beginning with the two-bodied monster of Plowden's constitutional theory, the argument of this chapter will follow the motifs of perfect wholeness, secular perpetuity, and "assimilation" from political into aesthetic theology, with special attention to the "negative moment," or crisis point, in the dialectical pattern they enact.[6]

---

crosse "pricking" across the plain: because his spurs, an emblem of imperial chivalry, end in a sharp point and not in a rowell (Churchill, *Story of the Coronation*, pp. 37–39).

[6] Gordon Teskey, "From Allegory to Dialectic: Imagining Error in Spenser and Milton," *PMLA* 101 (1986): 13, argues that "if error in *The Faerie Queene* works not through negation but through an array of oblique movements all tending toward or away from the truth, then we may suppose that absolute opposites lie outside the compass of Spenserian narrative and shape its hierarchical structures remotely." The matter is not so simple as a flat "not . . . but" implies, however; in rejecting what he regards as anach-

Having described this poetics we will pause to see it at work in the narrative of *The Faerie Queene*, Book I, before returning to the founding conceit of Arthur's quest for Gloriana/Elizabeth—which will lead back into some of the historical and political questions I have begun by suspending.

THE AESTHETIC THEOLOGY OF "THE FAERIE QUEENE"

Two aspects in particular of the legal fiction known as the king's two bodies are important for Spenser's poetics. The first is the body metaphor itself as a figure for integral wholeness. Like Christianity, Spenser's art fantasizes its own perfection in terms of access to a spiritual body replete with truth. *"The Faerie Queene,"* writes Leonard Barkan, "is a limitless landscape of the world, a vast number of men who are themselves multiple and subdivided, and finally a single, perhaps perfect, human being who contains in body and spirit all the virtues of the heroes and all the struggles necessary to gain and keep those virtues."[7] The single, perhaps perfect human being who fig-

---

ronistic readings of Spenser's moral tortuousness, Teskey also asserts, "it makes some difference that for Spenser all narrative unfolds between remote but absolute values on its horizon" (p. 20, n. 4). Teskey's placement of the Logos "outside the compass" of the text, coupled with an insistence that it nevertheless organizes the space of the text, is a familiar gambit: "Thus it has always been thought that the center, which is by definition unique, constituted that very thing within a structure which while governing the structure, escapes structurality. This is why classical thought concerning the structure could say that the center is, paradoxically, *within* the structure and *outside it*" (Derrida, *Writing and Difference*, p. 279.) My insistence on the dialectical negations that enable us to describe romance errancy in terms of "movements . . . toward or away from the truth" is designed to stress the way Spenserian narrative works not only to "teach by entangling" (Teskey, p. 13), but also to reconstitute the absolute values on which it depends, and to invest human desire in historically specific versions of these transcendental values.

[7] Barkan, *Nature's Work of Art*, p. 6.

ures the complex unity of the poem is figured in turn by the marriage of Arthur with Gloriana. In stressing Gloriana's shadowy but important role as "the Sovereignty itself," Rosemond Tuve reminds us that the separate quests of the poem begin and end in Fairy court because all adventures belong to the sovereign, who grants them as favors to individual knights and may therefore be said to act "through his fellowship as through an extended self." Arthur serves "as a combined figure for the dynasty, the all-inclusive virtue, the spouse-to-be of the personified realm, [and] the royal house through whom divine power flowed into country and people."[8] The pattern of his heroism in the poem further identifies Arthur with the completion of the several quests in that his critical interventions are typically pivot points in the developing action, analogous in a Neoplatonic scheme to the *conversio* that begins to return the Many back toward the One. The mystical union of Arthur and Gloriana in one flesh would perfect the divine image of sovereignty *and* give formal closure to the "ideal body" of Spenser's poem.

That union is both promised and deferred, and so is the ideal body it shadows forth. Nowhere present in the poem, this body is nevertheless diffracted into many signatures, from the "pressed gras" Arthur finds in the wake of his dream, or the image graven on Guyon's shield, to the numerological patterns that mimic celestial harmony, the "golden wall" that surrounds Cleopolis (II.x.72), the name "Telamond" at the head of Book IV, the veiled mysterious shapes of Venus and Nature, or the sacramental embrace in which Scudamour and Amoret become one flesh in the 1590 ending to Book III.[9] Ultimately perhaps

[8] Tuve, *Allegorical Imagery*, pp. 347–50 (hereafter cited parenthetically).

[9] For the wall of gold as an emblem of the monarchy, specifically in its function as protectorate, see Axton, *The Queen's Two Bodies*, pp. 103–5 (hereafter cited parenthetically). Thomas P. Roche, *The Kindly Flame: A Study of the Third and Fourth Books of Spenser's "Faerie Queene"* (Princeton:

all the words and things in the poem are synecdochic traces in quest of the wholeness they signify; even Spenser's image for his textual source, the "everlasting scryne" from which his Muse lays out ancient scrolls that tell of Arthur's quest, is a synecdoche for what we might call the "archive." Located as we eventually learn in Eumnestes' chamber, it represents for Spenser the commemorative power itself, sole basis and guarantee for the ongoing "translation" of Western imperial culture. As synecdoche, this image attributes a distinctly global unity to the scattered hoards of documents found, purchased, transported, translated, reread and otherwise recovered during the late medieval and early modern explosion of *translatio studii* in Western Europe. The "gentleman or noble person" Spenser seeks to fashion pursues an ego ideal that would integrate the imperial self with an encyclopedia of its culture's symbolic paradigms, from literary genres to chronicle histories, from legal fictions to theological doctrines. In Arthur's quest for Gloriana, then, Spenser may be said to recast the ur-narrative of his culture's hunger for totality, now in the millennial form of a Protestant world empire.

In addition to the body metaphor itself, we need to consider the relation between the bodies natural and politic. Jurists who developed the theory of the "king's two bodies" denied that the body politic was a living soul; acknowledging it as an artifact of human policy, they nonetheless maintained it to be innately perfect and imperishable, "utterly void of Infancy, and old Age, and other natural Defects and Embicilities, which the body natural is subject to." Most important, this ideal fictive body was legally empowered to "assimilate to its own excellence" all such defects and imbecilities arising from the monarch's natural body.[10] For an aesthetic corollary to these prin-

---

Princeton Univ. Press, 1964), p. 16, suggests that "Telamond" should be decoded "the perfect world."

[10] Kantorowicz, *The King's Two Bodies*, pp. 7–12. Axton, *The Queen's*

ciples of perpetuity and assimilation, we may turn to Spenser's
Amoretti 75:

> One day I wrote her name vpon the strand,
>   but came the waues and washed it away:
>   agayne I wrote it with a second hand,
>   but came the tyde, and made my paynes his pray.
> Vayne man, sayd she, that doest in vaine assay,
>   a mortall thing so to immortalize,
>   for I my selue shall lyke to this decay,
>   and eek my name bee wyped out lykewize.
> Not so, (quod I) let baser things deuize
>   to dy in dust, but you shall liue by fame:
>   my verse your vertues rare shall eternize,
>   and in the heuens wryte your glorious name.
> Where whenas death shall all the world subdew,
>   our loue shall liue, and later life renew.

The grandiose gesture of turning away from writing "that
reachest unto dust," to inscribe the soul as a "glorious name" in
the crystalline substance of heaven—this gesture and its prom-
ise depend on the easy confidence with which the poet assimi-
lates *saeculum*, the medium of empire and of fame, to eternity,
the medium of "later life." In this uninterrupted transition
from perpetuity to eternity, writing itself implicitly undergoes
a kind of aesthetic coronation, absorbed into an incorruptible
body void of misinterpretation, linguistic drift, and the trans-

---

Two Bodies, refers to instances of assimilation as "miracles" and stresses both
skeptical resistance to the doctrine and possibilities for using it to criticize
the queen. That it had more orthodox uses may be seen in Sir John Neale's
observation that the body politic could even "assimilate to its own excellence"
defective origins, a version of metalepsis: Elizabeth had been declared ille-
gitimate by statute at the time of Anne Boleyn's fall; Mary, in rehabilitating
her own legitimacy, left this statute on the books, but when Elizabeth suc-
ceeded to the throne "it remained unrepealed, on the constitutional ground
that the crown covered all such flaws" (*Elizabeth I and Her Parliaments*,
[London: Cape, 1953], 1: 34). It was the sovereignty's capacity in principal
to absorb all flaws that so complicated proceedings against Mary Stuart.

valuations of secular history, which the merely natural letter is subject to.

This assimilation of writing's natural body to its glorious risen form is reflected in the idea of poetic inspiration Spenser derived from Neoplatonic love theory. Love inspires the poet to transcendent inscriptions,

> For loue is Lord of truth and loialtie,
> Lifting himselfe out of the lowly dust,
> On golden plumes vp to the purest skie. . . .[11]

These "golden plumes" on which love ascends from dust to the sky also feather the "golden quill" of poetic inspiration:

> Deepe in the closet of my parts entyre,
>   her worth is written with a golden quill:
>   that me with heauenly fury doth inspire,
>   and my glad mouth with her sweet prayses fill.
>
>   (*Amoretti* 85, lines 9–12)

In these lines Spenser projects an idealized metaphoric image of his own writing as the ghostly origin from which that writing proceeds.[12] The golden quill of love writes "worth," or sheer value, not material letters. The sweet praises that darken the page are therefore secondary, derivative. Yet the "literal" debasement of the poet's word, its fall into letters, remains implicit, serving here to sponsor the reassimilation of that word into the poet's bodily interior, a privileged scene for the immaterial inscription of "heauenly fury." In the context of the whole sonnet, this reassimilation is set defensively against the

---

[11] Lines 176–79 of the hymn to earthly love. Hereafter citations from *Fowre Hymnes* will be given parenthetically with the abbreviations HL, "An Hymne in Honour of Love," and HB, "An Hymne in Honour of Beautie."

[12] See Derrida's remarks on metaphoric writing in *Of Grammatology*, trans. Gayatri Chakravorty Spivak (Baltimore: Johns Hopkins Univ. Press, 1976), pp. 14–16. And cf. the discussion of Alma's "royall arras" under "How to 'Avoid' the Genitals," in chapter 4 of this text.

world's misprision of the extruded or published word as flattery.

Passages like this one internalize the image of writing much as Spenser in the proems to *The Faerie Queene* internalizes and purifies the image of Elizabeth: through a discipline of erotic meditation whose tradition extends from Plato's *Symposium* to Spenser's own redaction of the ladder of love in the first two of his *Fowre Hymnes*. This discipline of "pure regard" (HB, 212) works by attenuating the materiality of a body image, abstracting from it the pure fire and symmetry said to be the essence of heavenly beauty. In the course of this meditative sublimation a natural body is first transformed into a mystical one by negation of its physical being. The flesh is then reinvested with the mystical essence derived from its shape and energy. Just as poetic beauty occurs when the poet assimilates mere letters to an idealized metaphoric version of themselves inhabiting his bodily interior, so natural beauty occurs when the pristine soul assimilates matter to its own native excellence. The ladder of love thus operates by a metaleptic reversal of origins; it might well be called the "ladder of the former" inasmuch as it turns on a negative moment in which the "latter" term (in the sequences language-meaning and body-soul) elevates itself by rejecting as ontologically belated the material original from which it was "formed."

Some version of this negative moment can be found in any narrative of transcendence, whether it appears as a humiliation of the self and personal body, as a visionary blindness to nature, or as a revulsion from the things of the natural world. In Spenser's "Legend of Holiness," to take an obvious example, we *expect* to find Contemplation blind to nature, just as we expect to find the Redcrosse knight's illumination accompanied by a necessary blinding of *his* natural eye. An equivalent moment in the affective (as opposed to cognitive) rhythm of ascent occurs when the visionary pilgrim looks back from the thresh-

old of beatitude in a fit of acute revulsion from the world be-
low. This moment is present, for instance, in *The Consolation
of Philosophy* (IV, metrum I) and in Petrarch's "The Ascent of
Mount Ventoux."

Petrarch's letter shows clearly how negation works in the
logic of transcendence. First he describes the "literal" ascent of
Mount Ventoux, although it does sound suspiciously allegori-
cal from the start, given its obvious indebtedness to the open-
ing of the *Inferno*. After much labor with little progress comes
a reflective pause: "My thoughts quickly turned," he writes,
"from the material to the spiritual."[13] He proceeds to extract
an allegorical tenor from the story as its disembodied simula
crum, but this appears less as something derived from the story
of climbing a mountain than as something informing it from
the start, like Providence—hence the "staged" quality of the
initial account. Of course the relation between allegorical tenor
and vehicle is not the only instance of metaleptic reversal of
priority in the letter, which evidently "was written some fifteen
years after its purported date of April 26, 1336, and a decade
after its addressee, the Augustinian canon Dionigi da Borgo
San Sepulcro, had died."[14] The letter's fictional date also places
it some seven years prior to the actual conversion of Petrarch's
brother Gherardo, who nonetheless figures as Francesco's
"straight man" in the ascent.[15] These reversals cooperate in
staging the letter's moment of revulsion: having reconciled
himself to the steep ascent and attained the physical summit of
the mountain, Petrarch lights by sortilege on a passage from

[13] *Letters from Petrarch*, sel. and trans. Morris Bishop (Bloomington: In-
diana Univ. Press, 1966), p. 47.

[14] Michael O'Connell, "Authority and the Truth of Experience in Pe-
trarch's 'Ascent of Mount Ventoux,' " *PQ* 62 (1983): 507, citing the work
of Pierre Courcelle and Giuseppe Billanovitch.

[15] Jill Robbins, "Petrarch Reading Augustine: 'The Ascent of Mount
Ventoux,' " *PQ* 64 (1985): 533–53, elucidates Petrarch's conversion of both
Gherardo and Augustine to his own narrative purposes.

Augustine's *Confessions*: "Men go to admire the high mountains . . . and they abandon themselves!" (p. 49; *Conf.* X.viii.15). This triggers in him a recognition that kicks the ladder, as it were, out from under the emergent tenor by repudiating its literal or narrative vehicle: "How eagerly we should strive," he reflects, "to tread beneath our feet, not the world's heights, but the appetites that spring from earthly impulses!" (p. 50).[16]

Versions of the moment of revulsion may be found throughout Spenser's work: in the hermit's irritation when Redcrosse arrives on the Mount of Contemplation, for instance, and in the knight's own later reluctance to descend; in Colin Clout's analogous distress when Calidore turns up on Mount Acidale, and in Calidore's desire to remain there; at the end of the *Mutability Cantos* when the narrator turns from the vanished epiphany of nature to look on the sublunary world; and, in a particularly revealing instance, at the conclusion to each of the heavenly hymns. The *Fowre Hymnes* is so useful an example because it doubles the structure found in Petrarch's letter. This structure appears once in the internal progress of each hymn, where scripture, the creation, and the human body each form the text of a meditation whose gesture of completion is to turn

---

[16] Robert Durling, "The Ascent of Mt. Ventoux and the Crisis of Allegory," *Italian Quarterly* 18 (1974): 7–28, reads the letter's complex structural relations to its Augustinian and scriptural pretexts with admirable subtlety, but his view of allegory is not entirely compatible with mine. I concur in regarding allegory as essentially typological, *contra* Auerbach (Durling pp. 7, 25 n. 1), but cannot accept the flat contrast between allegory (based on analogy) and irony as its "negative form" (pp. 7, 22–23). Allegory contains, and is constituted by, its negative form in the relation of letter to spirit. The same may be said of typology as Auerbach describes it, a point developed by Timothy Bahti in his analysis of the Hegelianism implicit in Auerbach's account of typology ("Auerbach's *Mimesis*: Figural Structure and Historical Narrative," in *After Strange Texts: The Role of Theory in the Study of Literature*, ed. Gregory S. Jay and David L. Miller [University: Univ. of Alabama Press, 1985], pp. 124–45).

on its text in revulsion. It appears a second time in the relation between the two pairs of hymns: the heavenly pair end in beatitudes accompanied by the moment of revulsion. But the earthly hymns end in what we might call by contrast moments of *reversion*, or erotic turning back to the pleasures of the embodied soul. Such a reversion is also staged in *Amoretti* 72 ("Oft when my spirit doth spred her bolder winges"), which concludes, "Hart need not wish none other happinesse, / but here on earth to haue such heuens blisse." Petrarch ends the letter to Dionisio by praying for strength to resist a similar turn, and Boethius's Philosophia warns against its temptations in closing Book III of the *Consolation*. Her warning reads the backward glance that lost Euridice as an emblem of reversion: whoever "turns his eyes to the pit of hell," she says, "loses all the excellence he has gained."[17] It is typical of the *contemptus mundi* underlying such moments that by "the pit of hell" Philosophia means the created world—a rhetorical shift designed to protect her errant ephebe from failures of blindness to the world, since backward glances of regret or desire would threaten her program for the absolute recuperation of value through religious ascesis.

The contrast between revulsion and reversion organizes *Fowre Hymnes*, for what appears at the close of each heavenly hymn as a moment of revulsion is replayed as a palinode both in the dedication and at the center of the sequence. This gesture has never quite made sense; it seems blind to the integrity of the four poems taken together. The *"former* two Hymnes," says Spenser, composed "in the greener times of my youth," have proven treacherous reading for others "of like age and disposition," who are moved rather to passion than "honest delight" (emphasis added). Unable to call in the poems "by reason that many copies thereof were *former*ly scattered abroad,"

---

[17] Boethius, *The Consolation of Philosophy*, trans. Richard Green (Indianapolis: Bobbs-Merrill, 1962), p. 74.

Spenser announces his present intention "[a]t least to amend, and by way of retractation to re*forme* them, making in stead of those two Hymnes of earthly or naturall love and beautie, two others of heauenly and celestiall" (*Works*, p. 586, emphasis added). The most obvious paradox is simply that Spenser then proceeds to publish all four hymns together. But even had he suppressed the "former" in printing the "latter" pair we would still have to wonder what it means to reform "by way of retractation," or to amend by substitution. Such self-contradictory phrasing perfectly expresses the metaleptic relation between the heavenly hymns and the earthly model they purport to imitate, correct, *and* supplant in a single gesture.

For this reason *Fowre Hymnes* is an especially revealing product of the poetics that informs it. The visionary hermeneutics of Neoplatonism was always a sort of epistemological romance, in which disciplined meditation on a signifying body—Nature, scripture, the beloved—produces the transcendental object of its own desire. Disciplined meditation, what Spenser in the hymn to beauty calls "pure regard and spotless true intent" (HB, 212), offers itself as a methodical return from the secondary, derivative, merely apparent object of regard to the source of its form, the Logos, which the object is then assumed to signify by the metonymy of effect for cause. Whatever its text, though, this hermeneutic systematically misreads its own procedure, offering as an act of decoding what is in fact the work of production. Soul, says Spenser, "is forme, and doth the body make" (HB, 133), but the ladder of the former is a recipe for making soul: beginning where all the ladders start and ascending through prescribed stages of abstraction, it derives the heavenly logos from an image of the body.

The negative moment is indispensable to epistemological romance because the dialectical elevations of this hermeneutic depend on a metaleptic inversion of priority which abases one term as ontologically belated and inferior. *The Faerie Queene* is vastly more complex in its metaphoric structure than the texts I have cited for comparison, but the same principle applies: the poem's vision of its incorruptible aesthetic body rests on a pervasively internalized principle of self-renunciation. What we find in *The Faerie Queene* is, after all, romance—the genre of unconstrained fabulation—in love with didactic allegory. The fiction has introjected a powerful cultural demand for truth, and can meet this demand only by striving to differ internally from itself as fiction. In the effort to secure within itself a *decisive representation* of this difference, Spenserian allegory becomes "otherspeak" in the most radical sense—generating itself out of internal contradiction in forever-divided form, at once the integral body of truth and its repressed "other." Much as the heavenly hymns depend equally on the informing presence of the earthly pair and on their unqualified renunciation, *The Faerie Queene* is able to summon its ideal form into representation only as a sublimated negative image of itself.

This is why in Book I, for instance, the Redcrosse knight's betrothal to the whole body of Truth can never finally cast out the demons of duplicity and illusion. Superficially the contrast could not be clearer: the One, "Who, in her selfe-resemblance well beseene, / Did seeme such, as she was," versus the Other, declaring just as flatly, "I that do seeme not I, Duessa am" (I.xii.8.8–9; v.26.6). Yet Spenser cannot represent Una except in divided form. Initially she is set apart by a veil, recognizable in that she is hidden. But even when she stands revealed in canto 12 Spenser's language can express Una's integrity only as a mediated relation, "self-resemblance." Like the truth of the heavenly hymns, Una emerges into representation through a differential repetition that sets her apart from herself and so makes her dependent on what she is not—dividing Truth against itself to assert its self-resemblance in a phrase that echoes, as it opposes, Duessa's counterepiphany. However deeply Spenser may desire to set his own poetic activity in opposition to Archimago's, structurally they are alike, for he must double Una to create her.[18]

THE RETRACTATION OF REDCROSSE

The Redcrosse knight's passage through the dialectical negation that elevates Truth and spirit by debasing falsehood, writing, and the body can serve to suggest both the complexity and the consistency with which Spenser uses blindness and revulsion to secure the metaleptic reversals crucial to his fable and his poetic. We have already noted the strategic appearance of these two motifs on the Mount of Contemplation in canto 10, where Redcrosse exchanges blindness for vision—and vision of a more ordinary kind for blindness to things of the world. His counter-Orphic reluctance to "look back" crystallizes a pattern that has been taking shape since his first encounter with Duessa, who describes her own regressive search for the "woeful corse" of her betrothed in terms that should have alerted Redcrosse to her spiritual blindness—had he not, as Spenser puts it, "More bus[ied] his quicke eyes, her face to view, / Then his dull eares, to heare what she did tell" (ii.26.6–7). The many-ways ironic "quicke" is a nice touch, partly because it plays into the contrast between life and death that organizes all these motifs: lively as well as hasty in adoring the body of death, these eyes blind the knight to the life-pre-

[18] My argument here approaches that of DeNeef, *Spenser and the Motives of Metaphor*, esp. pp. 95–96. DeNeef offers a generally persuasive demonstration of the poet's need for, and dependency on, "false" models of reading and writing. This pattern may be understood as another version of the allegory's dependency on a negative moment: Spenser can assimilate his own image-making to the spiritual body of truth only by negating, in such figures as Archimago, the instability inherent in representation.

serving risen body he is supposed to adore. Unlike Duessa, Una looks forward; in canto 3 when she encounters Archimago disguised as St. George, Spenser tells us

> She has forgot, how many a wofull stowre
> For him she late endur'd; she speakes no more
> Of past: true is, that true loue hath no powre
> To looken backe; his eyes be fixt before.
> Before her stands her knight, for whom she toyld so sore.
>
> (I. iii. 30.5–9)

The enjambments, unusual for Spenser, combine with insistent repetitions to force us fore-ward as we read, mimicking Una's desire. Her dwarf is a backward-looker; perennially lagging behind and prudent always a little too late, he represents that coming-to-knowledge of "fool-happie oversight" which Spenser evokes so finely in the ship simile that opens canto 6. As such the dwarf is a comically useless form of wisdom. Also part of this pattern is Orgoglio's butler Ignaro, keeper of the Papal keys who does not know how to use them, whose head is screwed on backwards in token of his spiritual blindness.

Having queried Ignaro four different times and received the same maddening answer, Arthur can go *forward* to rescue Redcrosse only through a minor instance of the insight these characters lack: he must read the body as a metaphor. In his fourth and final demand Arthur explicitly characterizes Ignaro's body as a legible text:

> . . . Old sire, it seemes thou hast not red
> How ill it sits with that same siluer hed
> In vaine to mocke, or mockt in vaine to bee:
> But if thou be, as thou art pourtrahed
> With natures pen, in ages graue degree,
> Aread in grauer wise, what I demaund of thee.
>
> (I.viii.33.4–9)

The reference to nature's pen, the equivocations lurking in "graue . . . grauer," the repeated verb "read," even the orthographic pun hidden in "pourtra*hed*," all flash like so many lights and buzzers: it is precisely the ability to *read* that sets Arthur apart from Ignaro, whose "name . . . did his nature right aread" (st. 31.9) as one incapable of reading, and therefore of knowledge. Since Arthur does not learn Ignaro's name from the narrator (as we do), he must read the body for himself.[19] His first reading focuses on the "reuerend haires and holy grauitie" (st. 32.1) that signify age and dignity, but by the time he returns to this theme in stanza 33 his reference to "that same siluer hed" is beginning to accumulate more than a little irony: a second look at what nature's pen has portray-head in Ignaro should suggest a more imaginative reading, one that focuses not on what is conventional in nature's text but on the *volte-face* that points Ignaro's gaze not in the direction his "feet . . . lead" (st. 31.6) but in that associated with a rather different part of the anatomy. Arthur himself can go forward only after having "ghest [Ignaro's] nature by his countenance" (st. 34.4).

The themes given comic treatment here are sublated into divine majesty on the Mount of Contemplation, where the full typological resonance of the distinction between forward and backward is made clear. There Redcrosse's own "glorious" name will be revealed to him along with its significance, for *Saint George* contains (in reverse sequence) the path from dust to heaven that the knight's transcendence must follow, glancing both forward to his canonization in the city of saints and backward to his "georgic" beginnings in the *geos*, or earth. There too, of course, the mount of poetic inspiration will be evoked as an analogue to Mount Contemplation along with the Biblical pair—Sinai, "where writ in stone / With bloudy let-

---

[19] For my own impulse to reread Ignaro I am indebted to a suggestion by Richard Rand.

ters by the hand of God, / The bitter doome of death" was handed down (x. 53.6–8), and the Mount of Olives, where the same writing was at once erased and reinterpreted by one who would fulfill its "bitter doome" (st. 54.1–5). Together with the vision of New Jerusalem, this simile makes explicit the knight's brief rising to a typological vision, a moment in which his limited awareness as a character converges asymptotically with the foreconceit that structures the narrative throughout.

In canto 8 the distance between those perspectives is mediated, as usual, by the elaborate intertextual networking of Spenser's style, with its dense allusions to the Bible and multiple symbolic motifs. Arthur's rescue of Redcrosse, which reenacts the harrowing of hell, requires him to imitate Christ in part by overcoming revulsion with charity, since "Entire affection hateth nicer hands" (st. 40.3). It also involves his assuming the burden of the law, indirectly, on the knight's behalf. As I mentioned in the Introduction, it is Arthur who sees no need to "renew" the memory of Redcrosse's sin, assuming the burden himself instead: "This dayes ensample hath this lesson deare / Deepe written in my heart with yron pen" (st. 44.7– 8). This Biblical simile anticipates Spenser's association of Sinai with "the bitter doome of death" written "in stone . . . by the hand of God," and is itself, significantly, an echo of the Hebrew scriptures (Job 19:24). Arthur will continue to identify himself charitably with Redcrosse in the next canto when he refers to them both as "mated" (checkmated) by love (ix. 12.2), and then pledges friendship with him in a binding oath (st. 18.6– 9). Not least among the ironies of the canto is Redcrosse's solemn gift to Arthur of a goldleaf Testament, the text that prevenient knight has already enacted in their dealings.

Spared a review of his errancy, Redcrosse must still take a second look at Duessa in what must rank among Western literature's grimmest mornings-after. Yet her "maple rind" skin and menagerie of extremities (st. 47–48) are only the visibilia of a far more inward unsoundness. Before he is nursed back to health in Coelia's hospital, Redcrosse must confront a still more powerful form of the backward glance associated with the law, death, the corpselike body, and the letter that kills. In canto 9 he confronts a figure who "to his fresh remembrance did *reuerse* / The vgly vew of his deformed crimes" (st. 48.5–6, emphasis added); whose "raw-bone cheekes" and hollow eyes (st. 35.7–9) mirror his own "pined corse," "rawbone armes," and "sad dull eyes deepe sunck in hollow pits" (viii.40–41); whose "hollow caue" resembles the dungeon he has just left, and the "greedie graue" he was craving (ix.33.2–4, 45.5); who knows, without being told, about the battles Redcrosse plans to fight, the sins he has committed, and the torments he has suffered (st. 43–46); and whose very name, "Despaire," puns on his disarticulation of the Old and New Testaments,[20] or of the backward from the forward gaze. It is no accident that Trevisan dashes madly onto the scene at the start of this episode with his eyes "*backward cast*, / As if his feare still followed him behind" (st. 21.5–6, emphasis added).

Spenser implies that despair is, in effect, a way of reading when he mentions in stanza 22 that Redcrosse and Una "might perceive [Trevisan's] head / To be unarmed" (lines 1–2). Not the awkward bodily pun, this time, but the Biblical allusion to the helmet as "hope of salvation" (1 Thess. 5:8) links correct reading to hope by way of recollection: memory (of the scripture) grounds hope (of salvation), forging just the articulation Despair aims to break down. Forgetting the "greater grace, / The which . . . that accurst hand-writing doth deface" (st. 53.7–9), Despair asks the knight whether God will forget sins and so become guilty of them (st. 47.3–4), neatly *reversing* the

<hr>

[20] Maureen Quilligan, *The Language of Allegory* (Ithaca: Cornell Univ. Press, 1979), pp. 36–40.

historical sequence in which God first assumed human guilt and only then forgot it.

Despair uncouples the forward from the backward glance by a literalizing countermovement to figural sublation. The episode bristles with marks of this literalness: when Trevisan is first questioned, for instance, he stares "as one that had aspide / Infernall furies, with their chaines vntide" (st. 24.4–5)—a simile that turns literal when Despair shows Redcrosse "*painted in a table plaine*, / The damned ghosts, that doe in torments waile" (st. 49.6–7, emphasis added). Because he so clearly represents the knight's unregenerate self, lack of self-knowledge, and decayed body, Despair literalizes Una's description of Redcrosse as "of your selfe . . . berobbed" (viii.42.8). The result of this literalizing is that the "yron pen" of divine memory, which Arthur deflected from Redcrosse in canto 8, now turns into "wounding words" (ix.29.4), "That as a swords point through his hart did perse" (st. 48.2). This metaphor is on the verge of becoming literal in its turn when Una intervenes to reassert the broken link between justice and grace.

Una brings Redcrosse to the House of Holiness. There they are greeted by a figure whose name looks forward or backward indifferently to the same point of divinity: "Dame *Coelia* men did her call, as thought / From heauen to come, or thither to arise" (x.4.1–2). In this respect Coelia anticipates Redcrosse's vision of the angels' "to and fro" passage between heaven and earth (st. 56.2).[21] Coelia's daughters break this double perspective down into distinct phases, for two anticipate heaven

---

[21] This moment of the knight's vision also depends on a figural reading of Genesis. It is based on John 1:51: "And [Jesus] said vnto [Nathanael], Verely, verely, I say vnto you, hereafter shal ye se heauen open, & the Angels of God ascending and descending vpon the Sonne of man." The Geneva gloss refers, as might be expected, to Jacob's ladder at Gen. 28:12, and the gloss there identifies the ladder as Christ.

while the third, Charity, represents heaven's descending grace
to man:

> Fidelia and Speranza virgins were,
> Though spousd, yet wanting wedlocks solemnize;
> But faire Charissa to a louely fere
> Was lincked, and by him had many pledges dere.
>
> (I.x.4.6–9)

In the House of Holiness, then, the pattern of forward and
backward glances is gathered into an image of divine circular-
ity. We encounter a historiographical analogue to the House in
Eumnestes' chamber, a natural analogue in the Garden of
Adonis, and a poetic analogue on Mount Acidale. Each of
these passages in its own way engages the lowest point of the
circle, "the middest" of earthly experience and fallen history,
for it is at this point that descent must be converted into ascent,
or the backward gaze converted into the forward.[22]

At the House of Holiness Spenser represents the dynamics
of this conversion as a set of reading skills opposed to the lit-
eralizing hermeneutics of despair. The eldest of Coelia's three
daughters, Fidelia, carries a Testament and a communion chal-
ice: the knight's vision of New Jerusalem and his assimilation
into the glorified body must begin under her tutelage. Like
Despair before her and Contemplation after, Fidelia personi-
fies a condition latent within the knight that is activated by her
mediation. Just as the lover must look "with pure regard and
spotlesse true intent" to perceive the soul of his beloved, so the
Christian must awaken the "inner light" of faith by which to
behold his espoused when taking communion.[23] Hence Fi-

---

[22] Compare the discussions of temporal perspective under "How to Read
History Prudently" and "The Double Threshold," in chapters 4 and 5 of
this text.

[23] "For he that eateth and drinketh vnworthily, eateth and drinketh his
owne damnation, because he discerneth not the Lords bodie" (1 Cor. 11:29,
Geneva text).

delia's enabling gesture is to clear the knight's "dull eyes, that light mote in them shine."

> And that her sacred Booke, with Bloud ywrit,
> That none could read, except she did them teach,
> She vnto him disclosed euery whit,
> And heauenly documents thereout did preach,
> That weaker wit of man could neuer reach,
> Of God, of grace, of iustice, of free will,
> That wonder was to heare her goodly speach:
> For she was able, with her words to kill,
> And raise againe to life the hart, that she did thrill.

> And when she list poure out her larger spright,
> She would commaund the hastie Sunne to stay,
> Or backward turne his course from heauens hight;
> Sometimes great hostes of men she could dismay,
> Dry shod to passe, she parts the flouds in tway;
> And eke huge mountaines from their natiue seat
> She would commaund, themselues to beare away,
> And throw in raging sea with roaring threat,
> Almightie God her gaue such powre, and puissance great.
>
> $\qquad$ (I.x.19–20)

The mediation of the letter is associated here with blood, death, and blindness; transcending the letter is the way to life and "puissance great," the power Redcrosse will need to triumph in battle.

Since Spenser has reiterated in so many ways that *reading* is the pivot on which the mind turns from memory to anticipation, a closer look at this reading lesson may be in order. To begin with, the passage itself is rhetorically impressive. Since Fidelia stands for the spirit that is prior to the letter, Spenser can take over events recorded in Hebrew scripture (st. 20.2–5) and re-present them together with Matthew's testament to the power of faith (lines 6–8) not as events that occurred in a historical past, but as typical or potential effects of the spirit that stands before us. Thus the trope of personification lets Spenser appropriate the New Testament's authoritative metalepsis, or reversal of priority over the Hebrew scriptures. A second metalepsis works to complement this one. The narrative scene depends on clear distinctions between the character, the book she holds in her hand, and the words she speaks about it, but the language of the passage effaces these distinctions. The word "documents," from *docere*, to teach, refers to speech rather than writing, and the phrase "her wordes" at the end of the stanza confirms a shift from the written book to the voice of the tutor, assimilating to Fidelia's speech the power of life and death vested in scripture. Then at the opening of the next stanza the act of exposition is named directly as an outpouring of spirit, as though the commentary now preceded its text. Through this gradual metalepsis, the sense first of written and then of all verbal mediation is deftly elided from the scene. The passage thus foregrounds the rhetorical illusion of a release of spirit, a leaping out of the frame of language, preparing us for the conversion of recorded miracles into what Wordsworth calls "something evermore about to be."

The whole passage is a local instance of the grand strategy St. Paul employed in designating the New Testament "writing on the heart" in contrast to the old law written in clay, "the ministration of death written with letters." The difference between letter and spirit is used to privilege the new covenant over the old, though of course it is a division reproduced within each—the Pauline trope actually derives from Jeremiah (31:31). Spenser's use of this strategy similarly stages the text of *The Faerie Queene* as a release of the spirit hidden beneath the letter of scripture. In one sense his verses clearly depend on the priority of the Biblical passages they refer "back" to; yet they also tacitly assert their own precedence in presuming to render the scriptural scene of instruction—in presuming access to the originary ground of knowledge about scripture. The rhetorical figures that produce the illusion of such access are self-occulting, however, insofar as their success depends on our inadvertence to them *as strategy*. The illusion succeeds because it appears within the shadow of its own effect, a rhetorical sleight-of-hand that kicks the ladder, or letter, out from under what then presents itself as a pure signified.

This reading lesson enters into the pattern of blindness-and-vision we encounter on the Mount of Contemplation, and inevitably produces its own moment of revulsion:

> The faithfull knight now grew in litle space,
> By hearing her, and by her sisters lore,
> To such perfection of all heauenly grace,
> That wretched world he gan for to abhore,
> And mortall life gan loath, as thing forlore,
> Greeu'd with remembrance of his wicked wayes,
> And prickt with anguish of his sinnes so sore,
> That he desirde to end his wretched dayes:
> So much the dart of sinfull guilt the soule dismaycs.
>
> (I.x.21)

"Such perfection" indeed: the knight's *contemptus mundi* festers into a self-loathing so acute he is almost back in the cave of Despair. Speranza takes over immediately. She and Fidelia had entered in stanza 12 "Ylinked arme in arme in lovely wise," and now we see why, for their pairing opposes despair: Speranza offers her anchor "as was meet; / Else had his sinnes so great, and manifold / Made him forget all that *Fidelia* told" (st. 22.3–5). Still the knight desires "leave to die." His recuperation comes only through an askesis made up of fasting, corrosives, the removal of "superfluous flesh" (from his already wasted body) with hot pincers, beatings with an iron whip, lancing of the pericardium, and saline immersion. This regimen of horrors is administered by the medical team of Patience, Penance, Remorse, Repentance—and "Amendment," whose name should alert us to the deep structural parallel between this episode and the *Fowre Hymnes*. Redcrosse is being amended in much the same way as the earthly hymns had to be: he is reformed "by way of retractation," his guilt displaced into a series of visually spectacular figurative assaults on the integrity of his natural body.

EPISTEMOLOGICAL ROMANCE

The amendment of Redcrosse is a powerful image of the negative moment intrinsic to Spenser's poetics. The negative moment is crucial because, as we have seen, it works to open the endless reversibility of specular relations outward into a dialectical progression. Lacan's notion of the "mirror stage" offers a paradigm for this conversion of specularity into dialectic. Just as the infant is physically the origin of the reflection it sees in the mirror, so it is cognitively the projective origin of the wholeness it sees and identifies with in that reflection. The dialectic of selfhood thus begins in a discrepancy between the infant's cognitive development and its motor skills. This discrepancy, mediated back to the infant through the mechanisms of projection and identification, makes possible the primordial metaphor through which physical wholeness and coordination are assumed as values of the psyche: what is projected as an attribute of the body image is reassumed as a telos for the ego. It comes back one step out of phase, and the circle once broken will not close again.

The tutelary figures of Spenser's allegory, such as Fidelia or Contemplation, mediate the subject to himself in displaced form. What our reading of Redcrosse's conversion has stressed is that this displacement depends on a negative moment it can never finally recuperate, though its dialectical progression is defined from the start by the promise, or mirage, of a closure that will restore all losses at a higher level. Such a progression may be understood in both epistemological and erotic terms. The infinite regress of mutual reflection is an epistemological

quandary venerable enough, and vexing enough in its impli-
cations, that it drove Plato to reinscribe the circularity of
knowing in the image of that larger circle which departs from
and returns to the godhead. The result was a doctrine of inte-
rior forms that spark (and are sparked by) re-cognition: what-
ever we see and know in the world, we saw before in heaven
and had forgotten. Perceiving a likeness between the variable
and obscure images of experience and the dimly remembered
forms of divine truth, we labor through dialectic to reconstruct
a finer knowledge of these forms. This doctrine of anamnesis
makes all knowledge déjà vu, and every philosopher therefore
a kind of sublime Narcissus, striving to resurrect the frag-
ments of a lost self-knowledge into perfect correspondence
with their imagined heavenly paradigm and origin.

The Protestant doctrine of "inner light" works in much the
same way, of course: this is why Fidelia and Heavenly Con-
templation must represent at once a condition to be achieved
by Redcrosse and a principle latent within him. Like Boe-
thius's Philosophia, they enable the subject's return to a divine
source he already contains. Allegory is the literary method ap-
propriate to a recognition theory of knowledge: as Rosemond
Tuve remarked, its fictions make us think about what we al-
ready know; they seek to awaken and charge with motive force
a knowledge that remains latent, passive, or merely implicit in
the reader. Presumably this is the reason medieval commentar-
ies on the *Consolation* (for example) identify Philosophia as
"sapientia Boethiae" and the work itself as a figurative dialogue
between two parts of the same person: Robertson cites the in-
troduction to a fifteenth-century manuscript of Chaucer's
translation where we find the *Consolation* described as "this dia-
logue in this oon persone as it were too, oon desolate and an-
other full of confortht."[24] By the end of the dialogue Boethius
has embraced his truth and once again coincides with him-

[24] D. W. Robertson, Jr., *A Preface to Chaucer: Studies in Medieval Per-
spectives* (Princeton: Princeton Univ. Press, 1962), pp. 358–59.

self—two persons as it were one, in his self-resemblance well-beseen.

What Plato must exclude from his dialectic, insofar as it pretends to a system of truth, is the possibility that ideal forms are derived not from heaven but precisely from the material objects he wants to call their copies. To insist as I do here that ideas are copies of objects is not simply to oppose idealism with materialism, however—it is to acknowledge the specularity in which each serves as origin to the other. To open a dialectic out of this infinite regression, Plato must denigrate the material world and elevate ideas in a twin gesture whose aspects I am calling negation and metalepsis. His special animosity to the lies of the poets (as poets like Sidney and Shelley realized) looks a bit like evasion by displacement of the radical poesis on which dialectic itself depends.

Philosophia repeats this gesture in banishing the theatrical muses from Boethius's prison cell. Of course, she is herself a trope of personification, and the *Consolation* as a whole conveniently illustrates the metaphoric or tropical system through which didactic allegory constructs Truth. As metalepsis, Philosophia represents Truth as an origin that precedes and authorizes all true representations, including the various philosophical schools Boethius tries to synthesize in the *Consolation*. As synecdoche she represents the whole body of this Truth, grasped only piecemeal (as she explains) by contending schools that have torn fragments from her gown. Finally, as personification she is a trope for the presence, within Boethius's language, of the whole body of Truth that precedes and authorizes all philosophical discourse. The *Consolation* thus represents itself as having gathered the diversity of philosophical schools into the total form of their common divine origin—a fiction powerful enough in its structural coherence and logical articulation to sustain a whole series of denials that serve its author's most urgent desires—converting imprisonment into liberty, poverty into wealth, death into life, and compulsion into perfect freedom of choice.

To call this underlying structure "epistemological romance" is a way of suggesting that its power derives from a consolidation of knowledge with masculine desire. This consolidation is what enables Truth to appear in a poem like Spenser's as a romance heroine. Viewed as a structure of desire, epistemological romance begins in the loss or denial of bodily presence, analogous to the philosophical denigration of material being. We see an early example of this myth of bodily loss in the April eclogue to *The Shepheardes Calender*, where the Ovidian episode of Pan and Syrinx becomes in Spenser's hands a fable of the poem's two bodies. Ovid tells of a god in pursuit of carnal ecstasy, intent on ravishing a river nymph. The nymph cries out to Diana, and just at the liminal moment—at the edge of the river, as the god's embrace gathers her in and his sigh passes over her lips—she is transformed into water reeds, and the breath of violent passion yields a harmonic chord. For Ovid as for Spenser this is not primarily a story of feminine protest against rape but one of masculine consolation, a story of loss made over into renunciation as it is replayed in the ludic register, where mastery and recuperation seem possible after all. "This union, at least, shall I have with thee" says Pan to the vanished Syrinx,[25] and he makes the reeds over into another syrinx, a shepherd's pipes—reasserting his baffled will and recovering, in symbolic form, the lost feminine body. Spenser works this narrative into the self-referential symbolism of his pastoral debut, making "Elisa," queen of shepherds, the fruit of an immaculate union between Pan and Syrinx. At once pastoral mask for the queen of England and metapoetic symbol for Colin's song, "Elisa" names the sublimated body that comes to occupy the space of loss.

[25] Ovid, *Metamorphoses*, trans. Frank Justus Miller, 2d ed. (Cambridge: Harvard Univ. Press, 1921), 1.710.

Elisa is a prototype for Gloriana, who also represents both the English queen and the aesthetic body of her visionary form. Arthur desires the fairy queen first in an adolescent dream of sex, but wakes to find her gone. He rises to pursue her displaced form as a comprehensive ethical and spiritual "Ideal-I," but meanwhile bears the loss of her presence as a grievous "secret wound" (1.ix.7.8)—the melancholy emptiness that persists in the aftermath of his dream, caused by his painful renunciation of carnal immediacy. This emphasis on the wounding renunciation of desire makes it seem inevitable that Gloriana's alter ego should be la belle dame sans merci and her avatars, predatory succubae who enervate their victims. Redcrosse melting in Duessa's arms is only the first of many such fearful images in the poem; the most remarkable, surely, is Verdant preyed on by the witch Acrasia in the Bower of Bliss:

> And all that while, right ouer him she hong,
> With her false eyes fast fixed in his sight,
> As seeking medicine, whence she was stong,
> Or greedily depasturing delight:
> And oft inclining downe, with kisses light,
> For feare of waking him, his lips bedewed,
> And through his humid eyes did sucke his spright,
> Quite molten into lust and pleasures lewd;
> Wherewith she sighed soft, as if his case she rewd.
>
> (II.xii.73)

Many readers have testified to the fascination of this passage, with its eerie transfusion of erotic and sadistic frissions. Its special horror lies in its uncanny affinity with the epic's scene of conception, Arthur prostrate and dreaming of Gloriana. In the Bower of Bliss this dream has become a lurid tableau of predatory metaphysical fellatio. Verdant, like Adonis later in the poem, shares Arthur's "secret wound": his recumbent passivity, his expense of spirit, and the erasure of his heraldic insignia (st. 79–80) all testify to his symbolic castration. Meanwhile Acrasia, in a wicked parody of Venus's pietà sorrow over the fallen Adonis, mocks pity for her enervated victim even as she battens on his soul. She is Spenser's fairy quean, secret sharer of the principle by which the succuba of the superego feeds on bodily energy, summoning desire to ends beyond its knowing.

This reading of Arthur's melancholy as the private wound of Spenserian poetics will seem like neo-Freudian critical fantasy only if we forget the mythic provenance of Arthurian romance. Behind Spenser's Arthur stands that of medieval romance, and behind him the shadowy image of the Fisher King, whose identity with the realm he governs is powerfully expressed in the mysterious wound or sickness that dries up his organs of increase and renders the land barren. Rosemond Tuve argues persuasively that Arthur's role in *The Faerie Queene* "is directly in line with what a reader of earlier Arthurian romance expects" (*Allegorical Imagery*, p. 345), with one major exception: "Spenser makes no important use of the motif of a land waste through a wound given the ruler, which is the form of a clear identification between King's and country's health most common in Arthurian romances" (p. 351). The reason may well be that Spenser had a different and far more sophisticated form of clear identification closer to hand in the legal theory of his own age, an extensively rationalized version of the ancient myth that had gained currency in the succession debates of the 1560s and 1570s: crown law had evolved a doctrine of incorruptible perpetuity, holding that sovereignty itself has neither defect nor mortality and assimilates the sovereign's nature to its own. Thus what Spenser seems to have accepted as the "authorized" version of this myth denies the burden of more archaic versions, precisely inverting their symbolism: instead of contaminating his realm, the king is purified by it.

We have seen how radically this doctrine depends on its negative moment. In this respect it has something in common not only with Platonism but with the Arthurian materials Tuve has studied, where the king's mysterious ailment is rationalized in all sorts of unconvincing ways. Beneath the explanations, writes Tuve, we glimpse "the more primitive conception of a *loss of sovereignty* or unexpected decline of power that cannot be countered in natural ways," "some sense of deep human inadequacy which must be expiated even though it is not understood" (*Allegorical Imagery*, pp. 353–54, emphasis added). If we look to still older forms of the legend we find this inadequacy expressed as impotence or castration—sent down by God, in one version, to punish the king's concupiscence.[26] This loss of sovereignty is just what the doctrine of the king's two bodies was calculated to economize, much as Philosophia teaches Boethius to economize against "loss of excellence." Yet if Spenser follows Plowden in rejecting the tragic myth of the king's mortality, it nevertheless returns to haunt his melancholy hero, whose first knowledge of Gloriana is that he has already lost her.

THE IDEOLOGICAL FORCE OF "THE FAERIE QUEENE"

Like Arthur, Elizabeth is a figure of *The Faerie Queene*'s ideal unity; unlike Arthur, she represents the achieved form of this unity, central and preeminent in her iconic splendor. In his proems to the poem Spenser identifies Elizabeth as the source of his inspiration, the object of his mimesis, and the first, most important reader for whom he writes. These are all conventional elements of the Petrarchan scenario in which love sonnets are inspired by the lady, describe the lady, and address the lady, but the unique political and historical status of the

[26] Jessie L. Weston, *From Ritual to Romance* (New York: Smith, 1920), pp. 20–21.

queen alters the force and value of such conventions, which became a political rhetoric during Elizabeth's reign and are a profoundly political rhetoric in *The Faerie Queene*. When Spenser offers his poem as a reflection of the queen's "true glorious type" (I.pr.4), of her face, realms, and lineage (II.pr.4), of her public rule and private virtue (III.pr.5), of her great justice (V.pr.11), and of her Princely courtesy (VI.pr.6), he is at once calling attention to the specific political context within which he writes and redescribing that context, with all its complex transactions, in terms of an essentially allegorical structure.

In one aspect of this situation Spenser offers himself to Elizabeth as a mediator of her own self-knowledge, a figure like Fidelia or Contemplation who returns a displaced image of her in "mirrours more then one." The negative moment here is expressed as a subject's political abasement, evident in Spenser's emphatic recurrence to the humility topos. Yet this self-abasement masks an extraordinary ambition to (as Ralegh puts it) "write [his] Queene anew" (*Works*, p. 409, line 8). The commendatory sonnet in which this phrase appears is itself a mirror image of Spenser's proem to Book III (see chapter 3, "Gloriana's 'Pourtraict'"). Ralegh appears to be expanding a hint (as well as returning a compliment) from the final stanza of the proem, which begins:

> But let that same delitious Poet lend
> A little leaue vnto a rusticke Muse
> To sing his mistresse prayse, and let him mend,
> If ought amis her liking may abuse.   (III.pr.5.1–4)

Ralegh's verses offer a perfect miniature of the specularity inherent in the poet's rhetorical and political relation to Elizabeth:

> If thou hast formed right true vertues face herein:
> Vertue her selfe can best discerne, to whom they written bin.

If thou hast beautie praysd, let her sole lookes diuine
Iudge if ought therein be amis, and mend it by her eine.
If Chastitie want ought, or Temperance her dew,
Behold her Princely mind aright, and write thy Queene
       anew.
Meane while she shall perceiue, how farre her vertues sore
Aboue the reach of all that liue, or such as wrote of yore:
And thereby will excuse and fauour thy good will:
Whose vertue can not be exprest, but by an Angels quill.

(lines 3–12)

Here as in the proems, the fiction of simple reciprocity is preserved. Elizabeth is divine in her perfection and the poet merely mortal in his mimetic craft: if he has made a few mistakes, let them be caught in revision, as line 8 wittily revises "Behold . . . *aright*" into "and *write* . . . *a*new."

Yet the chiasmic wordplay on which the sonnet pivots in its central couplet does not quite serve to conceal a more radical equivocation in the word "Queene," which suggests not only that Spenser may rewrite his *Faerie Queene* but that he may revise Elizabeth herself, noting what she lacks and supplying it in his recomposition of her image. This suggestion is barely discernible—much like the criticism implicit in Spenser's portrayal of Belphoebe, interestingly. The following lines obliquely praise the power of Spenser's verse, making it at once the measure of what human art can aspire to and, in its necessary inadequacy, a measure of how far the queen's "vertues sore / Aboue the reach of all that liue, or such as wrote of yore." This inadequacy is the political form of that self-renunciation through which the poem summons its ideal form to the threshold of representation as a sublimated negative image of itself. It is also, at the same time, a strategic alibi for passages critical of Elizabeth: we read that the queen will recognize the transcendence of her own splendor precisely in the poem's deficiency; we do *not* read, except by inference, that this deficiency is "assumed" by the poet as human limit to his craft for tactical political reasons, and that *some* flaws may equally well be understood as covert criticisms of one whom it would be dangerous to fault openly.

In a second aspect of his relation to the queen, Spenser justifies his mediating function by presenting himself as a reader of her iconic splendor. Here again a denial of initiative and authority serves to mask the constitutive force of his reading, for what Spenser claims to behold in Elizabeth's princely mind is no device of his own feeble wit but the various images of divine majesty and virtue faithfully inscribed in his allegory and returned to her own contemplative gaze as reader of herself. When Spenser also refers to *Elizabeth* as a mirror (I.pr.4, VI.pr.6), his imagery suggests an extremely dense network of reciprocal readings and writings; taken together with the image of the poem as mirror of Elizabeth, such statements imply a double-mirroring in which she mediates divine influence to the poet, who then mediates her mediation back to her. At the close of his final proem, Spenser represents this divine circularity as a process at once social and natural:

> Then pardon me, most dreaded Soueraine,
> That from your selfe I doe this vertue bring,
> And to your selfe doe it returne againe:
> So from the Ocean all riuers spring,
> And tribute backe repay as to their King.   (VI.pr.7.1–5)

Here the triple rhythm we find so variously reflected in *The Faerie Queene*[27] works serenely to mystify the complexities of the transaction in a deeply ideological closure of reflexivities: as the poet's images double back on their origin, the natural world confirms the inevitability of the social order, and both,

---

[27] See Alastair Fowler, "Neoplatonic Order in *The Faerie Queene*," in *A Theatre for Spenserians*, ed. Judith M. Kennedy and James A. Reither (Toronto: Univ. of Toronto Press, 1973), pp. 56–60.

at a deeply implicit level, borrow from and reconfirm the structure of man's relation to God.[28]

The point of reversal, the moment styled *conversio* in Neo-platonic versions of this pattern, coincides here with the figure of the poet. The first part of this chapter investigated the interplay of effacement and reinscription that enables this reversal within Spenser's text, but our concern now is with the ideological force of the *self*-effacement through which his text seeks to write itself into the larger social text. The purpose of this self-effacement is to claim an authority beyond rhetoric or inspiration for the poet's production of truth. Such self-effacement is a powerful force at work in all the "texts" of history, including those in and through which the reinscription of English sovereignty proceeded in the sixteenth century.

As a beginning example, we may consider the text with which this chapter opened, the coronation of Elizabeth. Its self-effacement appears most simply in the claim, still current when Elizabeth II was crowned, that its signifiers are all "outward and visible sign[s] of an inward and spiritual grace." What this claim effaces, of course, is the considerable extent to which details of ceremony and regalia *produce* the mysteries they signify. As Clifford Geertz observes in "Centers, Kings, and Charisma: Reflections on the Symbolics of Power," "if charisma is a sign of involvement with the animating centers of society, and if such centers are cultural phenomena and thus

[28] In *Endlesse Worke*, p. 124, n. 1, Goldberg qualifies my earlier comments on the proem to Book VI ("Abandoning the Quest," *ELH* 46 [1979]: 173–92) by stressing the serious ideological purport of the fiction set forth in these lines. It should be clear that I have found his argument persuasive. I have also profited from Goldberg's Foucauldian analysis of contradiction as the characteristic mode by which royal power uttered itself in early seventeenth-century England. See *James I and the Politics of Literature: Jonson, Shakespeare, Donne, and Their Contemporaries* (Baltimore: Johns Hopkins Univ. Press, 1983), e.g., pp. 6–7: "To adopt the voice of power is, in Foucault's definition, to speak beyond oneself, ascribing one's powers elsewhere, saying one thing and meaning another."

historically constructed, [then] investigations into the symbolics of power and into its nature are very similar endeavors. The easy distinction between the trappings of rule and its substance becomes less sharp, even less real; what counts is the manner in which, a bit like mass and energy, they are transformed into each other."[29] The transformation of a subject into the bearer of sovereignty is a striking example of authority recreating itself through a massive and energetic display of signifiers: as a contemporary witness of Elizabeth Tudor's coronation progress blandly noted, "In pompous ceremonies a secret of government doth much consist."[30]

This way of looking at the coronation ritual desacralizes it completely; on their own terms, ritual and ceremony are explicitly antihistorical. As Geertz suggests, to deconstruct the "inherent sacredness of sovereign power" by reading the constitutive as well as referential logic of its signifiers is precisely to restore such texts to history. In one sense, of course, this desacralizing gesture merely extends a process already well underway in 1559, for the iconoclastic drive of Reformation politics had already begun to take its toll on the ceremonies of majesty when Edward VI came to the throne in 1547. Henry VIII had revised the coronation *ordo* in his own hand to suppress any implication that the monarch received his power from the Church, but this ordo was never used, evidently because Cranmer took the process Henry had begun much further, denying *any* "direct force [or] necessity" in the rites. At his coronation, Edward VI was instructed by Cranmer:

> The solemn rites of coronation . . . be good admonitions to put kings in mind of their duty to God, but no increasement

---

[29] Clifford Geertz, "Centers, Kings, and Charisma: Reflections on the Symbolics of Power," in *Culture and Its Creators: Essays in Honor of Edward Shils*, ed. Joseph Ben-David and Terry Nichols Clark (Chicago: Univ. of Chicago Press, 1977), p. 152.

[30] J. E. Neale, *Queen Elizabeth* (New York: Harcourt, 1931), p. 59.

of their dignity; for [the kings] be God's anointed, not in respect of the oil which the bishop useth, but in consideration of their power, which is ordained, of their sword, which is authorised, [and] of their persons, which are elected by God. . . . The oil, if added, is but a ceremony; if it be wanting, that king is yet a perfect monarch notwithstanding, and God's anointed, as well as if he was inoiled.[31]

Yet Cranmer's remarks also clarify a sharp contrast between Reformation iconoclasm and the effects of modern historiography. To desacralize ritual by reading its constitutive force is very different from denying that force; Cranmer's arguments are in fact no more than a way of taking the negative moment in ritual's logic of self-effacement to its extreme, and they serve, therefore, to sacralize royal sovereignty itself all the more powerfully. In this respect they function like Spenser's strategic self-effacement in *The Faerie Queene*.

Cranmer's devaluation of the ritual on behalf of Edward was followed by Mary's efforts to rehabilitate its sacramental character. She even sent to Rome for the chrism—a higher grade, as it were, of holy oil, which unlike the "oil of the catachumens" in use since the twelfth century was reserved for the ordination of bishops (Schramm, *History of the Coronation*, pp. 99, 126–27). Thus by 1559 the coronation ceremony, whose fluctuations served as a kind of index to power struggles among the crown, clergy, and nobility, was intensely charged in all its details with polemical significance. Richard McCoy argues persuasively that in this context two aspects of Elizabeth's coronation service stand out. First is its enigmatic character: reports of what actually took place conflict with one another and with themselves, so that "Elizabeth's coronation is one of those events which recede from view as one learns more about it" (p. 6), and what we do know or can surmise of its

<hr />

[31] Schramm, *History of the Coronation*, p. 139 (hereafter cited parenthetically).

details suggests "a typical Elizabethan compromise with something to confuse and offend everyone" (p. 9). Second is its relative obscurity: the "disturbing implications" of ceremonial compromise "were finally muted by the event's essential obscurity. It was a rite muddled by liturgical controversy, witnessed by a small number, and inadequately recorded" (p. 10). McCoy contrasts the confusion and obscurity of this event with the spectacular success of Elizabeth's "skilled performance during the civic progress of the day before" to suggest that Elizabeth's reign was marked at its inception by what scholars are increasingly coming to see as the essentially "theatrical and secular nature of Tudor power and its rites" (p. 2).[32]

Spenser's poem is hardly theatrical, but it does belong to a class of secular, politically powerful representations of sovereignty that were displacing sacramental ritual in the sixteenth century. Looking back at these large-scale shifts in the corporate structure of England we have the advantage of three centuries' distance and several generations of increasingly sophisticated historical interpretation. One natural consequence of these advantages is a tendency to endow this past with a retrospective inevitability; in speaking of long-term processes and broad tendencies, we can never know and perhaps hardly imagine how indeterminate the past may have been in the successive instants of its emergence. In a justly celebrated or notorious passage at the end of his essay on Shelley's *Triumph of Life*, Paul de Man writes that "nothing, whether deed, word, thought or text, ever happens in relation, positive or negative, to anything that precedes, follows or exists elsewhere, but only as a random event whose power, like the power of death, is due to the randomness of its occurrence."[33] It is equally true to say

---

[32] Richard McCoy, " 'The Wonderfull Spectacle': The Civic Progress of Elizabeth I and the Troublesome Coronation," (Paper delivered at the Conference on Medieval and Early Modern Coronations, Toronto, 1985).

[33] Paul de Man, "Shelley Disfigured," in *Deconstruction and Criticism*,

that everything happens in a multiplicity of relations, positive *and* negative, to whatever precedes, follows, or exists elsewhere, and that all these relations are rhetorically constructed. The doctrine of royal supremacy may be said to have secularized ecclesiastical authority and sanctified the power of the crown, yet the very interdependence of the two meant that the process set in motion could not be arrested or securely controlled: if Henry was forced to strike at the roots of ecclesiastical power in order to assert his own, is it not also true that the reverberations of his blow circled back a hundred years later to shake the throne? As James I was to put it, "No bishop, no king." Elizabeth said as much in her closing speech to the 1584 Parliament: "And of [those who press for ecclesiastical reform], I must pronounce them dangerous to a kingly rule."[34] If the effects of a given event can diverge and collide in this way, at least part of the reason must be that subsequent competitors for power are able to *read* the event in opposite ways. The Act of Royal Supremacy meant something very different to the 1566 Parliament that defied the queen—and was *made by them* to mean something different—than it meant to, or was made to mean by, a man like Archbishop Whitgift.

The long struggle for power between crown and successive parliaments during Elizabeth's reign, especially between the crown and the lower house, offers countless illustrations of this principle. Consider a single example, the efforts of Commons to establish freedom of speech among the recognized "privileges of the house." The force of tradition placed setting the agenda for parliamentary debate among the prerogatives of the

---

Harold Bloom et al. (New York: Seabury, 1979), p. 69. The sentence I have quoted begins "*The Triumph of Life* warns us that," and is followed by another sentence stating: "It also warns us why and how these events then have to be reintegrated in a historical and aesthetic system of recuperation that repeats itself regardless of the exposure of its fallacy."

[34] Neale, *Elizabeth I and her Parliaments*, 1: 100.

crown; when Sir Thomas More succeeded in getting "freedom of speech" formally instituted, in 1523, it represented only the right of dutiful opposition to royal bills. In effect, what was then established was a rule of interpretation: all speeches delivered in parliament were to be understood within the assumption of a loyal intentionality, so that no member's opposition to the crown on a money bill, for example, could be taken as evidence of treason. Radical Protestant factions in subsequent parliaments seized on this precedent as an excuse for insisting on the Commons' right to set its own legislative agenda—despite the fact that royal prerogative comprehended the power to forbid discussion of certain topics, and despite the fact that Elizabeth struggled to exercise this prerogative throughout her reign.[35] This creative use of precedent is a form of metalepsis, or revision of origins: under a shaky mimetic alibi (the claim to be correctly interpreting constitutional history) it did eventually trope into existence the precedent it claimed merely to preserve.

The mimetic alibi says that the use being made of verbal signs answers to their referents. Political rhetoric offers a sustained demonstration of the reverse—that the referent of a phrase like "the privileges of the House" can be altered by the way the words are strategically deployed. Language is always to some extent performative, generating authority out of misreading, just as community, or the body politic, is always to some extent a project rather than an artifact, forever in the making as particular, strategically motivated utterances compete for authority. The historical effect, the consequential force, of any document or event is therefore always in an important sense "up for grabs." In our own time and place we have seen a conservative Republican president successfully stage himself in the public imagination as the heir to Roosevelt

[35] *Ibid.*, 1: 17–28.

and Kennedy, persuasive evidence if any was needed of the extent to which rhetoric generates power by producing history.

In terms of the structural argument I have used, what enables such cooptations of tradition is the endless circularity or reversibility of specular relations, including those fundamental pairs sign/referent and signifier/signified. Foucault proposes an analogous principle in his later efforts to sketch the relations of discourse and power. He calls it a "rule of the tactical polyvalence of discourses": "We must make allowance for the complex and unstable process whereby discourse can be both an instrument and an effect of power, but also a hindrance, a stumbling-block, a point of resistance and a starting point for an opposing strategy. Discourse transmits and produce power; it reinforces it, but also undermines and exposes it, renders it fragile and makes it possible to thwart it."[36] From this point of view the earlier history of the English coronation, reflected in a series of *ordines* or written protocols that goes back to the tenth century, might be read as an exemplary tale of the struggle for control over privileged signifiers. The principle of reversibility I am arguing for stands out with special clarity in the twelfth-century episode involving a nameless cleric, "the Anonymous of York," who argued for the king's right to interfere in ecclesiastical affairs. What makes his treatise interesting is not that he anticipated events of the Reformation, but that he offered a structural interpretation of the coronation *ordo*, comparing it point for point with the Church's episcopal confirmations. Initially the sacramental character of royal coronations had served to strengthen the arguments of Pope

---

[36] Michel Foucault, *The History of Sexuality, Volume I: An Introduction*, trans. Robert Hurley (New York: Vintage, 1980), pp. 100–101. Montrose, " 'Eliza, Queene of Shepheardes,' " borrows a comparable definition of social symbolism from Abner Cohen's *Two-Dimensional Man*: "It is indeed the very essence of the symbolic process to perform a multiplicity of functions with economy of symbolic formation" (cited by Montrose, p. 179).

against crown: the ceremonial anointing of the monarch tended to sanctify his claims to secular authority only by annexing the right of coronation to the Pope and his delegates. But as our modern historian of the coronation ceremony explains, the result was a specular structure that could easily be reversed: "It was . . . possible to draw up out of the old *ordo* a sort of 'Bill of Rights' in favour of the encroachment of the King on the administration of the Church. If in the tenth century the clergy had thoroughly clericalized the coronation, the wheel had now come full circle, and the argument of the Anonymous showed how the coronation service supplied the legal title for a regalization of the Church" (Schramm, *History of the Coronation*, p. 35). The rhetorical name I have suggested for this circling of the interpretive wheel is *metalepsis*, or reversal of priority.

The legal metaphor of the king's two bodies offers a somewhat more complex example of the reversibility of discursive formations through which power is exercised. Marie Axton argues in *The Queen's Two Bodies* that the theory was formulated through forced readings of legal precedent, and points out that it was first propounded in the *Duchy of Lancaster Case* (1561) by Catholic jurists who used it to "minimize the personal impact of the new sovereign" and who had strong political and economic motives for doing so (p. 16). She goes on to demonstrate that it was popularized by supporters of Mary Stuart for the succession, and later used in the Inns of Court Revels to direct implicit criticism and admonition at the queen.

Spenser's virtual absence from Axton's study is particularly interesting. Axton describes Plowden's technique for manipulating precedent as "the political adaptation of a much older scholastic device": typology (p. 36). When these precedents were popularized by John Leslie, Mary Stuart's chief polemicist in the succession debates, certain figures and moments in chronicle history, and even key figures and episodes in classical history and mythology, took on a loaded significance which

Axton demonstrates to be crucial to their meaning in popular drama, royal spectacles, and other cultural forms that served as displaced political discourse on topics banned from open debate. The reason she has little to say about *The Faerie Queene* is undoubtedly that Spenser so carefully avoids these figures in his chronicle passages—Arthur is a hero less likely to provoke the "gealous opinions and misconstructions" Spenser had hoped to forestall by writing allegorically ("A Letter of the Authors"). The second installment of the poem, especially Book V, suggests a poet at once more critical and more anxious, quicker to take offense and readier to risk giving it. But in the 1590 version his nearest approach to controversy is the allusion to Henry VIII's will at II.x.76; Leslie and others had argued at length against its authenticity. What is most striking about this reference, though, is what the poet leaves out—namely, any mention whatsoever of Edward VI or Mary I. The passage deals with fairy succession, and has Tanaquill directly succeeding Oberon "by his last will." Since the conflicts and controversies of the intervening regimes had seriously weakened the crown's position—for many reasons Elizabeth on ascending the throne enjoyed nothing like her father's effective power—the image of her rule that Spenser here gives back to Elizabeth "magnifies" royal power by eliding discontinuities in the dynastic succession.[37] The *Briton moniments* read by Arthur in canto 10 have repeatedly emphasized the disastrous consequences of failed or uncertain succession, but the admonition to Elizabeth (if one is intended) remains characteristically oblique. Meanwhile the fiction explicitly offered as an image

---

[37] In this respect Spenser's account imitates the genealogical tree that appeared in Elizabeth's coronation progress: it too excluded Mary and Edward. For a suggestive discussion of the representational strategies reflected in this exclusion, see Mark Brietenberg, " '. . . The Hole Matter Opened': Iconic Representation and Interpretation in 'The Quenes Majesties Passage,' " *Criticism* 28, no. 1 (Winter, 1986): 15. I discuss the lines further under "How to Read History Prudently," in chapter 4 of this text.

of her rule works a transformation of the past not unlike what Axton calls Plowden's "legal miracles," assimilating the conflicted and discontinuous history of the Tudor body natural to that unbroken fictive dynastic continuity known as the sovereignty.

Spenser's most powerful use of the legal metaphor Plowden formulated does not lie in the kinds of specific tactical exhortation or admonition Axton finds in pageants and entertainments, but in his deep structural adaptation of the metaphor itself. Speaking of Peter Wentworth's succession treatise, Axton observes: "In all Wentworth's historical examples supporting the miracles of the body politic, to quote Erich Auerbach on biblical history, 'the fact is subordinated to an interpretation which is fully secured to begin with.' A similar technique is apparent on the public stage where 'the event is enacted according to an ideal model which is a prototype situated in the future and thus far only promised' " (p. 91). The allegory of *The Faerie Queene* is typological in exactly the same sense, organizing a perspective on contemporary England by means of an etiological fiction that looks back to a set of origins most educated Englishmen knew to be fictive, and forward to an imperial marriage that prefigures the millennial kingdom. If this is also the implicit structure of a wide range of historical texts that generate persuasive force or legal authority by reinscribing the past in the image of a desired future, the reason may be that it is the irreducible temporal structure of language, where rhetoric converts referential logic into constitutive force the way combustion turns mass into energy.

THE CATACHRESTIC BODY

I will have more to say in later chapters about Spenser's images of the beginning and the end. In the meantime I will conclude with a further point, also to be elaborated later. I have suggested that Spenser's use of Arthur may be seen as a strategy for sublimating the mythic infirmity of kingship into an ideal form, a mirage of wholeness pursued through a moral-psychological dialectic that can build civilization but not cure its discontents. This pattern conforms to Kenneth Burke's description in *Attitudes Toward History* of the symbolic patterns through which an artist seeks to invest adult authority symbols with the emotional power of parental archetypes. Incest awe, or its political counterpart in the "taboo of the ruler," desexualizes female images of transcendence or authority through a symbolic castration of the male subject. The self-transformation in which this subject "assumes" his castration works through a symbolic regression that dialectically refigures castration as rebirth—a pattern clearly played out in the conversion of Redcrosse. This psychic "ritual" of rebirth-as-socialization is symbolized as a change in sex through which the libidinally "neutered" male attains androgyny.

Consider from this point of view the opening lines of Book I, canto 5, which introduce a description of Redcrosse on the eve of his battle with Sansjoy:

> The noble hart, that harbours vertuous thought,
> And is with child of glorious great intent,
> Can neuer rest, vntill it forth have brought
> Th'eternall brood of glorie excellent.

In context this is an almost excruciatingly ironic version of the transformation Burke describes, since Redcrosse is fighting the wrong battle in the wrong arena, and will end by pledging fealty to Lucifera. In these circumstances the simile tells us, in effect, that we are witnessing a disguised replay of the dreadful parturition of Errour's brood. Yet it is also one of the more explicit formulations the poem offers of a symbolic pattern that runs throughout: thus Redcrosse is held in Orgoglio's dungeon for *nine* months (viii.38.6), and will be rescued by Arthur in

stanza *40*; Arthur meanwhile performs this rescue *nine* months
after his vision of Gloriana, as we will learn in canto 9 (st.
15.9). It is interesting that these references make Arthur's
dream of Gloriana contemporary with Redcrosse's liquefaction
on the grass in canto 7—but more importantly, they form part
of a symbolic pattern that makes Spenser's male protagonists
spiritually androgynous by refiguring their noble hearts or
minds as symbolic wombs in which their own identities are
reborn in the image of some "glorious great intent."

In this way Spenser's male knights become types or *figurae*
of that cosmic perfection shadowed in the marriage of oppo-
sites: in the statue of Venus (IV.x), the figure of Dame Nature
(VII.vii), and the union of Scudamour with Amoret in the
1590 ending to the poem. Roche suggests that Scudamour's
canceled fusion with Amoret alludes to Eph. 5:25–32, where
man and wife are said to be "one flesh"; we are similarly in-
structed at Gal. 3:27–28 that "there is neither male nor fe-
male" in the *corpus mysticum*. The policito-religious symbolism
of marriage so pervasive in our culture rests partly on these
and related Biblical passages. Redcrosse's castration and re-
birth prepare him for his betrothal to Una in canto 12, which
in turn looks forward to the marriage of the Lamb. Arthur's
metaphoric femininity is similarly a typological anticipation of
his millennial-imperial union with Gloriana, and the mystical
hermaphrodite they become is Spenser's implicit figure for the
perfected spiritual body of his poem.

This ideal body has a plenitude of sexuality, for it embraces
both genders, and it has none at all, for it depends on a "literal"
or bodily erasure of the generative difference within human
nature. Hamlet plays on the sexual ambiguity of this body with
bitter literal-mindedness when he mocks Claudius as "my
mother—father and mother is man and wife, man and wife is
one flesh, and so, my mother" (IV.iii.51–2); Spenser's tone and
attitude could scarcely be farther from Hamlet's, yet the mys-

tical body of his poetry bears no less confused an anatomy. Pending our return to the subject, let a minor example suggest the confusion of anatomy Spenser's poetics projects as its ideal form. Lines 9–12 of *Amoretti* 85 were cited earlier to show that Spenser's myth of transcendent inscription depends on the implicit fiction of a spiritual body:

> Deepe in the closet of my parts entyre,
> Her worth is written with a golden quill:
> That me with heauenly fury doth inspire,
> And my glad mouth with her sweet prayses fill.

We know that in Petrarchan sonnet sequences writing typically unfolds in the interval of deferred sexual union, taking the place of the body like Elisa or Gloriana. This passage, while not quite sexual, is certainly erotic. Like the Venus-Adonis tableau that recurs so often in various guises (Redcrosse and Duessa, Arthur and Gloriana, Verdant and Acrasia, Malecasta's tapestries, Timias and Belphoebe, the Garden of Adonis), it suggests a symbolic regression into womblike intimacy or maternal domination as the means through which castration becomes rebirth. The phrasing suggests both hollow space and repletion, most strangely in the phrase "parts entyre," which sounds almost like a riddle with "synecdoche" for its answer. A profound and intimate interior is both hole and whole in these lines, filled by a powerful surge of spirit issuing in a sweet flow. Hallowed by its diction—"closet" with its connotations of secrecy and interiority, "entyre" with its mingled sense of completion, perfection, and health[38]—the rhetoric of

---

[38] *Oxford English Dictionary*, 1971 ed., s.v. "closet," 6a and b. Two anatomical senses were current for Spenser: "closet" as womb (cf. *FQ* III.ii.11) and as pericardium, for which the *OED* cites an example from *The French Academy* (1594, very close to the date of *Amoretti*). See also Fletcher, *Allegory*: "The word 'health,' suggesting wholeness, suggests the basic allegorical trope of the *whole body*, the untorn garment, the complete paradise, the *hortus*

inspiration is nevertheless underwritten here by a "former" bodily impression, representing inspired composition as a displaced and idealized consummation of desire. To anatomize body parts—the cavities of the chest and mouth, or the uterine depths of the mother and the phallic quill of the father—would be awkwardly literal. The poet, whose metaphoric language in these lines appropriates a complex system of body values, now synthesizes parts and genders in a consummation too devoutly wished.

In rhetorical terms this epicene hermaphroditic body might be variously described. Earlier I characterized "epistemological romance" as a tropological system that builds up allegorical truth out of the solidarity of personification, metalepsis, and synecdoche. When Spenser assimilates this scheme to a manifestly typological pattern, he defers its closure, temporalizing personification and synecdoche. Personifications enter into a dialectical pattern that subsumes lesser or more specific figures into increasingly comprehensive ones, as Redcrosse and the other protagonists are subsumed into Arthur; synecdoche thus becomes more clearly a horizon state. Insofar as this system solicits investments of desire in its prospective synecdoches, and predicates their *figurae* on a public ideology in which the dynastic fortunes of the state are assimilated to the Biblical promise of a millennial kingdom, it may be said to operate ultimately under a mimetic claim, however complexly mediated: what we now see through the dark glass of allegory bears a genuine likeness, a metaphoric relation, to what we will eventually behold face to face. This claim serves a political function, since it justifies the tendentious conflation of English imperium with Biblical millennium. Yet however mimetic the symbolic system may claim to be with respect to transcendent

---

conclusis" (p. 201n). I am suggesting that many of the same connotations are evoked by the word *entyre*.

reality, as an epicene hermaphroditic body it is anomalous with respect to nature.

To deny the mimetic claim that promises closure for this system is in effect to redescribe it under the sign not of metaphor but of catachresis. This term bears two distinct meanings: it is the "forced" or unnatural use of metaphor, and it is the "extensive" use. By "extensive" is meant the transfer of an accepted name from its right object to something otherwise nameless.[39] The difference, then, between a meaningful extensive figure and a flurry of language signifying nothing can depend only on whether a nameless referent does in fact wait patiently for its designation, preinscribed as the blank fourth corner of a neat, Aristotelian analogy already drawn in the Book of Nature. In other words, it is a difference based purely on belief and always therefore open to question, which is one reason Derrida, in his discussion of Aristotelian rhetoric, calls metaphor "the risk of mimesis."[40] Driving signifiers apart from their conventional signifieds, and signs from their accepted referents, metaphor opens a space of figuration that it does not control; there is no guaranteeing what anomalies may be troped into being through the constitutive force of language. Arthur and Gloriana, comprehending within themselves all lesser knights and virtues and combining to form a transcendental hermaphrodite, type of the Christian Apocalypse, may very well put mimesis at risk.

Insofar as epistemological romance tropes into being that superphenomenal totality which has been given so many names (the cosmos, the soul, the body politic, the *corpus mysticum*, Telamond, Arthur-plus-Gloriana), it may be seen as an elabo-

[39] See Joseph M. Miller, Michael H. Prosser, and Thomas W. Benson, eds., *Readings in Medieval Rhetoric* (Bloomington: Indiana Univ. Press, 1973), pp. 106–9.

[40] Jacques Derrida, *Margins of Philosophy*, trans. Alan Bass (Chicago: Univ. of Chicago Press, 1982), p. 241.

rate catachresis, constituting anomalies under a mimetic alibi and offering them to us as images of the world and our relation to it. Spenser may well have tried to select narrative materials far from "the daunger of envy, and suspition of the present time" ("A Letter of the Authors"), but his fable departs from the historical present of Elizabethan England in order to circle back, elevating romance quest into a typological summons to the Tudor Apocalypse. In this respect the poem, for all its fictive remove from the present, has something in common with political rhetoric; its explicitly mythic image of *translatio imperii* is only somewhat more fictional than the precedents Henry VIII manufactured in such texts as the preamble to the 1533 Statute of Appeals (24 Henry VIII, c. 12). This was the statute that restructured the ecclesiastical courts under royal authority. It is clear why Henry felt such a step necessary: the monarchy itself was a legal anomaly, a corporate office in its distinction from the body natural, but one that transferred by descent, unlike all other corporate offices in the realm, which under common law transferred by succession. To fulfill his corporate function as protector of the realm Henry needed to secure the descent. But descent depended on the body natural, which functioned as what Derrida calls a "dangerous supplement" to the body politic, irrelevant except that it was essential. To fulfill his responsibilities to the visionary body of state Henry needed male heirs of the body natural, and these had not been obtained from Catherine. The result was a preamble giving statutory dignity to the claim that England was an imperial state, a preamble W. S. Holdsworth calls "remarkable, partly because it manufactures history upon an unprecedented scale, but chiefly because it has operated from that day to this as a powerful incentive to its manufacture by others upon similar lines."[41]

---

[41] Holdsworth, *History of English Law* 4: 591.

During the sixteenth century the "statutory root" planted by Henry was fed and watered by lawyers, theologians, and ecclesiastical historians, as Holdsworth points out. Recent scholarship lets us appreciate more fully the extent to which it was also nurtured by spectacles, pageants, progresses, paintings, ceremonies, and poetry, including Spenser's *Faerie Queene*: a whole array of cultural discourses whose cumulative and collective project was to produce a glorious future by manufacturing the past it required. Despite frequently violent conflict between competing visions of this future, the imperial history fabricated by Henry's statute rhetoric went unchallenged for centuries. Not much more than fifty years ago, Holdsworth could still assert,

> Two great professions . . . have had and still have a direct professional interest in maintaining this thesis. The lawyers are tied to it by their statutes and cases; the ecclesiastics by the tradition and the authoritative declarations of their church. Naturally, therefore, its truth is still believed and maintained by a long array of imposing names. It was not till an historian arose who, besides being the greatest historian of this century, was both a consummate lawyer and a dissenter from the Anglican as well as from other churches, that the historical worthlessness of Henry's theory was finally demonstrated. (*History of English Law, 4:591*)

The historian to whom he refers is of course Maitland, whose researches paved the way for innumerable works of modern scholarship—including *The King's Two Bodies*.

The profession of literary criticism is equally rooted in a massive historical and ideological sedimentation of which it may recently have started to become more self-conscious. Rather like the lawyers and poets of Tudor England, we labor to rewrite literary history in the image of some future truth, whether humanist republic of letters, feminist or neo-Marxist utopia, or a prophecy of nihilism. Even deconstruction can trace the duplicities of this dialectic only by repeating it in a self-displacing form, and the alternative to such strategies of "double writing" is still some form of ideological investment. We may construct a countercanonical criticism, but for richer or poorer this revisionism will repeat the deeper structure of the literary canon whose authority it seeks to volatilize.

My argument in this chapter has been that Spenser's poem functions within a similarly specular relation to the visionary imperium it both sees and seeks in Elizabeth. In glorifying this synthetic social-political fiction, the poem tends indirectly to its own glorification—not just despite, but *because of* the self-renunciation we have traced. In the mystical body of empire we discern the risen body of the poem itself, a deeply idealized fantasy of its own perpetual and intact cultural authority. In chapter 3 we will examine Arthur's dream of Gloriana as an allegory of the poem's quest for this sovereign body. Retold in Book I, canto 9 (the number of both mind and gestation) this dream recounts the insemination of Arthur's fantasy by the cultural superego—an insemination which is also, in its negative moment, a castrative humiliation of the narcissistic ego. Like the poem in its self-renunciation, Arthur renounces pride of the flesh in the interest of a reversion of glory upon himself. This reversion offers a symbolic and therefore immutable magnification of status, restoring what was literally lost *to* the body as a ghostly supplement to the inevitable loss *of* the body. To rehistoricize that transcendental supplement by reading its ideological force is a way of stressing how speculative such investments in the symbolic economy of monarchy could be. Since there is no guarantee that any historically particular form and moment of civilized life will accrue an adequate rate of consolation on its discontents, we can be certain only that investments of adoration reflect a profoundly ambiguous mixture of motives.

. . . of whiche Veritee wast, trowe youe, that
thaye spake ytt? —*Respublica*, 1553

3. Arthur's Dream

t is said that Elizabeth's first response to the death
of her sister Mary was to quote in Latin the twenty-
third verse of Psalm 118: "This is the Lord's
doing, and it is marvelous in our eyes." If so, she
was also quoting a motto inscribed on the gold sovereigns
Mary had issued in reforming the coinage.[1] Accurate or not,
the story of this barbed thanksgiving reflects the pointed ri-
valry within which the royal sisters had all their lives been
eclipsing one another. As daughters of Henry's castoff queens
they traded roles in an alternation neither could control: by the
time of her younger sister's birth in 1533, the seventeen-year-
old Mary was already appearing in popular ballads as "the for-
lorn princess," the same role Elizabeth would play during her
sister's reign and in Book I of *The Faerie Queene*. After Henry
recovered from the shock of his new child's female sex, he at
first decided to name *her* "Mary," a peculiarly heavyhanded
way of insisting that, like his wives, his daughters existed to
supplant one another. Elizabeth, as she was finally christened,
was promptly exalted at the expense of her sister, whose reduc-
tion in status from "Princess Mary" to "The Lady Mary" was
reiterated daily in the smallest details of court etiquette. But
with Queen Anne's miscarriage two years later the whirligig
of time brought in his revenges, and Mary displaced her sister
as heir presumptive to the throne. This antithetical symmetry
played itself out as long as both were alive: during Edward's
reign, Mary as Catholic heir apparent became the focus of po-

---

[1] James Mackay, *A History of Modern English Coinage: Henry VII to Eliz-
abeth II* (London: Longman, 1984), p. 26.

tential rebellion and was therefore degraded in the royal favor, while after Mary succeeded her brother, Elizabeth played shadow queen. Not even Mary's death brought an end to the pattern, for Mary Stuart would resume the prototypical role of "second person" during Elizabeth's reign.[2]

RIVALS AND MIRRORS

The political rivalries that shaped the lives and deaths of competitors for power in Tudor England were defined by a structural dilemma inherent in the very idea of the *monos archos*, the single and unitary ruler. Monarchy can be defined in law only by the interior hierarchy of its two bodies. (Axton's stress on the hypothetical, tendential status of this "legal fiction" need not obscure its theoretical necessity.) This interior doubling of the sacred embodiment of unity maps itself onto the field of power relations organized thereabout, where it channels the struggle for wealth and power into a system of specular rivalries, whether for the unique position of royal sovereignty or for those places of lesser ascendancy whose relative status was gauged with reference to the crown.

The fascination such specular relations hold for recent theory has to do with their way of rendering origins undecidable. Each figure in a specular relation serves in some sense as the origin of the other. One of the dilemmas of specular relations between persons is that they beget rivalry within identification and produce identity out of rivalry.[3] In her own way Elizabeth understood this strange logic very well; it partly explains her

[2] For details in the preceding paragraph see Erickson, *First Elizabeth*, pp. 17, 20–24, 59, 163, 178, and 203.

[3] See Kojève's translation-with-commentary of Hegel's *Phenomenology of Spirit*, IV.A, in Alexandre Kojève, *Introduction to the Reading of Hegel: Lectures on the "Phenomenology of Spirit,"* assembled by Ramond Queneau, ed. Allan Bloom, trans. James J. Nichols, Jr. (New York: Basic Books, 1969; Ithaca: Cornell Univ. Press, 1980), pp. 3–30.

reluctance either to name a successor or to execute Mary
Stuart. The specularity that binds rivals to competing shares in
a single destiny, and that makes the "second person" of the
realm always potentially a focus for rebellion, also tends to
make any blow struck at a rival recoil upon its perpetrator.
Elizabeth resisted executing Mary Stuart for so many years—
and seems toward the end to have dropped some broad and
rather desperate hints about wanting Mary assassinated—at
least partly because she understood that no matter how danger-
ous Mary became, to execute an anointed sovereign by the au-
thority of the English crown would be to weaken the divine
absoluteness of monarchy as such. A similar recoil threatens
the security of the usurper, as Shakespeare so powerfully dem-
onstrates in the career of Bollingbroke. From the moment of
Richard's fall, the king in Shakespeare's *Henriad* is hedged not
with divinity but with speculation—with mirrors, rivals, tav-
ern impersonations, battlefield doubles, and Prince Hal's
deeply internalized sense of the monarchy as a performance,
an imitation of itself. True or false, then, the image of Eliza-
beth reversing her rival's motto with a well-timed repetition
bears witness to a symbolic formation that shaped history as
well as fiction in the sixteenth century.

The symbolic formation reflected in this private, perhaps
fictitious glimpse of Elizabeth's reaction to the death that made
her queen is also reflected in the elaborate and carefully unified
series of public spectacles staged for her coronation progress,
and painstakingly documented for immediate publication by
Richard Mulcaster, later Spenser's schoolmaster. Although the
progress itself was a custom of some antiquity, the staging of
individual pageants had only begun with Mary. The most
prominent pageants in her progress, however, were offered by
Italian communities in the city; the elaborate spectacles that
greeted Elizabeth were therefore conceived partly as a way of
overgoing those unpopular signs of foreign influence, as her

chronicler implies in stressing that the city "without any foreign person, of itself beautified itself."[4]

The fourth of these pageants, mounted at the Little Conduit in Cheapside, offers a striking public equivalent to Elizabeth's ironic remark. Accompanying Mary through London on the coronation progress of 1553, Elizabeth had witnessed a pageant illustrating the humanist commonplace *veritas filia temporis*, "Truth the daughter of Time." The same phrase would appear in Mary's marriage festival, in a royal interlude celebrating her return (the source of my chapter epigraph), on her crest, and on her seal of State; and when "this is the Lord's doing" made its way from Psalm 118 to the reverse side of Mary's newly issued sovereigns, *veritas filia temporis* appeared as the reverse motto inscribed on most of her other coins.[5] Both mottos proclaimed the triumphant return of Catholicism as the religion of state in England, and were therefore "marked" for rhetorical appropriation when Protestantism was restored.

At the fourth stage of Elizabeth's progress, before the assembled aldermen of the city, two artificial mountains were erected, each bearing a tree. The mountain on the north "was made cragged, barreyn, and stonye," its tree "all withered and deadde" (Osborne, *Quenes Maiesties Passage*, p. 46); the one on the south was green and flourishing, covered with flowers, its tree "very freshe and fayre" (p. 47). On the north side a crudely dressed personage labeled "Decayed commonweale" sat despondently under the withered tree, while over his head

---

[4] James M. Osborne, ed., *The Quenes Maiesties Passage through the Citie of London to Westminster the Day before her Coronacion* (New Haven: Yale Univ. Press for the Elizabethan Club, 1960), p. 11 (hereafter cited parenthetically as Osborne, *Quenes Maiesties Passage*).

[5] See Fritz Saxl, "Veritas Filia Temporis," in *Philosophy and History: Essays Presented to Ernst Cassirer*, ed. Raymond Klibansky and H. J. Paton (Oxford: Clarendon, 1936), p. 207, n. 2; and Donald Gordon, " 'Veritas Filia Temporis': Hadrianus Junius and Geoffrey Whitney," *JWCI* 3 (1939–40): 228–40.

the branches were hung with "Tables" listing the causes of public ruin; to the south a well-dressed counterpart, "Flourishing commonweale," stood erect under placards listing the causes of public prosperity. A cave with a locked door was placed between the two mountains. At the queen's approach, a winged old man bearing a scythe issued from the cave, leading forth a smaller figure whose placard read "*Temporis filia*, the daughter of Tyme" (p. 47). *Temporis filia* carried an English Bible labeled "*Verbum veritatis*, the woorde of trueth," which was lowered on a silken strand for presentation to the queen's delegate. Mulcaster's account suggests that Elizabeth may have been especially pleased with this pageant, for not only did she receive the English Bible with a broad pantomime of rapture—kissing it, then elevating it before the crowd with both hands and finally clasping it to her breast—but in her eagerness to get there she nearly overran Time itself, sending one of her knights ahead to accept the Bible before she had fully arrived in place to crown the moment with another of her supposedly improvised remarks: "Tyme," she said, with more than the intended irony, "and Time hath brought me hether" (p. 44).

In appropriating Mary's Catholic motto to stage the presentation of an English Bible to her rival and successor, the Cheapside pageant reverses its pretext emphatically to produce a doubtless gratifying compound of aggressive irony, righteous self-congratulation, and prophetic solicitude.[6] Its schematic allegory, based on common motifs from late medieval and Renaissance religious art,[7] suggests how utterly intermin-

---

[6] Breitenberg, " '. . . The Hole Matter Opened,' " analyzes the pageant as formulating and inculcating an Elizabethan political rhetoric.

[7] See Robert Kellogg and Oliver Steele, eds., *Edmund Spenser: Books I and II of "The Faerie Queene," "The Mutability Cantos," and Selections from the Minor Poetry* (Indianapolis: Bobbs-Merrill, 1965), pp. 11–15. See also Irwin Panofsky, *Studies in Iconology* (New York: Harper, 1962), p. 64 (cited by Kellogg and Steele, p. 12).

gled the motives of religious reform and national sovereignty
had become, for the trees of life and death, the dying and re-
born landscapes, and the symbolic parturition of a purified
verbum veritatis tend at once to sanctify the godly common-
wealth and to secularize the religious iconography, borrowing
the prophetic force of Biblical typology to hail the advent un-
der Elizabeth of the *Respublica bene instituta* (Osborne, *Quenes
Maiesties Passage*, p. 47). In this respect the pageant offers a
crude formal analogy to the typological structure of *The Faerie
Queene*. More specific comparisons are possible as well, though
they probably reflect no more than a common inheritance of
traditional symbolism: the living and dying trees, for example,
appear in Fradubio (i.ii), the withered stump outside the cave
of Despair (ix), and the Edenic tree of life (xi); the figure of
Time and his daughter are interestingly redistributed in Time,
Genius, and the flock of babes in the Garden of Adonis (iii.vi);
and the landscape of the flourishing commonwealth anticipates
the regreening of Arlo Hill in the *Mutability Cantos*.

There is, however, one scene in *The Faerie Queene* that may
allude more directly to the Cheapside pageant. In it the patron
saint of England greets the royal infant of Welsh descent who
has just rescued him from the oppressions of Catholicism, and
who now sojourns in quest of the ideal British sovereignty.
Like the pageant, the scene culminates in the gift of a Bible,
presented to Arthur by Redcrosse: in both scenes the gift serves
at once to acknowledge a deliverance performed and to proph-
esy the godly kingdom still to come. In both scenes, too, the
gift is linked with Mary's transvalued motto—for Arthur's ac-
count of himself in canto 9 of Book I not only alludes conspic-
uously to the phrase *veritas filia temporis*, it juxtaposes *two* cru-
cial allusions to the phrase, each of them implicitly a prophecy
of the ideal kingdom. After explaining to Redcrosse and Una
that he was stolen at birth and raised by fairies, Arthur recalls
what Merlin told him about his ancestry:

Him oft and oft I askt in priuitie,
Of what loines and what lignage I did spring:
Whose aunswere bad me still assured bee,
That I was sonne and heire vnto a king,
As time in her iust terme the truth to light should bring.

(1.ix.5.5–9)

In describing his dream of Gloriana, Arthur recalls her similar promise:

Most goodly glee and louely blandishment
She to me made, and bade me loue her deare,
For dearely sure her loue was to me bent,
As when iust time expired should appeare.   (1.ix. 14.1–4)

As Hamilton observes in his gloss on these passages, "Obviously the two moments will become one."[8]

The chain of repetitions that leads from Mary's coronation through Elizabeth's to Book 1 of *The Faerie Queene* begins when the seed phrase *veritas filia temporis* is appropriated and invested with Catholic resonance.[9] It is reappropriated in Elizabeth's name and "unpacked" into a prophecy of the reformed commonwealth, which Spenser in turn appropriates for more radical transformation. Of course what Spenser actually receives is less a detachable verbal formula (despite the prominence of the *veritas filia* phrase in his text milieu) than a cluster of associated verbal and pictorial elements that more or less signify one another, and among which various transformations and recombinations occur. *Veritas filia temporis* was part of a matrix that included *tempus omnia reuelat* (time reveals all),

[8] Since Hamilton's glosses are keyed to the text in the Longman annotated *Faerie Queene*, I cite them without additional reference.

[9] The textual origin of this commonplace is unknown: the Roman grammarian Aulus Gellius, in Book 12 of *Attic Nights*, attributes it to "another ancient poet, whose name escapes me." In 1526 Erasmus added it to his proverb anthology, and from there it passed quickly into broad circulation—serving as a printer's mark, as Mary Tudor's personal motto, as the motto for a popular woodcut (later an emblem in Hadrianus and Whitney), and as a standard theme of late Renaissance painting. See the articles cited in n. 5.

veritas odium parit (truth gives birth to hatred), *veritas de terra orta est* (Ps. 85:11, "Truth shall bud out of the earth"), and *nihil enim est opertum* (Matt. 10:26, "Nothing is covered that shall not be discovered"); as visual elements the matrix also included a cave or abyss and an antithetical, demonic figure, Calumny or Hypocrisy, attacking Truth. In appropriating the proverb, Spenser extends this field of transformations: thus Falsehood and Hypocrisy both appear in the action of Book 1, not only attacking Truth but, more insidiously, impersonating her and her knight. Errour, lurking in her cave and spewing out books when attacked, resembles a parodic *Veritas*, while ironically it is Una who twice delivers Redcrosse from a cave.[10] Meanwhile the figure of Time as a revealer is shifted from Una to Gloriana, where instead of hailing the emergence of Truth it reconciles Arthur to an indefinite delay.

This last transformation gains further complexity from the genealogical foreconceit of *The Faerie Queene*. This foreconceit makes the narrative and symbolism of the poem doubly typological, for it elaborates them with reference to two distinct moments, the one in which Arthur acts and the one in which Spenser writes. As both the object of Arthur's quest and an honorific name for Elizabeth, "Gloriana" links these two moments typologically: just as events in Hebrew scripture anticipate events in the life of Christ which in turn refer to events that will occur at the end of history, so Arthur's career is fulfilled in Elizabeth's reign, which nevertheless looks forward to the millennial kingdom, since "yet the end is not." This double time scheme is clearly marked by the breaches in Spenser's chronicle history (II.x.68, III.iii.50), and it governs the references to *veritas filia temporis* in canto 9, glossing the "daughter of time" first as Arthur's destined accession and then as the substantial revelation of the fairy queen.

Spenser's transformation of the Latin motto and of the sce-

---

[10] For this observation I am indebted to Professor John N. King.

nario unfolded from it during Elizabeth's progress begins, then, with a doubling of perspective that complicates and enriches the secular typology inherent in the religious politics of the age. This doubling leads to a role reversal, for in Spenser's scene the Bible is presented to Arthur, not Elizabeth. The significance of this reversal once again lies in the reflexive relation between the two. Gloriana-Elizabeth appears to Arthur as the dim figuration of a well-instituted republic; the New Testament is the Truth on which that godly republic, still forming itself in the womb of time, will be firmly grounded at its advent. The time scheme implicit in this fiction sets up Elizabeth's accession as a typological fulfillment of the Arthurian *figura*, although this structure is qualified by the margin that still separates Elizabethan England from millennial glory. Hence the prophetic force of the coronation pageant, which stages the moment of Elizabeth's succession as a crisis, or turning point, between two symbols of the commonwealth that are braced in mere static opposition until the queen's arrival opens the locked door of Time to deliver the Truth of the moment into her hands.

The *verbum veritatis* thus serves to exhort as well as to glorify Elizabeth. The symbolic structure of Spenser's poem balances identical motives, for Arthur is both the once *and future* king, an image of golden antiquity that serves to prophesy the age just coming to birth. In choosing to give us *Prince* Arthur—a character, in other words, who is not yet the figure we know from romance, chronicle, and myth, but who shows us that legendary magnificence in the making—Spenser intensifies the aura of expectancy surrounding his protagonist. The double chronology that structures the narrative works to suspend this charge of expectancy between praise and exhortation—praise insofar as Arthur looks forward to the Elizabethan present, but exhortation insofar as he looks just beyond the present to an end that is not yet, offering Elizabethan readers a model of imperial self-fashioning that invests all energy and desire in the *figurae* of a Protestant millennium. In this second sense Arthur appears *to Elizabeth* as a dreamlike promise of the well-instituted republic.

Spenser complicates this already complex structure in yet another way, for the mirroring that turns antique narrative into a speculation on the historical "present" is itself mirrored by yet another doubling *within* the moment of antiquity, as Spenser recasts the chronicles to make Arthur's reign overlap with that of Britomart and Arthegall. This doubling appears to be determined by Spenser's androgynous model of ideal sexuality, for if his first doubling-and-reversal substitutes a male Arthur for a female Elizabeth, this second one substitutes a female quester and a male dream image, at least until its narrative loop is closed off by the decisive reassertion of masculine authority in Book v. In the meantime Spenser develops the theme of androgyny through Arthur's symbolic femininity and Britomart's symbolic masculinity. Britomart wears armor, does battle, quests after an ideal image of her beloved, and is mistaken for a man. Arthur makes a womb of his imagination, inseminated with glory by his visionary copulation with the fairy queen, he gestates and gives birth to the noble deeds that constitute a comprehensive exemplum of magnificence. In the allegory of Book I Arthur, as a figure of descending love, is oddly like Charissa.

The allegory of Arthur's "pregnancy" is developed partly through references to the numbers of gestation: nine (months) and forty (weeks). Arthur lifts Redcrosse out of Orgoglio's dungeon in stanza 40 of Book I, canto 8; in canto 9 he recounts his dream of Gloriana, which occurred "Nine monethes" prior to his rescue of Redcrosse. This pattern in turn activates the resonance of words like "terme" and "labour," as in "time in her iust terme the truth to light should bring" (st. 5.9) or "From that day forth I cast in carefull mind / To seeke her out with labour, and long tyne" (st. 15.6–7). Orgoglio's dungeon may look more like a grave than a womb, but this is in keeping with the theological symbolism that converts death into rebirth, "delivering" Redcrosse to the parental figures who will supervise his spiritual parturition in the heavenly hospital of canto 10.

A fuller exploration of Spenser's gender symbolism and its complex dialectic awaits us in chapters 4 and 5. For the present it will be enough to observe that this pattern too is implicit in the seed phrase *veritas filia temporis*, and may account for the fact that Spenser's twin allusions to the phrase, cited above, are placed exactly nine stanzas apart in canto 9. The Elizabethan regime's exfoliation of this seed phrase in the pageant of 1559 has been gathered into a far more complex structure of symbolic transformations, but it still plays a seminal role, for out of it Spenser has developed what we may call with some precision his allegory's scene of conception.

ARTHUR'S DREAM

Canto 9 of Book I is divided between two scenes, one in which Arthur takes his leave from Una and Redcrosse and a second in which they enter the cave of Despair. Our concern is with the first of these, in which Arthur recalls his upbringing and describes his dream of the fairy queen. Since we take Gloriana to be a synecdoche for the ideal unity of the poem she appears in, we may begin by noticing that the passage describing Arthur's dream is carefully framed between explicit images of the wholeness projected by masculine desire. These images help to define the symbolism of the dream.

First is the "goodly golden chaine, wherewith yfere / The virtues linked are in louely wize" (st. 1.1–2); as Hamilton's gloss implies, this golden chain of concord is in effect a synecdoche of synecdoches. It represents the chain of analogies linking the several virtues and their quests in the structure of the poem, and it links this structure in turn to its cosmic paradigm, the loving harmony among the elements that serves as a comprehensive model for conservative notions of social, political, psychological, and aesthetic unity. The second image comes eighteen stanzas later, when Redcrosse and Arthur solemnly join hands to forge an initial link in the projected chain that will bind the twelve virtues into an image of the magnificence that "conteineth them all" ("A Letter of the Authors"). Subsequent links in this same chain will be forged whenever the protagonists of separate quests bind themselves into "that golden chaine of concord" (III.i.12.8, where Arthur, Guyon, and Britomart pledge allegiance); such passages are strategically placed to help forge the armature of the poem's allegorical unity. Thus when Arthur passes from cantos 8 and 9 of Book I to the same cantos in Book II—an itinerary our reading will also follow—he travels a circuit whose only "map" is the metaphoric structure of the poem itself, not traceable (as Spenser teasingly reminds us in the proem to Book II) by the "blunt and bace" sense of those who read with bloodhounds. When the links of this figurative chain are all in place, Arthur presumably will be complete, no longer a mere torso or "memberless" trunk.[11] The elusive body of *The Faerie Queene* should also be completed at this hypothetical moment, which I have called a vanishing point for the allegory; and indeed the difference between Arthur and Gloriana will in principle have vanished: the hero will have achieved his quest in becoming the thing he sought.

The allegory of Arthur's dream offers a psychogenetic ac-

---

[11] The analogy to "a torso in sculpture" comes from Northrop Frye, "The Structure of Imagery in *The Faerie Queene*," *UTQ* 30 (1961): 153. My understanding of Arthur's role as composite protagonist is indebted to Nohrnberg's learned dilation of the master's sentence in "Arthurian Torso," *Analogy*, pp. 35–58, as well as to Fletcher, *Allegory*, pp. 35–38.

count of the human need to project such images of perfect wholeness. The scene opens with a springtime pricking of the "corage" that may recall the opening of *The Canterbury Tales*:

> It was in freshest flowre of youthly yeares,
> When courage first does creepe in manly chest,
> Then first the coale of kindly heat appeares
> To kindle loue in euery liuing brest.   (I.ix.9.1–4)

What was literally April in Chaucer now seems figurative, however, a season in the same calendar of sexual awakening we have met before in Colin's "December" complaint:

> Whilome in youth, when flowrd my joyfull spring,
> Like Swallow swift I wandred here and there:
> For heate of heedless lust me so did sting,
> That I of doubted daunger had no feare.
>
> ("December," lines 19–22)

Various echoes of "December" are audible in Arthur's reminiscence: compare "Love they him called that gave me checkmate" (line 53) with "myself now mated, as ye see" (I.ix.12.2), or "thy sore hart roote / Whose rankling wound as yet does rifelye bleede" (lines 93–4) with "that fresh bleeding wound, which day and night / Whilome doth rancle in my riven brest" (I.ix.7.3–4). We need not overemphasize such verbal parallels, since Spenser's characteristic diction and his sustained concern with erotic experience tend to create an almost omnipresent echoic effect that contributes to the distinctive "feel" of his poetry. Here, though—whether calculated or incidental—they reflect a larger pattern in which Arthur's quest for Gloriana figures as a retractation of Colin's erotic experience—as if Colin had "cult"-ivated Elisa from afar instead of pursuing Rosalind. What Arthur narrates in the passage at hand is a sublimation Colin never imagined.

Flushed with adolescent libido, Arthur at first recalls Chaucer's doomed and mocking Troilus:[12]

---

[12] Cf. Kellogg and Steele, *Edmund Spenser: Books I and II*, I.ix.10n.

That idle name of loue, and louers life,
As losse of time, and vertues enimy
I euer scornd, and ioyd to stirre vp strife,
In middest of their mournfull Tragedy.   (I.ix.10.1–4)

This animosity seems to stem from "old Timon's wise behest, / Those creeping flames by reason to subdew" (st. 9.5–6). But Arthur's naive exuberance turns this caution inside out; his shallow contempt of lovers betrays an un-self-conscious narcissism, a failure to distinguish self-restraint from ardent self-love:

Their God himselfe, grieu'd at my libertie,
Shot many a dart at me with fiers intent,
But I them warded all with wary gouernment.

(I.ix.10.7–9)

"Wary gouernment" *should* be an image of vigilant self-restraint—we will witness a retractation of this image when Arthur defends Alma's castle—but in Arthur's adolescent imagination the figure retains a carnal sense of self-delighting athletic skill in combat. It is almost as though his imperfect sublimation of erotic and aggressive energy involved a failure to rise from literal to figurative reading of his own experience.

Psychoanalysis sometimes distinguishes between the "ideal ego," an infantile fantasy of omnipotence, and the more familiar "ego ideal," an agency of the superego created when the narcissistic ideal ego converges with an internalized parental image.[13] (To avoid confusion I will refer to the first as the "fantasy" or "infantile" ego.) The Arthur we see in stanza 10 has not yet perfected the conversion of infantile ego into ego ideal, and appears to be ethically infantile, so to speak.

Stanza 12 betrays Arthur's narcissism in the full sweep of its innocence. Spurred by an energy he does not comprehend,

[13] On the difference between the ideal ego as narcissistic fantasy and the ego ideal as agency of the superego, see J. Laplanche and J.-B. Pontalis, *The Language of Psychoanalysis*, trans. Donald Nicholson-Smith (New York: Norton, 1973), pp. 144–45, 201–2.

glorying in the illusion of his freedom and autonomy, Arthur
has been seduced by a fantasy ego before he ever couches on
the grass:

> For on a day prickt forth with iollitie
> Of looser life, and heat of hardiment,
> Raunging the forest wide on courser free,
> The fields, the floods, the heauens with one consent
> Did seeme to laugh on me, and fauour mine intent.
>
> (I.ix.12.5–9)

The tone of these lines is a finely balanced comic irony. Ar-
thur's restless energy may not be explicitly sexual, but the lan-
guage of "pricking" and "iollitie," "looseness" and "heat,"
clearly suggests the unconscious eroticism sustaining his sense
of freedom and power. "Raunging the forest wide on courser
free" Arthur seems master of his own desire, yet something is
amiss. Transferred epithets are so common to Spenser's fluid
style that we might almost read over these lines without notic-
ing that the "courser" is "free" and the rider "prickt." Arthur
himself does not notice, and things conspire to indulge his for-
getting as if "with one consent." The asyndetic linking of
"heavens" with the rest of nature fosters the illusion: even as
"heavens" yields its metaphysical weight to the simple natural-
ism of field and stream, the scene as a whole quietly reabsorbs
the connotations thus released, all outdoors resolving itself into
the countenance of an indulgent Fate.

Basking in the reflection of his self-love writ large on the
face of nature, Arthur is perilously close to the swelling pride
of Braggadocchio, newly mounted on the steed he has pur-
loined from Guyon:

> Now gan his hart all swell in iollitie,
> And of him selfe great hope and helpe conceiu'd,
> That puffed vp with smoke of vanitie,
> And with self-loued personage deceiu'd,

He gan to hope, of men to be receiu'd
For such, as he him thought, or faine would bee.

(II.iii. 5.1–6)

The sonorant consonants of the first line roll in and out of elongated vowel sounds (especially if "all" and "ioll-" are heard as back vowels), subtly mocking the tumescence of Braggadocchio's anima. That anima is a cruder version of Arthurian "Prays-desire." The difference between Gloriana and *gloriosus*, at once vast and precarious, may be glimpsed in one of the differences between the two passages quoted. There is no "I" in Arthur's memory of the day he dreamed of glory—as though his separate ego had been elided in all innocence by an unconscious narcissism just too powerful for it, and existed only in the reflex of nature's benign gaze. As Lacan would say, Arthur's fantasy ego "is given to him only as *Gestalt*."[14] In contrast, the narrator's comment on Braggadocchio flourishes the personal pronoun five times in six lines, ending with the awkward cadence of "he him thought." Braggadocchio's gestalt is given to him only as ego.

The Arthur who looks back on his younger self in canto 9 of Book I seems only too ruefully conscious of the fall that came after his pride, even comparing himself to the devastated Redcrosse as "one now mated" (st. 12.1–2). This layering of perspectives accounts in part for the subtlety of tone that marks the passage, for we feel distinctly the pressure of a larger yet curiously unspecified point of view that comprehends how much is excluded from the happy blur of Arthur's pubescent "intent." A comparison with stanza 7 suggests that the "final" name for this elusive widening of perspective must be God or Providence:

For whither he through fatall deepe foresight
Me hither sent, for cause to me vnghest,

<hr>

[14] Lacan, "The Mirror Stage," p. 2 (hereafter cited parenthetically).

> Or that fresh bleeding wound, which day and night
> Whilome doth rancle in my riuen brest,
> With forced fury following his behest,
> Me hither brought by wayes yet neuer found,
> You to haue helpt I hold my selfe yet blest. (I.ix.7.1–7)

Tortuous syntax evokes the sense of laborious wandering that haunts Arthur, even as the dogged faith that sustains him emerges in the way supposed alternatives turn out to be indistinguishable: either God has sent Arthur here for unguessed reasons, or his own wounded heart has brought him here at God's command by "ways yet never found." The Providence that directs Arthur's wandering coincides, of course, with the analogical structure of the poem itself, which typically produces him in time for an eighth-canto rescue of the legend's protagonist. Arthur can never comprehend this design, but in principle at least he can converge with it at the vanishing point of the allegory. Meantime, the difference between Arthur now and Arthur before his dream is not simply that his awareness has grown, but that he knows its limitations. Before, he intuitively confounded himself with the visible world around him; now, mortally wounded by a sense of his own incompleteness, he struggles to identify himself with an ideal he can barely imagine.

Arthur's struggle resembles the story of the infantile ego's "assimilation" by its second body, the ego ideal. It will be useful at this point to recall the argument of Lacan's essay on the mirror stage, which focuses on the emergence of human subjectivity in infants. This takes place through identification: the infant, "still sunk in . . . motor incapacity and nursling dependence" (p. 2), focuses on its body image in a mirror—or identifies with the image of any (m)other body—and "assumes" the coherent unity of that image as an attribute of the infantile ego. The immediate relevance of such a theory to didactic allegory is evident in the fact that such allegory typically defines itself as a mirror offered to its readership, one whose images are to be assumed as components of an ego ideal through the specular mechanism of identification. Identification in the mirror stage is preverbal and infantile, since the fantasy ego has not yet been universalized by way of the first person pronoun nor subjected to the demands of a superego; by contrast, the assimilation of the fantasy ego by the ego ideal appears to work through a kind of internalized, second-order mirror stage. The ego ideal results from identification with parents or with collective ideals, and serves as a model to which the subject demands that his infantile ego conform. In this sense every human subject is, like Boethius, "oon persone as it were too."

Yet if "the important point" about the mirror stage, for Lacan, "is that this form situates the ego, *before its social determination*, in a fictional direction" (p. 2, emphasis added), then the important point about didactic allegory is that it seeks to influence the social determination of the ego, and that it does so through complex strategies for resuming the ego's orientation "in a fictional direction" in order to extend it. As Burke would say, didactic allegory seeks to invest public symbols of social and political authority with residual infantile attachments. Between them, then, the mirror stage and the internal specularity to which it gives rise trace the psychogenesis of "social repression," and may be seen as inaugurating the ideological construction of the historical subject.[15]

[15] "Social repression" is a term used by Gilles Deleuze and Felix Guattari to mark their Reichian modification of the Freudian theory of repression; see *Anti-Oedipus: Capitalism and Schizophrenia*, trans. Robert Hurley, Mark Seem, and Helen R. Lane (Minneapolis: Univ. of Minnesota Press, 1983), pp. 8–9, 120–21. The potential value of *Anti-Oedipus* for literary history is demonstrated by Richard Halpern, "John Skelton and the Poetics of Primitive Accumulation," in *Literary Theory/Renaissance Texts*, ed. Patricia Parker and David Quint (Baltimore: Johns Hopkins Univ. Press, 1986), pp. 225–56.

In the story of Arthur's dream, Spenser inscribes this inaugural moment as the psychogenesis of *The Faerie Queene*. Arthur's vision of Gloriana arises from his adolescent assumption of an ego ideal dreamed in the fictional guise of a succuba.[16] This ideal establishes Arthur's relation to the world in Lacanian terms as "a temporal dialectic that decisively projects the formation of the individual into history. The *mirror stage* is a drama whose internal thrust is precipitated from insufficiency to anticipation—and which manufactures for the subject, caught up in the lure of spatial identification, the succession of phantasies that extends from a fragmented body-image to a form of its totality that I shall call orthopaedic" (p. 4). This "orthopaedic," or structurally corrective, fantasy of wholeness remains fictive, and "will rejoin the coming-into-being of the subject asymptotically, whatever the success of the dialectical syntheses by which he must resolve as *I* his discordance with his own reality" (p. 2).

It is sometimes assumed that if the poem were finished Arthur would find the fairy queen. But Spenser nowhere indicates that this is so. In "A Letter of the Authors" he suggests that the poem was to end with an image of its own beginnings at the court of Gloriana, but says nothing about the marriage of his principals, and in the proem to Book I, where Arthur's story is introduced, he says only that Arthur "suffered so much ill" while seeking her "so long . . . through the world . . . That I must rue his undeserved wrong" (st. 2.6–8). The poem itself is structured according to the pattern of dialectical syntheses through which Arthur approaches the moral and spiritual condition Gloriana signifies; but the poem remains incomplete. The idea that Arthur and Gloriana are both synecdoches for its completion—Arthur for its becoming complete and Gloriana for its being complete—suggests an alle-

[16] See Fowler, "Neoplatonic Order," pp. 72–74.

gorical structure for which their union in marriage is less an achievable telos than, as I suggested earlier, a kind of vanishing point. The fairy queen is thus *The Faerie Queene*, a gestalt constituted by Arthur's ego ideal and realized progressively as he transforms that ideal into heroic action.

Through the figure of Arthur, the poem's two bodies engage those of the ego, projecting an image of the subject's quest for his ego ideal as an asymptotic approach to the full assimilation of, or glorious marriage to, his own cultural gestalt. The "first" ego pursues its double through a dialectically organized network of displacements or sublimations which it can never fully master, and whose closure is therefore always deferred: a marriage that is also a mirage. In one sense Gloriana appears to resolve the conflict in Arthur between "kindly heat" and reason, since she represents the substance of his education by Timon in the guise of libidinal gratification. She is a chaste succuba, though, witholding the final proof of her love "until iust time expired." As a figure of delayed gratification, she serves at once to draw Arthur's narcissistic libido outward into a world of objects and to prevent its settling there: Gloriana thus both represents and consolidates the deflection of masculine desire from determinate objects like the feminine body into the endless circuitry of those cultural and symbolic systems out of which we articulate visions of moral, social, and political good.

Her desirability and her terminal elusiveness combine to make Gloriana what we might call a topos of ectopia, or being-out-of-place, the radical of chivalric errancy. Presented to Arthur's desire as a vision of *u*topia (a sexual embodiment of the once and future kingdom), the fairy queen draws his "intent" out of the chaos of will and libido in which she finds him. Yet she does so only to set him off in quest of the horizon state where will and libido finally coincide, with no guarantee that "iust time" will expire before Arthur does. The quest itself, meantime, pits Arthur against his own libido "Till liuing moysture into smoke do flow" (1.ix.8.4), dissolving contradiction into death.

Yet despite the emphatic contrast between Arthur before and Arthur after his dream, there is a sense in which Gloriana's intervention is already, at its first and only occurrence, a revision of Arthur's earliest memory:

> For all so soone as life did me admit
> Into this world, and shewed heauens light,
> From mothers pap I taken was vnfit:
> And streight deliuered to a Faery knight,
> To be vpbrought in gentle thewes and martiall might.
>
> (1.ix.3.5–9)

Throughout the paternal "nouriture" that follows, Arthur retains a pointed curiosity about his natural origin. Yet he receives from Merlin only the vague assurance of his royal blood, together with a promise that "time in her iust terme the truth to light should bring." Merlin's and Gloriana's promises will converge in the same way that quest, quester, and goal become one at the vanishing point of the allegory: Arthur will discover his true origin and identity when he finds Gloriana.

Morally this means that Arthur should discover his essential self (and heavenly origin) in the deferred embrace of an ethical imperative, the patriarchal "behest" that lifts him out of maternal nature into the symbolic order of culture. Historically it means that when Arthur assumes his dynastic heritage, ascending to Uther Pendragon's throne, he will wed himself literally to Guinevere but figuratively to the ideal body of the sovereignty. Anagogically it must signify the millennial wedding of the ideal ruler and realm—prefigured by Arthur as well as Elizabeth—when human history will collapse its typological distances in the annihilating fulfillment for which they are doctrinally scheduled. None of these fulfillments is imminent in the poem as we have it, though: they remain mirages of a condition in which the subject would recover oneness of being with the source of life—a sublime projection of the infantile fusion of self with maternal breast. Arthur's mortal ectopia may "begin" with his dream of Gloriana, then, but it has also already begun with his weaning, and it proceeds by retractations of the infant's inchoate desire for bodily completion. His anima, or imaginary feminine complement, is named for this process of displacement in which desire for the maternal body refigures itself as desire for the father's approbation: weaned to virtue, like Guyon at II.vii.2.4–5, Arthur nurses inwardly on the "comfort" of "prayse-worthy deedes."

This reading of Arthur's history suggests that as the poem's most conspicuous image for wholeness and completion, Gloriana promises transcendence of the split between maternal nature and patriarchal culture that leaves Arthur mortally riven. Hence she figures the mandate of patriarchal authority in precisely the form of what that authority comes to replace and forbid: access to the maternal or feminine body. We may say of her what Derrida, in his now classic essay on "the structurality of structure," says of the idea of a "centered" or "grounded" structure as such: Gloriana is "contradictorily coherent. And as always, coherence in contradiction expresses the force of a desire."[17] Because she figures the resolution of an irreducible contradiction, Gloriana has no positive essence: her "essence," if we may call it that, is the essentially *negative* fact that she never returns in the body. As a lure that enables the cultural superego to depasture masculine desire, Gloriana promises a recovery of infantile experience on the far side of human culture and history. And yet her return, like the fabled return of Arthur or the Second Coming on which both are patterned, is visionary or symbolic—and therefore, in terms

[17] *Writing and Difference*, p. 279.

of the psychosexual symbolism we have been examining, masculine rather than feminine.

GLORIANA'S "POURTRAICT"

Within the horizon of Spenser's narrative, the program of transcendence to which Gloriana summons Arthur may be an open-ended series of erotic displacements (romance ectopia without end), or it may be a teleologically ordered quest for glory (romance ectopia informed by Providence). What we saw in stanza 7 was that this Providence appears as the object of Arthur's faith but not of his knowledge. From a point of view that remains firmly in "the middest," the difference between randomness and design will always be undecidable, and this is as true for the reader as it is for the protagonist: the final form, or "centered structure," of the poem itself is never more than an attempted sublimation of copious textuality into meaning, a conjectural grid by which we seek to invest interpretive errancy with the illusion of inevitability.

One such grid leads from the passage we have been examining to its numerical equivalent in Book II, the opening of canto 9. Whether by Providential design or romance serendipity, it is once again in the seventh stanza that Arthur describes his quest:

> Now hath the Sunne with his lamp-burning light,
> Walkt round about the world, and I no lesse,
> Sith of that Goddesse I haue sought the sight,
> Yet no where can her find: such happinesse
> Heauen doth to me enuy, and fortune fauourless.
>
> (II.ix.7.5–9)

Guyon replies that he'd gladly lead Arthur "through all Faery land" if he weren't already bound to another quest. First-time readers often ask half-seriously why Arthur never just gets directions to Fairy court. But what directions could be given in a poem notorious for its "true imaginative absence of all particular space or time"?[18] Arthur's emphatically solar quest might circumambiate the globe forever without locating "So faire a creature [as] yet saw neuer sunny day" (I.ix.13.9).

Our literal-minded desire to read the story for its own sake is often a target for the poker-faced Chaucerian irony so common in *The Faerie Queene*. The proem to Book II is one such exercise in drollery. As the scene of invocation and address to his "mighty Soueraine," Spenser's proems generally strike a lofty tone; certainly nothing in the proem to Book I prepares us for the way Spenser's stately verses slip here into mocking evasion. First he anticipates that "some" will doubt the veracity of his "antique history"—projecting an idiot questioner who responds to Fairyland like the Irish bishop who, to the amusement of Swift and his coterie, said *Gulliver's Travels* "was full of improbable lies, and, for his part, he hardly believed a word of it."[19] Spenser at first replies by citing Peru, Virginia, the sphere of the moon, and the recent discovery of new stars as comparable instances of unknown worlds discovered. But in the fourth stanza he teases the cartographic imagination more openly:

> Of Faeric lond yet if he more inquire,
> By certaine signes here set in sundry place
> He may it find; ne let him then admire,
> But yield his sence to be too blunt and bace,
> That no'te without an hound fine footing trace.
>
> (II.pr.4.1–5)

In the proem to Book VI we will learn that to travel Fairyland one needs no hound except the Muse (st. 2.8–9), though if we

---

[18] Samuel Taylor Coleridge, "A Course of Lectures," 3rd lecture, excerpted in MacLean, *Edmund Spenser's Poetry*, p. 580.

[19] Jonathan Swift, *Gulliver's Travels*, ed. Martin Price (Indianapolis: Bobbs-Merrill, 1963), p. xiv.

haven't figured it out by then the information may not be much use. Spenser tells us clearly enough in the stanza already before us that Fairyland is an image of the queen's person, realm, and ancestry (lines 6–9). To pursue Gloriana, then, is to follow a metaphor—even for Arthur; it is to seek out a comprehensive vision of moral and political virtue, the glorious ideal form of sovereignty. Since Arthur re-creates himself in the image of this vision by participating in each of several knightly quests to perfect its component virtues, turning back the way Guyon has come would amount to a regressive search for the mere bodily form of glory. As Donne was later to write of Elizabeth Drury, "Because since now no other way there is / But goodness, to see her, whom all would see, / All must endeavour to be good as she" ("The First Anniversary," lines 16–18). Arthur does not "know" this in the way a reader does, and on the face of it his response to Guyon suggests little more than a concurrence between chance and chivalry:

> Grammercy Sir (said he) but mote I weete,
> What straunge aduenture do ye now pursew?
> Perhaps my succour, or aduizement meete
> Mote stead you much your purpose to subdew.

$$(\text{II.ix.9.}1–4)$$

What looks like changing the subject, though, as the conversation wanders from Arthur's quest to Guyon's, is no accident but an "intendment" within the providential foreconceit that undergirds the apparent randomness of the narrative and constitutes the ideal body of *The Faerie Queene*.

Arthur proceeds, then, in the same way as the poem itself, "precipitated from insufficiency to anticipation" through an open-ended series of displacements, a series that repeatedly abandons what is literal or bodily in quest of a higher unity whose closure is terminally deferred. At the beginning of canto 9 we encounter another figure of this higher unity, analogous to the dream vision of Book I: the image of Gloriana on Guyon's shield. The familiar pattern of displacement emerges as Arthur questions Guyon:

> . . . why on your shield so goodly scord
> Beare ye the picture of that Ladies head?
> Full liuely is the semblaunt, though the substance dead.
> (II.ix.2.7–9)

Guyon responds by dispraising the portrait in comparison with its original:

> Fair Sir (said he) if in that picture dead
> Such life ye read, and vertue in vaine shew,
> What mote ye weene, if the trew liuely-head
> Of that most glorious visage ye did vew?   (II.ix.3.1–4)

The portrait is Gloriana's, of course, and so to be treated with reverence: when Pyrochles in canto 8 took refuge behind Guyon's shield, Arthur "His hand relented, and the stroke forbore, / And his deare hart the picture gan adore" (II.viii. 43.4–5). Still it is *only* a portrait, and therefore not a proper object of adoration. As Spenser insists in *Fowre Hymnes*, true love passion is a response to "celestiall powre" and "life-full spirits" (HB, 50–52), not just to the blending of color and symmetry of line; otherwise, "why do not faire pictures like powre shew?" (HB, 82). To love Gloriana's picture would be only somewhat less absurd than to love the "pressed gras" Arthur found on waking from his dream.

Guyon's response at II.ix.3 implies as much in its form as well as its substance. Arthur's questioning comes to rest in an ornamental symmetry not unlike that "proportion of the outward part" Spenser dismisses in the hymn (HB, 75). Guyon picks up the chiastic pattern of Arthur's alexandrine (lively semblant / substance dead) in the first line and a half of his response, which superimposes a second chiasmus (lively / dead / dead / life) and then a third (picture / life / virtue / show), displacing closure each time by overlapping the patterns. Lines 3–4 shift the word "liuely" from the semblance of the "picture dead" to the "trew liuely-head" of the original (with emphasis on "trew" and a pun on "head"); thus the symmetry of chiastic repetition, at first associated with a closed and literal mimesis of the sort that regularly adorns the bowers and palaces of lust in Spenser's poem, eventually projects the contrast between "liuely" and "dead" into the open-ended form of a rhetorical question.

In the Hymn to Beauty the portrait is offered not in contrast to the face but by way of analogy to it, for the "glorious visage" itself is also a copy and no true original, bright with a glory borrowed from within and above. Love responds not to what the face and portrait have in common, the merely formal "features" art can duplicate, but to the unrepresentable, purely spiritual difference between them: the presence in the face of "life-full spirits" that "quickneth with delight" (HB, 51). And so Guyon pauses but does not come to rest in the truth of Gloriana's lively head, resuming immediately with a further qualification:

> But if the beautie of her mind ye knew,
> That is her bountie, and imperiall powre,
> Thousand times fairer then her mortall hew,
> O how great wonder would your thoughts deuoure,
> And infinite desire into your spirite poure!   (II.ix. 3.5–9)

What was "liuely" in comparison to the picture is "mortall" now in comparison to the mind's own hue, and this self-revising progression gives us a rhetorical portrait—or to use Spenser's finer term, "retrait" (st. 4.2)—that is twice redrawn, suggesting the successive stages by which the soul ascends the ladder of love. No physical "trait" or track can serve as a resting place for desire, not the pressed grass, the portrait, the fugitive glimpse of Florimell that Arthur pursues in Book

III—not even the "mortall hew" of Gloriana herself, could he see it. The proper end of desire is "infinite" and therefore ineffable, realized if at all not in satisfaction but in the annihilation foreshadowed by line 8, when wonder will "deuoure" thought to the last morsel. So close an approach to the godhead devours fiction too, though, and Spenser is careful not to overleap Gloriana in the direction of too full an epiphany. He keeps us in "the middest" of things with Arthur and Sir Guyon, patiently devouring ourselves "Till liuing moysture into smoke do flow."

We may note, however, that by leaving the progression open-ended Spenser seems implicitly to be demonstrating the superiority of poetic to oil-based portraiture. The *paragone* among the arts was a standard topos of court poetry, as witness Elizabeth's entertainment at Mitcham in 1598: "The occasion was graced by costly gifts and splendid revelry, in the midst of which a dialogue between a poet, a painter, and a musician was prominent"; the artisans debated the aptness of their respective media for "depicting [Elizabeth] as an object of worship."[20] Spenser tells Elizabeth in the proem to Book II that she can behold her face in the mirror of his verse; then he places it on his hero's shield where an earlier generation would have expected the Virgin Mary, and has Arthur lower his sword in adoration of the "Faery Queenes pourtract" (II.viii.43.3). In this context his handling of the dialogue between Arthur and Guyon implies an argument in favor of writing, which can defer the illusion of presence, over painting, which more obviously relies on the same illusion. The Latin verb *trahere*, to draw, opens into a knot of terms related to the contrast between visual and verbal art: "pourtraict," "retrait," "retractation," and (from the proem, st. 4.5) "trace." In canto 8 we are told that the "pourtract was *writ*" on Guyon's shield (st. 43.3, em-

[20] Roy Strong, *Portraits of Queen Elizabeth I* (Oxford: Clarendon, 1963), p. 33.

phasis added), and in the passage at hand Arthur *reads* life and virtue (II.ix.3.2) in it. Both functionally and etymologically, then, there seems to be little difference between one sort of trace and another; yet Spenser wants to insist on their distinctness, "redrawing" or revising their indifference by claiming the movement of displacement-and-revision for his own art in contrast to the mimetic closure of a portrait (to which one presumably responds, "Ah, that is she"). It is precisely by staging his poetic "retrait" as a displacement-and-revision of the picture that Spenser sustains the tracking movement which leads from trace to trace toward infinity; the commentary Guyon offers on his shield's image is at once an implicit challenge to pictorial art and a lesson in tracing the fine footing of the Muse. That Arthur may need such a lesson is suggested by the wound he receives—not from the irascible Pyrochles, but from the concupiscible Cymochles, a wound occasioned, as Hamilton notes in his gloss, by "Arthur's failure to strike [the] shield because it bears his love's image."

In these passages Spenser treats the controversial subject of royal imagery with indirection and considerable subtlety. Arthur's baldric is set with a precious gem in the shape of Gloriana's head (I.vii.30), and of course it was fashionable among Elizabeth's courtiers to wear "the royal image as a kind of talisman."[21] The Tudor proliferation of royal icons replaced traditional religious imagery, much as the cult of the virgin queen took over the symbolic trappings of Mariolatry,[22] and the more radical Protestant iconoclasts attacked it openly. Nicholas Sanders, in *A Treatise of the Images of Christ and His Saints* (1567), taunted Bishop Jewel, "Breake if you dare the Image of the Queenes Maiestie, or Armes of the Realme . . . or token belonging to the honorable Knights of the Garter."

[21] *Ibid.*

[22] Wells, *Cult of Elizabeth*, emphasizes the poet's tendency to endow the queen with Marian attributes.

Strong observes that the Anglican position on royal imagery was typically awkward, "for on the one hand the use of religious images was denounced as a popish superstition, while on the other, the sacred nature of the royal portrait image was to be maintained"; thus Thomas Bilson argues that "the images of Princes may not well be despited or abused, least it be taken as a signe of a malicious hart against the Prince, but bowing of the knee or lifting up the hand to the image of a Prince is flat and inevitable idolatrie."[23] In this context Spenser's handling of the battle scene offers a fine discrimination: Arthur hesitates between striking the image and doing reverence to it; outwardly he does neither, although the incipient motion in his heart is toward adoration, and for this he sustains a minor wound from the concupiscent Cymochles. In another passage cited by Strong, Bilson justifies homage to the royal image, arms, or regalia as "rendred to [the monarchs'] owne persons, when they can not otherwise be present in the place to receive it" (p. 38). Spenser's strategy extends this reasoning indefinitely: homage is rendered via many different traces to a power whose presence is terminally deferred, and who can never therefore be "in the place to receive it."

Spenser takes up the theme of royal portraiture again after Guyon has destroyed the artwork of Gloriana's erotic double Acrasia. In the proem to Book III, Spenser responds to Guyon's devastation of art by questioning his own poetic mimesis of Elizabeth. Art and nature in the Bower were tangled in delectable rivalry; the proem resumes that rivalry in mock patriotic terms reminiscent of Elizabeth's coronation progress, asking why "Forreign ensamples" of virtue should be imported from Fairyland when a fine domestic paragon sits on the throne:

> It falls me here to write of Chastity,
> That fairest vertue, farre aboue the rest;

[23] Strong, *Portraits*, pp. 38, 39, 38.

> For which what needs me fetch from Faery
> Forreine ensamples, it to haue exprest?
> Sith it is shrined in my Soueraines brest,
> And form'd so liuely in each perfect part,
> That to all Ladies, which haue it profest,
> Need but behold the pourtraict of her hart,
> If pourtrayd it might be by any liuing art. (III.pr.1)

The language of the couplet at once rounds out the stanza's rhetorical question and evokes a wider context that begins to transform the question, recalling the "pourtract" on Guyon's shield, the "royall arras" in Alma's parlor (II.ix.33.7–9), Arthur's puzzlement over just what was "pourtrahed" in Ignaro's physiognomy, and the *pour-traict*, or drawing out, of Amoret's heart in Busirane's inmost chamber. In this context the conditional tense of the alexandrine ("*If* pourtrayd it might be") displaces the simple terms of the opening question by reintroducing the problem of representation on the side of the "natural": we may not need fictive paragons if we already have a real one, but how can we apprehend this "liuely" reality if it escapes representation?

Stanza 2 of the proem to Book III turns sharply on the phrase "liuing art." Initially the words suggest something simple: any artistic technique now practiced or the technical skill of anyone currently alive. But stanza 2 drops the word "any," and repeats the phrase in apposition to "life-resembling pencill": "But liuing art may not least part expresse, / Nor life-resembling pencill it can paint." Here "liuing art" suggests something closer to "art of counterfeiting life." This subtle modulation in the meaning of the key phrase accompanies a strong rhetorical turn from "if" to "but," from qualification to flat denial— shifts whose combined effect is to reverse the force of interrogation: what the poet now calls into question are not fictions that acknowledge their foreignness to reality but those that claim to portray it directly.

From this reversal, stanza 2 moves quickly into a version of the *paragone* among art forms:

> But liuing art may not least part expresse,
> Nor life-resembling pencill it can paint,
> All were it Zeuxis or Praxiteles:
> His daedale hand would faile, and greatly faint,
> And her perfections with his error taint:
> Ne Poets wit, that passeth Painter farre
> In picturing the parts of beautie daint,
> So hard a workmanship aduenture darre,
> For feare through want of words her excellence to marre.
>
> (III.pr.2)

Zeuxis and Praxiteles are evoked as representatives of painting and sculpture respectively, and are linked as classical exemplars of an art that rivals nature through its fidelity to sensuous appearances—exactly the kind of art that insinuates itself everywhere in the Bower of Bliss. Since the object of imitation here is the heart of Elizabeth herself, there can be no question of successful rivalry between original and copy, regardless of the medium involved. Spenser's handling of the *paragone* is complicated by the supplementary distinction he introduces between sensuous and allegorical modes of representation, for this creates an asymmetrical pattern in which painting and sculpture are opposed to poetry on the basis of differing media and to allegory on the basis of differing representational strategies. Thus *poetry* can cap the sequence of forms that are inadequate to their original while still leaving open a space for the emergence of *allegory* as an alternative to the poetics of sensuous realism.

Stanza 3 thus turns on the proem's opening question by importing allegorical fictions as an alternative to direct description:

> How then shall I, Apprentice of the skill,
> That whylome in diuinest wits did raine,

> Presume so high to stretch mine humble quill?
> Yet now my lucklesse loth doth me constraine
> Hereto perforce. But O dred Soueraine
> Thus farre forth pardon, sith that choicest wit
> Cannot your glorious pourtraict figure plaine
> That I in coulourd showes may shadow it,
> And antique praises vnto present persons fit.　　　(III.pr.3)

The errancy of sensuous imitation can only "taint" its original; allegory makes a virtue of this deficiency by converting "error," or wandering, into a deliberate strategy.[24] Just as chance and wandering at the narrative level always appear to be provisional, played off against the promise of their final conversion into providence, so, at the level of poetic technique, mimetic displacement appears comparably provisional, played off against the promise of its final retractation into a comprehensive vision of Elizabeth's corporate splendor.[25]

The proem goes on to suggest in stanza 4 that the best possible portrait "in liuing colours" is already available from Ralegh, if that is what Elizabeth wants:

> That with his melting sweetnesse rauished,
> And with the wonder of her beames bright,
> My senses lulled are in slomber of delight.　　(III.pr.4.7–9)

Such praise, however, can hardly seem unambiguous while the memory of Verdant is still so fresh. And indeed, stanza 5 qui-

---

[24] Spenser invokes the limits of mortal craft also as an alibi for tacit criticism of Elizabeth; see "The Ideological Force of *The Faerie Queene*," in chapter 2 of this text.

[25] Patricia Parker, *Inescapable Romance: Studies in the Poetics of a Mode* (Princeton: Princeton Univ. Press, 1979), pp. 54–113, offers a perceptive account of the poem's narrative movement as "regression from Apocalypse" and of the poem as "all middle" (p. 76). Her argument is persuasive, but I think it slightly underestimates the extent to which the motif of errancy is dialectically engaged by traces of a beginning and ending that frame the action though they never appear within it, and which are therefore just as omnipresent as they are unapparent (see chap. 2, n. 6 of this text).

etly, almost inadvertently erases "that same delitious Poet" from view:

> But let that same delitious Poet lend
> A little leaue vnto a rusticke Muse
> To sing his mistresse prayse, and let him mend,
> If ought amis her liking may abuse:
> Ne let his fairest Cynthia refuse,
> In mirrours more then one her selfe to see,
> But either Gloriana let her chuse,
> Or in Belphoebe fashioned to bee:
> In th'one her rule, in th'other her rare chastitee. (III.pr.5)

The stanza carefully parallels two "let" clauses: let the poet of melting sweetness "lend / A little leaue vnto a rusticke Muse," and let that poet's Cynthia be content "In mirrours more then one her selfe to see." If the parallelism were sustained, the two mirrors would turn out to be Ralegh's verse and Spenser's, but as the stanza moves to its close Ralegh drops out of the picture: "Either Gloriana let her chuse, / Or in Belphoebe fashioned to bee: / In th'one her rule, in th'other her rare chastitee." In this apparently casual transition, Ralegh, the poetry of melting sweetness, and the royal body natural have all disappeared together—for the second "person" Spenser discloses is not his monarch's private body but her private virtue.

THE IDEOLOGICAL SOLIDARITY OF "THE FAERIE QUEENE"

The pattern we have been tracing precipitates the poem, the protagonist, and the reader in their various ways from insufficiency to anticipation. So far my description of this pattern has been mainly formal, but it should be clear that Spenser's retractation of Elizabeth is no adoring transcendence of world and flesh in the visionary beauty of her mind. The difference between mimesis and textuality cannot be used to privilege words over paint and stone, or poetry over travel literature, for it is a difference at play *within* each medium or discourse. Spenser, however, feigns to internalize and transcend within his own fiction such competing forms as the literature of empirical discovery or the art of royal portraiture. His reiterated critique of visual representation is by no means disinterested, then—especially since the neo-Burgundian magnificence of court culture under the Henries had given way to a considerable reduction in royal patronage under Edward VI, Mary, and Elizabeth. In this context Spenser's critique of representation both redefines the object of royal patronage—"magnificence"—and asserts the superior value of his own medium in the magnification of the prince.

The politics of patronage and career provide one example of the ideological investments we encounter in Spenser's poetry, and of the way his visionary, spirit-centered poetics is inextricably caught up in imperial enthusiasm. *The Faerie Queene* is infinitely richer than a social text like the Cheapside pageant, but not fundamentally different in its interests and allegiances. The first stanza in canto 9, typical of Spenser's canto openings in its sententious moralizing, sets forth a politics of bodily form:

> Of all Gods workes, which do this world adorne,
> There is no one more faire and excellent,
> Then is mans body both for powre and form,
> Whiles it is kept in sober gouernment:
> But none then it, more fowle and indecent,
> Distempred through misrule and passions bace:
> It growes a Monster, and incontinent
> Doth loose his dignitie and naiue grace.
> Behold, who list, both one and other in this place.

(II.ix.1)

Especially in its formal apposition to the beginning of canto 9 in Book v, poised between Adicia's misrule and the sober government of Mercilla, this stanza offers what might be thought of as Menenius Agrippa's fable of the belly in reverse. It naturalizes an authoritarian image of restraint, fulfilling one of the classic functions of ideology: to derive political structures from nature or God. At the same time, it appropriates the aesthetic qualities of the human body, converting them into a "natural" sign of virtue, and so by reflex into a sign of "healthy" politics. Presumably the fact that all this is quite conventional, familiar from Castiglione, Elyot, La Primaudaye, and a hundred other writers, does not diminish its significance. Nature, God, idealized imperial monarchy, and the aesthetic properties human artists imitate from "Gods workes" are all functioning members of an ideological solidarity, a conventional network within which they mutually signify one another. They are interconnected through the human figure itself, "as though meaning were merely the ulterior predicate of a primal body." This network, or primal body—the most inescapable of ideological formations—is itself the "nature" Spenser's poetry imitates.

The ideological work performed by Spenser's poetry is well exemplified in stanza 3, where Guyon identifies the beauty of Gloriana's mind as "her bountie, and imperiall powre." Hamilton glosses "bountie" in this line as "goodness," but how can it fail to suggest munificence, especially in such close proximity to imperial power and to the *paragone* that advances poetry as a means of producing royal-imperial splendor? From whose point of view shall we say that an empress's generosity appears so neutrally as her "goodness"? As Englishman, poet, bureaucrat, colonist, and political subject, Spenser was himself *constituted* by Elizabeth's "imperiall powre," and was economically dependent on her "bountie." He therefore has reason to idealize both money and power as spiritual essences like the "grace and chastitie" he attributes to Elizabeth in stanza 4: all belong to her divine endowment, a "Thousand times fairer then her mortall hew."

The most powerful resource of this discourse is the metaphysical belief in a hierarchy of body and soul. The soul's ontological privilege is typically expressed as a form of the authority to govern. Guyon's rapturous praise of the fairy queen in the fourth stanza extends this implicit reliance on a metaphysics of spirit: more beautiful than her glorious visage by a thousand times, her glory proper "shineth as the morning starre, / And with her light the earth enlumines cleare" (st. 4.6–7). Only such a profound mystification of authority—no perfunctory or merely decorous ceremony of speech, but the necessary fiction by which that authority works—can account for the passionate compounding of political allegiance with idealized desire reflected in Guyon's rapid sequence of epithets, "My liefe, my liege, my Soueraigne, my deare" (st. 4.5).

Arthur's response in the next stanza further suggests the worldly interests that underlie what Montrose calls "the erotic idealization of a power relationship."[26] Guyon is "thrise happy," says Arthur, to labor in the service

> of that Princesse bright,
> Which with her bounty and glad countenance
> Doth blesse her seruaunts, and them high aduaunce.
> How may straunge knight hope euer to aspire,
> By faithfull seruice, and meet amenance,
> Vnto such blisse? sufficient were that hire
> For losse of thousand liues, to dye at her desire.
>
> (II.ix.5.3–9)

Varying Guyon's formula, Arthur unfolds the royal effulgence into "bounty and glad countenance"—and with the word "countenance" we are clearly in the world of patronage. The

[26] Montrose, " 'The Perfecte Patterne,' " p. 42.

term functions euphemistically, by way of a peculiar meta-phoric idealization of the "visage" (Latin *videre*, to see, + nominalizing suffix) depicted on Guyon's shield: the spiritual form of Gloriana's visage is her backing, her sanction, her approving gaze—a valuable commodity in the royal court, where it was linked to a "bounty" that included the distribution of lucrative patents and offices. The same euphemistic double-ness lurks in the paired verbs of the next line, where "blesse" is coupled with "high aduaunce," while the peculiarly sexual charge that ignites chivalrous allegiance breathes unmistakably in Arthur's talk of bliss, loss, death, and desire. Hamilton notes that Arthur's lines contrast with Mammon's offer to Gu-yon of Philotime: "Thy spouse I will her make, if that thou lust, / That she may thee aduaunce for workes and merites iust" (vii.49.8–9). The name "Philotime," meaning "love of honor," echoes the names of Arthur's tutor and his squire, and resembles that of his anima, "Prayse-desire." The details of her description, especially the catalogue in stanza 47 of "wrong wayes" by which her courtiers seek advancement, also corre-spond with the tenor of Spenser's complaints about Elizabeth's court in "Mother Hubberds Tale," *Colin Clovts come home againe*, "Prothalamion," and the last lines of the 1596 *Faerie Queene*, as well as with what we know of court politics. If, then, there is a troublesome discrepancy between Mam-mon's promise of "iust" reward and this description of the po-litical system, is it really very different from the discrepancy between Spenser's erotic idealization of Elizabeth and the Macchiavellian realism with which she actually governed? The differences Spenser *wants* to treat as schematic antitheses, be-tween *merce* and *mercede*, Philotime and Gloriana, or immod-erate "lust" for "high degree" (vii.49.8, 47.1) and Arthurian desire for praise, are all differences within his own poetics and career, not differences between himself and some hypothetical Malfont.

Hamilton's notes to these passages seek to locate a decisive point of difference between Gloriana and Philotime in a sort of political analogy to divine election. Philotime "offers salvation by good works contrary to the Protestant emphasis on faith rather than works. . . . Cf. the Faerie Queene's freely offered grace to advance her servants, ix.5.4–5, and Arthur's free act, viii.56.1–6." Yet if we venture into the network of cross references that establishes this distinction, what we find is a more elaborate version of the strategy we have already observed, which projects difference within as difference between.[27] At II.vii.46 Spenser describes the "great gold chaine ylinked well" familiar from Homer's *Iliad* as a symbol for divine control over the creation (*Iliad*.viii.18–27), and familiar from canto 9 of Book I as a symbol for *The Faerie Queene*'s projected unity. Here, though, the golden chain functions as an emblem of "Ambition," a social structure characterized by ruthless infighting:

> Those that were vp themselues, kept others low,
> Those that were low themselues, held others hard,
> Ne suffred them to rise or greater grow,
> But euery one did striue his fellow downe to throw.
>
> (II.vii.47.6–9)

The contrast with Arthur's "free act" is exact. Arthur has raised the fallen Guyon by defeating his enemies, yet refuses to acknowledge any obligation binding Guyon to reward or repay him (viii.56). The opening of canto 9 then brings us to the passage discussed above, in which Arthur turns from lamenting the literal failure of his quest for Gloriana to offer Guyon yet further aid, thus forging another link in the golden chain of concord and (presumably) climbing another rung in the ladder of true glory. In his delicate question to Guyon about entering royal service, Arthur has carefully avoided im-

---

[27] Cf. Barbara Johnson, *The Critical Difference: Essays in the Contemporary Rhetoric of Reading* (Baltimore: Johns Hopkins Univ. Press, 1980), p. x.

plying that one climbs this ladder by calculated reward, asking instead about how faithful service and due "amenance," or subjection to authority, might enable one "to aspire . . . Unto such blisse."

Guyon replies in stanza 6 that Arthur might well aspire to the "meed" or "grace" (a typically ambiguous pairing) of any earthly prince whatsoever—but that he could certainly expect "Great guerdon" and "favour high" from Gloriana should he desire to join the knights of Maidenhead. At this point Arthur avows before God that since he first pledged knighthood, his "whole desire hath been, and yet is now, / To serve that Queene with all my powre and might"—and complains that he's circled the globe in search of her. We have seen where the conversation goes from there: averting the literal ceremony that would assimilate his protagonist to an existing order of knighthood, Spenser has Arthur enact the spiritual significance of such orders in an apparently ad hoc fashion, lending fraternal aid to Sir Guyon in the quest at hand. The poem anticipates that such episodic confirmations of knightly solidarity will eventually complete a pattern whose symbol is the golden chain of concord, introduced proleptically at the first of Arthur's providential interventions:

> O Goodly golden chaine, wherewith yfere
> The vertues linked are in louely wize:
> And noble minds of yore allyed were,
> In brave poursuit of cheualrous emprize,
> That none did others safety despize,
> Nor aid enuy to him, in need that stands,
> But friendly each did others prayse deuize
> How to aduaunce with fauourable hands,
> As this good Prince redeemd the Redcrosse knight
>   from bands.   (1.ix.1)

In its emphasis on the advancement of another's praise, this passage stands diametrically opposed to the golden chain of ambition that structures the court of Philotime. Hamilton notes its function as a synecdoche of the poem's unity when he observes that "the linking of the virtues is shown by the relationship of the Books and the structure of the whole poem"—one example of which would of course be the ninth-canto positioning that links Arthur's fellowship with Redcrosse to his fellowship with Guyon, and so by a series of parallels and echoes links it as well to its antithesis in Mammon's cave.

The symbol of the golden chain is proleptic in that it looks forward to the completion of Arthurian magnificence as a gold-link fellowship of virtues, whose structure will coincide with the allegorical unity of the narrative's romance multiplicity. What remains uncertain is the relation between this projected fellowship and the already existing Order of Maidenhead. It appears to be another instance of the pattern we have been examining, of displacement-and-revision: Arthur's assertion in stanza 7, for instance, that his "whole desire" has been to enter Gloriana's service "sith I armes and knighthood first did plight," implies that the dream recounted in Book I may figure his assumption of knighthood, and that the object of his quest may in one of its aspects be a visionary retractation of the Order of Maidenhead.[28] If this were so, the comparison of Gloriana's grace to divine election would indeed be exact, not only because it is something one may aspire to but may never deserve, but also because it is something Arthur has always enjoyed but cannot know, except indirectly, until "iust time expired."

It would be a mistake, however, to dissolve the chivalric symbolism of knighthood too quickly into its otherworldly equivalent. Michael Leslie's recent study of chivalric symbolism in *The Faerie Queene* reemphasizes the political function of

[28] The argument of Michael Leslie, *Spenser's "Fierce Warres and Faithfull Loves": Martial and Chivalric Symbolism in "The Faerie Queene"* (Totowa, N.J.: Barnes and Noble, 1983), hereafter cited parenthetically as Leslie, *Spenser's "Fierce Warres."*

the ceremonial forms by which Elizabeth's regime sought to consolidate its authority and to solicit faith in its higher qualities. More specifically, Leslie demonstrates how closely the Order of Maidenhead in Spenser's poem is connected to the Order of the Garter, "the rituals of which consciously sought (and still seek) to recreate those of the Round Table" (*Spenser's "Fierce Warres,"* p. 26). St. George was patron of the Order, and its annual feast was held in celebration of St. George's day; moreover, "the device of the red cross, borne by St. George, and that of the 'heavenly Mayd,' borne by Sir Guyon, form also the two greatest badges of the Order" (p. 189). Its most conspicuous device, of course, was the Garter itself. The *Register* of the Order elucidates the symbolism of the Garter as follows:

> For by that honourable and orbicular Garter . . . the Knights were reminded, whatever they undertook to go thorow it with Piety, Sincerity, and Friendship, Faithfulness and Dexterity: That they Should not undertake, or attempt any Thing contrary to the Oath and Institution of their Order . . . That they should not stir a Foot contrary to their Fidelity, or what their Union and Band of Friendship required And that one Friend should not in the least Derogate from another. (Leslie, *Spenser's "Fierce Warres,"* p. 148)

As an emblem of mutual solidarity, signifying through its "orbicular" form the "Union and Band of Friendship" which declares "that one Friend should not in the least derogate from another," this Garter seems directly allied to the "Goodly golden chaine" celebrated at I.ix.1.

Leslie suggests, in fact, that Spenser planned an extensive structural analogy between *The Faerie Queene* and the Order. Recalling C. Bowie Millican's observation that "the sum of the books of Spenser's two projected poems equals the number of seats, with the king's own, on the famous Winchester Round Table," Leslie adds that there is no precedent for this number in the Arthurian tradition—whereas the Order contained, in addition to the Sovereign, his heir apparent, and certain others, a core of "twenty-four 'elected' knights, each of whom has his appointed stall in St George's chapel, Winsor Castle" (*Spenser's "Fierce Warres,"* p. 188). As "the principal chivalric institution of England, and arguably of Europe; and . . . a crucial element in the pageantry and state propaganda of Spenser's period" (p. 138), the Order may well be a historical "focal point, at which the fictional, legendary world of heroic and triumphant Arthurianism intersects with the Elizabethan world, and through which the qualities of the one can be attributed prophetically to the other" (p. 194). The specific importance of the Order as a diplomatic instrument of Elizabethan foreign policy—and above all its association, through Leicester and others, with the mirage of a Protestant League and the aggressive foreign policy that accompanied it—tend to confirm its prophetic function in Spenser's symbolism. The impatiently militaristic politics of Book V, especially in the Belge and Sir Bourbon episodes, suggests some very close parallels between the contemporary Order of the Garter and "the new, reformed order to which the virtuous knights-patron of *The Faerie Queene* will belong and which is to be revealed in triumph at the end of the poem" (p. 195).

To the extent that Leslie's hypothesis works by projecting a closure for the poem's proleptic structure, it once again precipitates our reading from insufficiency to anticipation. Yet it serves to emphasize the ideological burden this open-ended structure assumes in Spenser's poem, which seeks at once to represent (in Arthur) and to enact (in the reader) a sustained conversion of erotic energy to political and religious ends. This conversion is effected through a mystification of the poem's ideological investments: worldly and interested, they are nevertheless represented as ultimately spiritual, authorized by God. This dehiscence at the heart of Spenser's poetics means we must read him in two ways at once: even as the projected transcendence that authorizes the quest commits the quester to a program of idealization that strips the images of desire of all worldly and fleshly entanglements, the historical and political allegiances implicit in Spenser's conception of that transcendent form tend to invest desire in the *figurae* of a Protestant English imperium.

This confusion of ends does not often seem to bear directly on our reading of the poem, perhaps because both seem so distant from the medial perspective we share with Arthur. The more pressing danger seems rather to be the despair of achieving either. This is why Arthur complains so bitterly, and why he continually associates his quest with a self-destructive drive toward death: the crucial difference between transcendence and annihilation—an absolute metaphysical antithesis that underwrites all the provisional moral polarities needed to sustain the quest—is always still to be achieved. In the meantime the various contrasts that organize the poem, including that between the poem itself as quest for the perfect image of virtue and as competitor for "just" reward in the court of Philotime, remain objects not of knowledge but of an expectant faith that grows increasingly difficult to sustain. Arthur's hunger for the "blisse" of Gloriana's blessing, consciously intended as a soldier's prospective *morituri salutant*, is not completely free of either concupiscence or thanatos, for in *The Faerie Queene* the opposites of satisfaction and annihilation are impossible to separate. We can never purge Spenser's language of its eroticism, its overtones of patronage, its political implications, or its shadow of a wish for death—any more than we can purge these things from our own language and experience.

The only major human organs absent from the House of Alma
are the sexual ones. . . . —*Maurice Evans*

4. Alma's Nought

ueen Elizabeth swore frequently and, one pre-
sumes, with some relish. Like authority itself, oaths
were a masculine prerogative she could flourish.
Her male counselors naturally disapproved—the
younger Cecil once wrote that "she was more than a man, and,
in troth, sometimes less than a woman."[1] But they disapproved
of so much: her reluctance to submit to the yoke of honorable
matrimony, her galling presumption in expecting to be "the
ruler or half-ruler" of the kingdom,[2] her strategic preference
for misdirection and delay in foreign policy, her refusal to set-
tle the succession, her flirtations with a string of "favorites"—
the list of her privy counsel's exasperations was a long one, and
most of them stemmed either directly or indirectly from the
deep-seated feeling that it was radically inappropriate for a
woman to hold sway as the "Supreme Head" of anything, let
alone the mystical body of Church and State. St. Paul had been
quite explicit on this subject (Eph. 5:22–24), and what was
true for Church and family held true for the godly common-
wealth: the distinctively masculine organ in these supernatural
bodies was the head. No wonder then if the queen's favorite
threat against patronizing or subversive counselors was to
make them "shorter by the head."[3] Emasculating political sub-
ordinates who regarded themselves as her natural superiors
was undoubtedly one of the small consolations afforded by
Elizabeth's royal office.

[1] Neale, *Queen Elizabeth*, p. 404.
[2] Erickson, *First Elizabeth*, p. 241.
[3] *Ibid.*, p. 251.

164

THE VIRILE MEMBER

The mystical body of Tudor ideology is an ancient, thoroughly conventional image of corporate authority. Yet from an anatomical point of view it seems peculiar, if not aberrant, to regard the head as a gender-specific organ. This peculiarity serves an obvious political function, since it capitalizes male supremacy through the symbolic substitution of one body part for another. Perhaps, then, the special privilege of the *caput* in this system should be seen as dialectically related to a taboo on naming the penis.

No proper word for the genitals existed in sixteenth-century English. The *OED* shows the first use of "penis" late in the seventeenth century, and the first use of "phallus" in 1613. This is not conclusive evidence, in part because the cultural taboo against naming this organ is reflected by, as well as in, the dictionary, which defines but does not use the word "penis," relying instead on the quaint Victorian periphrasis "virile member." But corroboration may be found in contemporary expositions of the body natural, which show a significant gap in terminology. For example, the second volume of La Primaudaye's *French Academie* contains a "naturall history of the body and soule of man,"[4] an anatomical survey that begins with the face and head and follows the structure of the body downward, combining lessons in anatomy with sententious annotations on the moral wisdom emblematically inscribed therein. The testicles and ovaries receive brief treatment together under the name of "kernels," those organs "that are in more secret partes which serve for seede, namely to keepe it, to dresse it, and to prepare it for generation" (La

[4] Pierre de La Primaudaye, *The Second Part of the French Academie*, tr. Thomas Bowes, STC 15238 (London, 1594), (hereafter cited parenthetically as La Primaudaye, *Second Part French Academie*).

Primaudaye, *Second Part French Academie*, p. 53). The subject is treated more extensively in chapters 69–72, which include a thorough discussion of the "offices, sundrie partes and many members" involved in human reproduction—except that where we expect some mention of the virile member, we read instead: "But our meaning is not to make any long particular narration [this on p. 389 of the second volume], both by reason of the matter which would be very long, as also because sinne hath made the Generation of man so full of shame, that men can hardly speake of it, or of those members that serve thereunto, especially of one part of them, without shame." Neither shame nor the coy fear of "matter which would be very long" keeps the author from discussing "that slymie seede of man" (p. 396), or what he thought was a mixture of blood, sweat, and urine in the womb (p. 400). The taboo he observes has little to do, then, with squeamishness, and it is very specific. A similar pudicity may be observed in the 1597 translation of Aristotle's *Problemata*.[5] After a first, miscellaneous group of topics the volume proceeds anatomically, starting with the details of the face and head and working its way through such delicate subjects as "Piles or fluxe of blood in the fundament" (sig. D^{r-v}). All these chapters are headed by concrete nouns, names for either organs or humors, until we come to the genitals—at which point the heading style shifts to "Of carnall copulation."[6]

La Primaudaye once goes so far as to mention the body's need for "peculiar vessels" to serve the godly ends of reproduction, including "some to expell" the seed: "And as this ex-

[5] Anonymous, *The Problems of Aristotle, with other Philosophers and Phisitions. Wherein Are Contained Divers Questions, with Their Answers, Touching the Estate of Mans Bodie*, STC 764 (London, 1597).

[6] Although the chapter contains no designation for the penis, randomness takes its own revenge against erasure in the page signature on which the chapter begins: E, recto.

pulsive is necessary in Generation on behalfe of the male, So in regarde of the female it is requisite that there should be a vertue to containe and preserve" (*Second Part French Academie*, p. 389). The nonce euphemisims "expulsive" and "vertue" suggest that, "properly" speaking, the semantic space of the genitals is a vacuum in Elizabethan English. For this very reason, though, it becomes a vernacular carnival ground, where slang terms, nonce locutions, and innuendos ply garish trade. A glance through *Shakespeare's Bawdy*, while hardly the last word on the subject ("O what an endlesse worke have I in hand"), nevertheless can serve to suggest something of the semantic fertility of the *arvis genitalibus*, or what we might call the elision fields. According to Partridge, "In the approximate period 1590–1780, *yard* was perhaps the most generally used literary term for 'penis' "; but in Shakespeare he also finds, among others, bauble, cock, cod, carrot, dead men's fingers, distaff, dribbling dart of love, eel, erection, horn, hook, instrument, lance, little finger, needle, Pillicock, pipe, point, poll-axe, potato-finger, roger, standard, stump, sword, tail, tale, thing, thistle, thorn, three-inch fool, tool, and weapon.[7]

The most profound and consequential substitution made possible by a taboo on naming the penis is not found in anyone's bawdy, however: it is an ideological transformation of the body that grounds patriarchy in a catachrestic image called "Nature." If this ideological body is the nature imitated by Spenser's poetry, as I argued in chapter 3, then it should be possible to explore the literary workings and transformations of that ideology through a commentary on gender symbolism in *The Faerie Queene*. Such is the assumption of my next two chapters, which comment on sections of Books II and III in response to a series of questions about gender symbolism in

[7] Eric Partridge, *Shakespeare's Bawdy: A Literary and Psychological Essay and a Comprehensive Glossary*, rev. ed. (London: Routledge, 1968), p. 222. See also pp. 22–24, and the glosses of individual words.

Tudor ideology. What kind of metaphoric system substitutes the head for the penis? How does it reinscribe the female organs? How are such transformations involved in the system of specular relations that joins the poet and his monarch? And how does this metaphoric system use its body images to articulate vast and complex fields like the history and politics of empire? Spenser's allegory of the temperate body in II.ix will be our starting point because its symbolic structure offers a number of possibilities for examining the larger role of the human body as an ideological form in *The Faerie Queene*. The construction of the castle itself raises questions about the relation of the body to flesh on the one hand and to spirit on the other, about the relation of masculine to feminine, and about the relation of anatomical gender to the images of wholeness considered in earlier chapters. The discussion of feminine symbolism leads into a separate chapter anchored in readings of Book III, as might be expected. Meanwhile the relation of the body castle in II.ix to the chronicles of canto 10 shows how the corporal image serves to organize an imperial historiography.

Because the chronicles temporalize what emerges first as a static, architectural form, they return us to the prophetic concerns of chapters 2 and 3, centered on the figure of Arthur. It is through Arthur, then, that we will approach the body of Alma's castle. This epicene body appears to reinscribe Arthur's symbolic castration, for while its architecture incorporates any number of *heimlich* details, including the lips, tongue, nose, beard, and even "Port Esquiline," there are no sexual organs. No reader familiar with the cartoon monster Lust in Book IV— "his huge great nose . . . Full dreadfully empurpled all with bloud" (vii.6.5–6)—will suppose that Spenser could not for shame have allegorized the penis: the figure of Lust does exactly that—it allegorizes the penis *for shame*.[8] The first ques-

---

[8] Since the description of Lust also includes "a wide deepe poke" in his

tion Alma's castle raises, then, is why the genitals are not alle-
gorized *in the same way* as the other body organs, within the
same metaphysical conceit or figurative "frame"—and through
what reinscriptions they do find their way into representation.

HOW TO "AVOID" THE GENITALS

In Alma's heart, or parlor, Cupid sports among personified
affections:

> And in the midst thereof vpon the floure,
> A louely beuy of faire Ladies sate,
> Courted of many a iolly Paramoure,
> The which did them in modest wise amate,
> And eachone sought his lady to aggrate:
> And eke emongst them litle Cupid playd
> His wanton sports, being returned late
> From his fierce warres, and hauing from him layd
> His cruell bow, wherewith he thousands hath dismayd.
>
> (II.ix.34)

The comic tone of the ensuing "sophisticated courtly scene out
of medieval romance"⁹ is set from the beginning by the dimi-
nution of Cupid, who has turned from war to sport and laid
aside his bow. Spenser's reader has encountered this last ges-
ture three times before—in the proem to Book I, in Arthur's
account of himself to Una, and in the description of Guyon's
protecting angel—and will encounter it a fifth time in the Gar-
den of Adonis. Each time, the reference to Cupid's voluntary
disarmament indicates the sublimation of eros. Here, too, al-
though the language—"iolly" "Paramoure," "amate," "ag-
grate," "wanton," "dismayd"—resonates with sexual innu-
endo, its connotations are limited "in modest wise" by the

---

lower lip (st. 6.2), his physiognomy may travesty the androgyny of the risen
body.

⁹ Walter Davis, "The Houses of Mortality in Book II of *The Faerie
Queene*," *SpStud* 2 (1981): 124.

signals of eros tamed. Indeed the allegorical framing, or ana-
tomical *mise en scène*, of this modest courtship has already en-
acted the sublimation of eros inasmuch as it involves the stra-
tegic displacement of sexuality from the anatomical center of
the body to "the midst" of the chest cavity.

The ensuing comedy of self-consciousness and misrecogni-
tion begins with a typically Spenserian ambiguity: Alma enters
with Arthur and Guyon, and each of the knights "a Damsell
chose: / The Prince by chaunce did on a Lady light" (st. 36.5–
6). We saw in chapter 3 how pervasively Spenser's narrative
hovers between the apparent randomness of chivalric errancy
and the providential guidance of an allegorical foreconceit;
here that momentous uncertainty is scaled down, like "litle
Cupid," to a question of self-consciousness: is it purely by
chance that Arthur's choice turns out to be an image of himself?
She is an image, more precisely, of Arthur's repressed melan-
choly, as his own questions to her imply:

> Gentle Madame, why beene ye thus dismaid,
> And your faire beautie do with sadnesse spill?
> Liues any, that you hath thus ill apaid?
> Or doen you loue, or doen you lacke your will?
>
> (II.ix.37.5–8)

Arthur's questions echo tellingly against his own experience,
as the lady observes with some starch in response to his misdi-
rected reproach. Like the confounded alternatives of his an-
swer to Una at I.ix.7, the paired questions Arthur asks in line
8 turn out on reflection to be one: to love *is* to lack one's will.
To love as Arthur does is to lack it utterly and to be constituted
out of this radical lack, "precipitated from insufficiency to an-
ticipation" (Lacan, "Mirror Stage," p. 4). To be constituted
in this way is indeed to be dis-made by Cupid, and at its most
painful Arthur can scarcely distinguish his desire from death.

The scene at hand keeps these darker reflections in the mid-

dle distance but cannot completely exclude them. In the proem
to Book I, for instance, Spenser describes the "Heben bow" as
deadly (st. 3.5), and asks Cupid to lay it aside following a de-
scription of Arthur's quest for the fairy queen,

> Whom that most noble Briton Prince so long
> Sought through the world, and suffered so much ill,
> That I must rue his vndeserued wrong.   (I.pr. 2.6–8)

We next hear the request that Cupid lay aside his bow from
Arthur himself, when Una asks what "secret wound" could
grieve "the gentlest hart on ground":

> Deare Dame (quoth he) you sleeping sparkes awake,
> Which troubled once, into huge flames will grow,
> Ne euer will their feruent fury slake,
> Till liuing moysture into smoke do flow,
> And wasted life do lye in ashes low.
> Yet sithens silence lesseneth not my fire,
> But told it flames, and hidden it does glow,
> I will reuele, what ye so much desire:
> Ah Loue, lay downe thy bow, the whiles I may respire.
>
>   (I.ix.8)

The repetition of this phrase in II.ix.34, where Cupid has
"from him layd / His cruell bow," is intended to exclude love's
"feruent fury" from the parlor, yet it can scarcely fail to evoke
the suffering and the shadow of death that have haunted Arthur
like "vndeserued wrong." Small wonder then if his desire for
praise appears "somwhat sad, and solemne eke in sight, / As if
some pensiue thought constraind her gentle spright" (st. 36.8–
9).

   Arthur is a proleptic fiction, seemingly unrelated to the fig-
ure familiar from romance and legend because he is *not yet* the
Arthur we know, in a manner of speaking not yet himself.
This essential lack-of-self is the "breach" revealed (against his
will) by the action of Arthur's flesh and blood, "now seeming

flaming whot, now stony cold" when the lady turns his questions back upon him (st. 39.5). What the incident dramatizes in its comic mode is Arthur's thoroughly human will to misrecognition. His anima knows him better than he knows himself because she is something the heroic will refuses, "turning soft aside" from every encounter with its own castration: precipitated to anticipation by the reinscription of insufficiency as "Prays-desire," Arthur will always resume his quest for phallic self-completion.

Arthur turns aside "with chaunge of colour." His blushing carries over into the next scene, where we explore its implications in his subcharacter Guyon, whose parley with Shamefastnesse is parallel to and simultaneous with Arthur's courting. Prays-desire, we are told, "was right faire and fresh as morning rose, / But somwhat sad, and solemne eke in sight" (st. 36.7–8); Shamefastnesse is described as "right faire, and modest of demaine, / But that too oft she chaung'd her natiue hew" (st. 40.3–4). If the first description recalls the awakening of desire in Arthur, linking it to his postvisionary *triste* in the following line, then "modest of demaine" suggests Gloriana's other aspect, her deferral of full self-disclosure. That deferral is Gloriana's minus value, the denial of sexuality that sets her apart from Acrasia. Perhaps, then, Shamefastnesse is blushing over what she has in common with Acrasia, or with the immodest bathing beauties against which she and Prays-desire are so obviously counterpoised. Stanza 41 elaborates an ornamental simile for her passionate blushing that links Shamefastnesse curiously to the painted ivory gate of Acrasia's bower: "That [blushing] her became, as polisht yuory, / Which cunning Craftesmans hand hath ouerlayd / With faire vermilion or pure Castory" (lines 5–7). Hamilton glosses the passage with Donne's reference to "the creation of Adam from red earth: 'a rednesse that amounts to a shamefastnesse, to a blushing at our own infirmities, is imprinted in us by God's hand' (*Sermons* ix

64)." Guyon's suggestion in the next stanza that Shamefast-nesse fears some "ill . . . / That in the secret of your hart close lyes" (st. 42.3–4) may carry a similar suggestion. The ill she fears lies "close" in both senses, at once hidden and nearby: it could hardly be closer, since the heart's closet, the pericardium, is where they stand as they speak; and what that placement conceals, as I suggested earlier, is the dis-placement of desire from its earthier location.

If Guyon's question does inadvertently strike too "close," it makes sense for the lady's blushing to redouble itself: "The flashing bloud with blushing did inflame, / And the strong passion mard her modest grace" (st. 43.3–4). The blush, after all, is not only an indication of embarrassment; as the immediate bodily trace of "strong passion" it also partakes of the cause or source of embarrassment, and so leads into a metonymic vertigo of self-consciousness. The language of the scene works in an analogous way, not only because the more Guyon asks what is wrong the worse he makes it, but also because the source of embarrassment keeps flashing around inadvertently at the periphery of everyone's diction, from Guyon's question to Shamefastnesse about "the secret of your hart" to the narrator's remark just quoted, with its swishing and bubbling alliteration and its talk of blood, inflammation, and strong passion. Given the hysterical delicacy of the moment, Alma's question to Guyon, "Why wonder yee / Faire Sir at that, which ye so much embrace" (st. 43.6–7), seems certain to set off another furious round of blushing.

This *mise en abŷme* of blushing extends into the next stanza, where Guyon colors "in priuitee" (another loaded phrase) and then repeats Arthur's evasion by turning "his face away" from the abyss that has opened beneath his effort to make small talk with an image of himself. Such anima-adversion is the only tactful escape from the infinite regress, and we find Alma gamely pitching in: "She the same / Dissembled faire, and faynd to ouersee" (st. 44.2–3). So too does the narrator, who concludes with a straight face, "Thus they awhile with court and goodly game, / Themselues did solace each one with his Dame" (st. 44.4–5). And while it emerges within the scene's decorum as a kind of bemused tact, this voluntary misrecognition appears to "lie at the heart" of Guyon's virtue in both senses of the phrase: the "fountaine of [Guyon's] modestee," the originary principle of his *verecundia*, is the action of feigning to overlook, here confounded by a direct reflection of itself.

The displacement through which genital eros finds its way into representation within the temperate body is enacted silently by this allegorical "framing" of sexuality in the heart. There it emerges in an unstable ratio of shamefastness, which denies access to the genitals, and desire for praise, which reinscribes libido as ambition. Feigning to oversee is thus an integral part of the representational strategy by which the reinscription of sexuality proceeds. Spenser opens this strategy to deconstructive reading because he doubles the frame: he brings his knights into the human heart to confront the displacement and reinscription of their desires. The result is a momentary dehiscence of the representational frame, in which Arthur and Guyon glimpse the castration out of which they are constituted and quickly turn aside, reenacting *within* the scene the invisible framing gesture that first summoned it into representation.

One of the more baffling features of Alma's castle is the "royall arras" that hangs in the heart's parlor, "In which was nothing pourtrahed, nor wrought, / Not wrought, nor pourtrahed, but easie to be thought" (st. 33.8–9). Perhaps these lines are intended to refer to the "preimaginal" nature of the sensitive soul's apprehensive power, as Berger suggests; or as Mills has argued, to simple "sensory forms awaiting conceptualization."[10] But clearly the arras stands in complete contrast

[10] Harry Berger, Jr., *The Allegorical Temper: Vision and Reality in the "Faerie Queene" II* (New Haven: Yale Univ. Press, 1957), p. 77n (hereafter

to the tapestries and other artifacts that decorate Spenser's places of lust. The unforgettable image of Busirane "figuring straunge characters of his art" with the "liuing blood" that runs from Amoret's transfixed heart (III.xii.31.2–4) combines and gruesomely literalizes two thoroughly conventional figures of speech, that of writing in the heart and that of love as a piercing arrow; it is a striking and self-conscious *abusio* of these topoi. Since Busirane's power turns out to be based on illusion, and since the power of illusion is, thematically, what distinguishes Spenser's allegorical figurings from sensual verse and *trompe l'oeil* painting, it seems reasonable to assume that the arras in Alma's heart participates in a contrast with the idolatrous imagery of the carnal imagination.

As an interior screen where almost anything may appear but where no image remains fixed, the arras corresponds suggestively to the representational space of the allegory itself. We saw in chapter 3 that Spenser's ideology of representation involves something like a highly sublimated iconoclasm, a sustained movement of displacement-and-revision that keeps undoing the premature or provisional closure which enables mimetic representation. We also saw that Spenser uses the anti-representational force of writing to imply a questionable distinction between the pictorial arts and his own form of allegorical portraiture. Walter Davis has pointed out the way Spenser's mode of representation shifts, as we tour the castle with Alma, from a graphic physical allegory of the vegetable soul's functions to a social comedy of the sensitive soul's affections, and finally to the "general and abstract terms" of the intellectual soul.[11] This description makes the representational space of the poem itself a kind of mystic writing pad, like the arras in Alma's heart. It may also be significant that the arras makes

cited parenthetically as Berger, *Allegorical Temper*); Jerry Leath Mills, "Symbolic Tapestry in *The Faerie Queene*, II. ix. 33," *PQ* 49 (1970): 568–69.

[11] Davis, "Houses of Mortality," pp. 124–25.

its appearance in stanza 33—just at the threshold between the vegetable and sensitive souls. This threshold marks the conceptual border that "frames" discontinuous spaces of figuration; if one representational mode is to give way to its successor, it must do so through a sort of implicit self-erasure, and this self-erasure is figured not only *in* the arras, but *at* the point of transition between modes of figuration. Spenser thus introduces the paradoxical logic of reinscription just at that point in the allegory where we are called upon to perform a comparable operation, relinquishing the concreteness of the kitchen scene for a more complex, more fully "sublimated" image of the body.

We have already seen how the heart's comedy of *méconnaisance* seems to extend the protagonists' unsettling self-consciousness into a structural principle, so that the allegory verges on a glimpse of the erasure that makes it possible. If we look back to the kitchen allegory of the vegetable soul, what we find is a correspondingly cruder version of this meta-allegory. The governing metaphor here is not coupling, or subli-mating, but digestion: with Guyon and Arthur, we enter the body through the mouth, descend the throat to the stomach, and survey the mechanics of excretion, as though we had been allegorically swallowed. Actually, though, the metaphor works the other way around: unlike Polonius, we arrive not where we are eaten, but where we eat. Spenser's name means "steward," and Hamilton glosses the last two lines of stanza 27—"He Steward was hight *Diet*; rype of age, / And in demeanure sober, and in counsell sage"—as "witty praise of the poet's own name." This reading gains further support from the description in stanza 29 of the kitchen as "a vaut ybuilt for great dispence." At least one of Spenser's contemporaries must have read this as a pun, for in a 1598 poem attributed to Carew the same wordplay occurs—unmistakably—together with an explicit echo of stanza 47's resonant opening, "Ne can I tell, ne can I stay to tell / This parts great workmanship":

> But neither can I tell, ne can I stay to tell,
> This pallace architecture, where perfections dwell:
> Who list such know, let him *Muses despencier* reede. . .[12]

As the figure presiding over an allegorical repast, Spenser signals our metaphoric repletion just where we would expect him to—in stanza 33, as we cross over into another mode of figuration:

> Which goodly order, and great workmans skill
> Whenas those knights beheld, with rare delight,
> And gazing wonder *they their minds did fill.*
> (II.ix.33.1–3, emphasis added)

There is yet another sense in which stanza 33 represents a turning point in Spenser's representation of the body, for in order to reach the parlor Alma and her guests must literally turn and retrace their steps: "Thence back againe faire Alma led them right." Anatomically speaking, the point at which they turn is at or very near the center of the body, and of course the line in which they turn is the fifth, the structural pivot of Spenser's nine-line stanza. I mentioned earlier that we enter at the mouth and descend, tracing in a quite literal way the path of swallowed food; the larger itinerary we are following returns us symmetrically from the midpoint of the body through the heart back to the head. Our return trip, however, grows increasingly complex, as the allegorical modes we encounter grow progressively more abstract, sublimating their physical tenor through increasingly sophisticated representational strategies.

These progressively more ambitious retractions of the

---

[12] Cummings, *Spenser: Critical Heritage*, p. 95. In commendatory verses to *The Faerie Queene*, "H. B." refers to Spenser as "this rare dispenser" of the Muses' graces (*Works*, p. 409).

anatomy depend on erasures to frame them. At the level of the vegetable soul this erasure should be expressed in its most literal or physical form. It does not appear directly, however, for even at this level the erasure of the genitals is what *frames* the space of representation, not what appears within it. Thus our tour of the vegetable soul ends with a physical turning aside at precisely the point where we might have expected to encounter the genitalia, and proceeds to a sublimated image of human sexuality in the parlor of the heart. There the knights confront allegorical personifications of their own desires, feminine figures who turn out on closer inspection to represent as well the very process of sublimation whereby the knights' desires are precipitated from physical insufficiency to symbolic anticipation. This uncanny doubling of themselves leads the knights into a self-consciousness they cannot sustain, a vertiginous glimpse of the essential lack on which their questing selves are founded. With help from Alma and from the narrator himself, they turn aside from what they see, feigning instead to "ouer-see"—and so repeating in a different mode the physical turning aside that occurs in stanza 33.

The term "sublimation" is itself an example of what it means, a metaphor abstracted from a physical process that uses heat to purify solids. Digestion (Spenser's "concoction") is a kind of sublimation through which the body assimilates nutriment from food; it is Spenser's most physical image of the movement from matter to spirit on which his fiction and his poetics are based.[13] The "negative moment" in this vegetable

---

[13] Compare Donne: "Now, as the end of all bodily eating, is Assimilation, that after all other concoctions, that meat may be made *Idem corpus*, the same body that I am; so the end of all spirituall eating, is Assimilation too, That after all Hearing, and all Receiving, I may be made *Idem spiritus cum Domino*, the same spirit, that my God is." *Sermons*, VI, p. 223, cited in Frank Manley, ed., *John Donne: The Anniversaries* (Baltimore: Johns Hopkins Univ. Press, 1963), pp. 141–42. William Kerrigan, "Ego in the English Renaissance," writes that "the best academic medicine of the Renaissance

dialectic is its expulsion of waste material, represented in stanza 32 with an engaging combination of frankness and wit:

> But all the liquor, which was fowle and wast,
> Not good nor seruiceable else for ought,
> They in another great round vessell plast,
> Till by a conduit pipe it thence were brought:
> And all the rest, that noyous was, and nought,
> By secret wayes, that none might it espy,
> Was close conuaid, and to the back-gate brought,
> That cleped was *Port Esquiline*, whereby
> It was auoided quite, and throwne out priuily.[14]   (II.ix.32)

As we move from the body's plumbing back up to its sitting room, the process of sublimation begins to double and redouble itself, refining the allegory by purifying it more and more of fleshly contamination. Reminders of the physical basis and origin of sublime allegorical figures are thus a structural embarrassment, an inopportune return of what should have been "auoided quite." It would be perverse, therefore, to point out that the words "close," "secret," and "priuily," which occur

---

invested the real anatomy with features that modern dreamers attribute to their imaginary anatomies" (p. 294). Among these is the Galenic use of digestion or "the separation of nourishment" as a model for other body processes, including those of the brain: "imagination gathered, reason cooked, memory assimilated: the human mind ate, digested, and incorporated the external world" (p. 295).

[14] Arthur and Guyon may behold the "goodly order, and great workmans skill" on display in this scene "with rare delight, / And gazing wonder" in part because they, like Spenser, live before the invention of indoor plumbing. Describing Hampton Court in the days before Harrington's water closet, Carolly Erickson remarks that its stench "must have been at least as awe-inspiring as its architecture, and detectable from nearly as far away. . . . [T]here was no sewage system. Combined with the overpowering odors from the discarded kitchen garbage and stable sweepings and foul-smelling rushes, full of spilled food and sour wine and animal droppings, the stink of the servants' privies must have made an alarming assault on the senses" (*First Elizabeth*, p. 223).

together in stanza 32, occur together again in stanzas 42 and 44, where Guyon asks Shamefastnesse what "in the secret of your heart close lyes," and blushes "in priuitee" when he finds out. The words have been cleansed, refined by that framing strategy otherwise known as "reading in context," and so can have no relevance to the obviously strained interpretation of blushing as an unwelcome reminder of the personification's "person."[15]

In his gloss on stanza 29, Hamilton summarizes the path of this "Cook's tour" through the body, noting that it "*avoids* the sexual organs" (emphasis added). Professor Hamilton is not above the occasional bad pun, as his comment on "fundamental matters" in stanza 32 indicates, and it is difficult not to wonder whether he intends another one here. If not, he should have. The urinary tract and bowels bring us to just the point at which we should encounter the genitals, but instead they are treated as "nought"—naughty, and therefore nothing; they are "auoided quite," excluded "priuily," and so become the figurative excrementa of this first "digestion" of the body into allegory. The body is thus doubly refigured: as flesh—for which the genitals are a kind of negative metonymy—the body is repudiated, refigured as excrement; while as coherent form (synecdoche, symbolic wholeness, phallic self-sufficiency) it is displaced into an open-ended series of transformations. We have already encountered the first of these transformations in the structure of the tour itself, which turns aside from the instruments of copulation to discover an allegorical coupling in the heart.

[15] The displacement of the literal toward the symbolic may be experienced at the level of close reading through a variety of cues that evoke a sense of double perspective or widening of context. The negative moment of this rising movement is experienced as a sense of sharp contextual limit on the connotations of words and images; my readings frequently call attention to this limiting principle by transgressing it. My purpose is neither to ignore the poet's intentions nor to violate them capriciously, but to read those intentions within a critical frame of reference that does not coincide with them, and that will allow their strategic exclusions to become manifest.

Our first overview of Alma's castle introduces this splitting of the body between form and substance. Stanza 21 exemplifies a conventional cluster of associations linking the flesh of the body with matter, and thus by a series of metonymies with mortality, pride, and the vanity of wordly pretensions—all in opposition to the spirit and its works:

> First she them led vp to the Castle wall,
> That was so high, as foe might not it clime,
> And all so faire, and fensible withall,
> Not built of bricke, ne yet of stone and lime,
> But of thing like to that *Aegyptian* slime,
> Whereof king *Nine* whilome built *Babell* towre;
> But O great pitty, that no lenger time
> So goodly workemanship should not endure:
> Soone it must turne to earth; no earthly thing is sure.
>
> (II.ix.21)

Hamilton notes that "king Nine," or Ninus, is "a parody of the nine from which the temperate body is constructed, 22.8." Babel is likewise a negative type of "that heauenly towre, / That god hath built for his owne blessed bowre" (47.4–5). By a slight extension of these analogies we may see Ninus and his doomed construction as antitypes of the poet and the poem: Ninus worked in the medium of death, but Spenser's poesis refines the material of the body in the direction of pure spirit. Stanza 21 thus looks backward to the House of Pride, where Ninus languishes with other scriptural types of wordly tyranny in close proximity to the "shamefull end" or posterior exit, with its "donghill of dead carkases" (I.v.48.3–4, 53.6–8); and it looks forward by antithesis to the triumphant opening of canto 12, "Now gins this goodly frame of Temperance / Fairely to rise," where Spenser salutes the erection of his own allegorical edifice.

Stanza 22 again refigures the division between form and matter, this time as a distinction within the body's architecture:

> The frame thereof seemd partly circulare,
> And part triangulare, O worke diuine;
> Those two the first and last proportions are,
> The one imperfect, mortall, foeminine;
> Th'other immortall, perfect, masculine,
> And twixt them both a quadrate was the base,
> Proportioned equally by seuen and nine;
> Nine was the circle set in heauens place,
> All which compacted made a goodly diapase.　　(II.ix.22)

The contrast between form and matter, already assimilated in stanza 21 to the difference between mortality and immortality, is now extended to include the differences between masculine and feminine, circle and triangle, and—in terms of the body's vertical axis—between the head that approaches heaven and the legs that reach to the ground. Hamilton reads the resulting structure as symbolically hermaphroditic; Fletcher reads it as epithalamial.[16] But within this image of transcendence and reconciliation we find masculine authority hierarchically privileged. We also find what may be Spenser's most explicit reinscription of the human genitals: the privileged signifier of masculinity is a divine circle and that of femininity an earthly delta—geometrical analogue to the Nile river delta, source of Egyptian slime and recurrent image in *The Faerie Queene* of natural fecundity. Thus what is offered as an explicit image of the higher unity of man and woman in a single body, *figura* of the risen body "in which there is neither male nor female," also represents the castration of both genders.

Woman is symbolically castrated in that she is at once excluded from the perfect closure of the divine circle and subordinated within a deceptively symmetrical unity. Her bodily specificity is in effect converted into a sign of all that is fallen in nature, just as man's is converted into a sign of the self-

[16] Hamilton's reference occurs in his gloss to II.ix.22. Cf. Angus Fletcher, *The Prophetic Moment: An Essay on Spenser* (Chicago: Univ. of Chicago Press, 1971), p. 20.

sufficient perfection from which we fell. This allegorical rein-
scription of the body is repeated in our tour of the castle, which
begins and ends in the divine masculine circle of the head and
traces yet another image of that circle in its descent and return.
The lowest point of our allegorical itinerary is the lacuna that
marks the body's castration and forms the apex of the feminine
delta: the subwaistline regions that are symbolically associated
with femininity and the earth lie outside the representational
"frame" constituted by this ideal circle. Thus while the ascend-
ing movement that leads back up to the head pursues increas-
ingly sublime refigurations of the male organ, the female or-
gan disappears except in its negative form, becoming "nought"
in every sense. No wonder shame is personified as a hysteri-
cally blushing woman.

THE INTENTIONAL TURRET

If the turning aside and feigning not to see of the parlor
scene really are allegorical retractations of physical "avoid-
ance" in its multiple senses, then as we pass from the parlor to
the turret we should expect to cross another threshold between
modes of representation. We climb the spinal vertebrae with
Alma and her guests at the end of stanza 44; in stanza 45, true
to form, a new dimension is introduced into the symbolism:

> That Turrets frame most admirable was,
> Like highest heauen compassed around,
> And lifted high aboue this earthly masse,
> Which it suruew'd, as hils doen lower ground;
> But not on ground mote like to this be found,
> Not that, which antique *Cadmus* whylome built
> In *Thebes*, which *Alexander* did confound;
> Nor that proud towre of *Troy*, though richly guilt,
> From which young *Hectors* bloud by cruell *Greekes*
>   was spilt.   (II.ix.45)

This stanza reemphasizes the vertical orientation we noted in stanza 22, likening the turret to heaven and stressing its distance from the "earthly masse" on which it stands. But here we also encounter a temporal dimension to the symbolism in the negative simile that denies likeness between the *caput* and such antique capitals as Troy and Thebes. These cities, like the tower of Babel in stanza 21, are seen as types of fallen pride, emblems of the mortality to which every edifice *on ground* is doomed. As human antitypes of the divine craftsmanship on display in the structure of the body, they further explicate the earlier pun on "Nine."

Together with the reference to "highest heauen" in line two, these antitypes of God's workmanship anticipate the anagogical symbolism of stanza 47:

> Ne can I tell, ne can I stay to tell
> This parts great workmanship, and wondrous powre,
> That all this other worlds worke doth excell,
> And likest is vnto that heauenly towre,
> That God hath built for his owne blessed bowre.
>
> (II.ix.1—5)

The dimension added to the allegory as we move from the sensitive to the intellectual soul is here clearly identified as a kind of typology. Like the Redcrosse knight on the Mount of Contemplation, we attain a vantage from which time itself may be "suruew'd," and from this privileged perspective we see the human head as *figura* of the New Jerusalem. This privileging of perspective rises on the back of yet another doubling of the representational frame, for the head is both what we see and the position from which we view it. Thus the allegorical space of the brain is distributed among three faculties—memory, judgment, and imagination—and these compose the temporal dimension added to the allegory, their separate gazes trained on what is past, and passing, and to come.

One feature of Spenser's craft which has often been re-
marked is the sense of timing with which he witholds or re-
veals names. It seems curious that while imagination and
memory are christened with names derived from Greek, the
personage located "in the middest" goes unnamed. He is de-
scribed in stanza 54, however, as "a man of ripe and perfect
age" whom long meditation has made "right wise, and won-
drous sage" (lines 2, 5). These phrases echo the earlier descrip-
tion of Diet as "rype of age, / And in demeanure sober, and in
counsell sage" (st. 27.8–9), the same words Hamilton glosses
as "witty praise of the poet's own name." The calculated reso-
nance of stanza 54 may be a discreet way of suggesting that the
faculty of judgment is, as it were, the "Muses dispencier" or
Despencer.[17] Certainly there is an analogy between the func-
tions performed by Diet and judgment: each within his own
sphere chooses and directs, and so shadows the poet's respon-
sibility for the allegorical dispensation of his narrative.

From this point of view it seems especially significant that
neither memory nor imagination comprehends a principle of
discrimination. Phantastes "mad or foolish seemd" (st. 52.7);
his chamber is abuzz with flies that encumber the senses, inter-
fering with our efforts to know (st. 51.1–3). As emblems of
the fantasy's susceptibility to false knowledge, these buzzing
flies appropriately recall the gnat similes Spenser has used to
characterize Maleger's troops (II.ix.16) and Errour's brood
(I.i.22–3), as well as the "Legions of Sprights . . . like little
flyes" that Archimago summons to encumber the Redcrosse
knight's fantasy (I.i.38.2). Phantastes and his chamber confuse
the functions of the good and bad Genii described at xii. 47–48,
mixing visions and prophecies with dreams and unsound opin-
ions (st. 51.7–8), images "such as in the world were never yit"

[17] Given Spenser's habits of composition it may well be significant that
these paired allusions to himself appear in stanza 27 and its "double," stanza
54.

with others "daily seene, and knowen by their names" (st. 50.4–6), or "leasings, tales, and lies" with poetic fictions, which must surely be included in "all that fained is" (st. 51.9). This radical inability to recognize pattern and order is evoked in the asyndetic list that closes stanza 50: "Infernall Hags, Centaurs, feendes, Hippodames, / Apes, Lions, Aegles, Owles, fooles, louers, children, Dames." Hamilton notes that "at first reading, all seem lumped together"; he then breaks the list down into three sets of four ("fantastical creatures"; "animals"; "inferior humankind") and observes that on "second reading" the human types come into focus as those in whose "idle fantasies" the rest of the list may be found. But second reading, the mental activity of classifying and deducing relations, is a function of the middle chamber; the most significant thing about Spenser's list is precisely its failure to indicate the distinctions Hamilton reads in.

Eumnestes' chamber is filled with books instead of pictures, and Berger suggests a progression from the fantastic images of the first room through the murals of the second to the written documents of the last (*Allegorical Temper*, p. 83). This is not, however, another version of the *paragone* among artistic media, for Eumnestes sits "tossing and turning" his records "withouten end" (st. 58.2)—that is, without any principle of closure to direct his research. As usual, "end" is an anal pun, for this "man of infinite remembrance" (st. 56.1) is like Nietzsche's intellectual dyspeptic: "What we experience and absorb," writes Nietzsche, "enters our consciousness as little while we are digesting it (one might call the process 'inpsychation') as does the thousandfold process, involved in physical nourishment—the so-called 'incorporation.' The man in whom this apparatus of repression is damaged and ceases to function properly may be compared (and more than merely compared) with a dyspeptic—he cannot 'have done' with anything."[18] As

[18] Nietzsche, *Genealogy of Morals*, pp. 57–58.

pure memory, Eumnestes lacks a principle of elimination. His work is culturally essential—he is, after all, the keeper of the "immortal scrine" from which the poem itself is derived (st. 56.6; compare I.pr.2.3). But his work is also literally interminable, since he records events "still, as they . . . pas" (st. 56.3). In effect he embodies yet another form of infinite regress, since every gesture that might intrude to shape and limit his records takes its place immediately *among* them.[19]

There is a sense, if we push this logic far enough, in which Eumnestes could well overburden the function of the middle chamber, and a sense likewise in which judgment can bring perspective to "infinite remembrance" only through what Nietzsche calls an "apparatus of repression." This apparatus produces what I have called in varying contexts the "negative moment" or castrating gesture intrinsic to Spenser's poetics: in terms of historical ordering it involves displacing selected elements from the welter of the past and, through a version of dialectical *aufhebung* (sublation), refiguring them as types of the first and the last, the idea of an origin and the sense of an ending. Such temporal boundaries are an irreducible condition of meaningfulness; they are yet another version of the "frame" without which representational space cannot emerge. The repression that erases persons and events at the "literal" level on which Eumnestes operates means that their dialectical elevation must "fayne to ouersee" the infinite regress from which, strictly speaking, it cannot escape. This is what it means to say, as I did earlier, that the typological perspective Spenser associates with the human head as a figure of eternity gains its "suruew" of history by rising on the back of an infinite regress.

The walls of the middle chamber are painted with images of memorable deeds, with texts and scenes of legal and political deliberation, and with "All artes, all science, all Philosophy, /

---

[19] My comments on Eumnestes in this paragraph are indebted to work in progress by Elizabeth J. Bellamy.

And all that in the world was aye thought wittily" (st. 53.8–
9)—in short, with just about the full sum of human knowl-
edge. Berger stresses that these images have been "intellec-
tually judged" (*Allegorical Temper*, p. 83), and what sets the
unnamed figure in their midst apart from Eumnestes and
Phantastes is precisely that his activity comprehends a princi-
ple of discrimination: he alone is said to *meditate* the images
that surround him (st. 54.3). Angus Fletcher's seminal work
on the Spenserian conception of poetic prophecy stresses its his-
toricism: "The prophet," says Fletcher, "thinks in terms of
continual emergencies, if not crises, since for him the past and
the future are gathered into an overloaded present."[20] In the
passage we are examining, the middle chamber figures that
"overloaded present," and the meditative function of the sage
who operates there implicitly gathers memory and imagination
into itself, composing a radical allegory of Spenserian *poesis*.

Spenser explains in *Fowre Hymnes* that meditation involves
the reduction of images to ideal essences (HB, 211–17); it is
therefore another name for what I have called their elevation
or sublation. As a form of *historiography* it must refer to the
dialectical processes that establish value and duration. Such
processes are inherently projective, even tendentious, yet with-
out them there is no representational space, no frame of refer-
ence, within which we can meaningfully speak of the "pres-
ent." Thus if Eumnestes' chamber suggests the infinite regress
into which this historicism intervenes (and which it cannot ac-
knowledge as such), the chamber of judgment likewise sug-
gests the specular doubling of representational space whereby
perspective is established: the meditative activity of judgment
not only takes place in, and focuses on, the present; it also *con-
stitutes* that "present" as its sphere of concern. The function of
judgment, in other words, summons itself into representation

[20] Fletcher, *Prophetic Moment*, p. 5.

and constitutes its own authority on the basis of a deep, unacknowledged circularity. This circularity is the specular double, or uncanny "other," of the divine circle in whose image the head and its privileged perspective on time are inscribed.

What does it mean to say that the *mise en abŷme* and the image of God are specular doubles? For one thing, it means that the relation between them is at once indispensable and undecidable. We have seen repeatedly how Spenser plays on the difference between randomness and providence, chance and choice, or romance errancy and the patterning of an allegorical foreconceit. The poem continually evokes this indefinite doubling of perspective; the more closely we read its surface, the more pervasive the effect seems to be. The various technical means by which this effect is achieved are all ways of keeping us suspended in "the middest" while sustaining the impression of a larger perspective. What we have seen repeatedly, however, is that this larger perspective is a retreating horizon, constituted by a closure for which Gloriana herself is the image. It is everywhere foreshadowed, yet nowhere finally present.

We find a typical instance of this effect in stanza 59 when Spenser tells us "There chaunced to the Princes hand to rize, / An auncient booke, hight *Briton moniments*." Berger notes the subtlety of phrasing by which these lines evoke an oblique sense of Providence at work (*Allegorical Temper*, p. 80); and when we learn in the next stanza that Guyon "chaunst" on the *Antiquitie* of Fairyland, there seems little doubt that we are witnessing a refiguration of the chance choices that paired the two with their animas in the chamber of the heart. Yet if chance is one possible name for the force that directs the knights to just these books, and just these women; and if divine Providence, and "Gloriana," are other possible names; we can scarcely forget that another set of names is equally pertinent: from "A Letter of the Authors," for instance, we might cite "the generall intention and meaning, which in the whole course [of the allegory] I have fashioned"; "my generall intention"; "a pleasing Analysis of all"; or "the whole intention of the conceit." These are phrases for what Sidney calls the poet's "foreconceit," and as the letter makes clear, they figure that strategic intervention in which the poet "thrusteth into the middest, even where it most concerneth him, and there recoursing to thinges forepaste, and divining of thinges to come, maketh a pleasing Analysis of all." In other words, they figure the poet's relation to the man in the middle chamber, who has at once no name and many names, including the name "Spenser."

This middleman of the mind represents the domain of purposive action, of concern and intentionality, as the language of the letter implies. When we move from canto 9 to canto 10, "recoursing to thinges forepast," we move into the domain of memory, but we do so according to a program devised in the middle chamber. This program—the poet's intention—"thrusteth into" Eumnestes' chamber not on the basis of absolute knowledge, but on the basis of *concern*, or desire. This concern aspires to coincide with Providence, but it arises *within* history, generated, as we saw in chapter 2, by the imperial etiology fabricated in Henry VIII's statutory preambles and elaborated by Tudor lawyers, martyrologists, genealogists, and historians. This concern can rise above its arbitrary origin in Catherine's infertility only by asserting an alternative etiology, yet no such assertion can appear as meaningful or purposive except within the teleology it must first assert.

Spenser situates this allegory of intentionality within an image of the temperate body. This is one reason psychoanalysis proves useful in framing a critical reading: it summons into representation what Spenser's poetic intentions necessarily exclude from view. What Spenser's intentions exclude are the genitals; what his allegory shows but cannot say is that the poet, protagonist, and reader are alike precipitated into anticipation—into a series of ever more abstract, ever more sublime, ever more "universal" reinscriptions of the Logos—by an initial refusal of the literal facts of the flesh. This refusal is in turn implicated in the sexual politics of patriarchy, for the castrative reinscription that "thrusteth into the middest" of the body "even where it most concerneth *him*" is one that turns aside from the literal penis in order to erect the symbolic privilege of the phallus. In discussing stanzas 21 and 22 I had occasion to remark that this gesture involves the castration of woman as well as that of man, but the symbolic ascendancy of the masculine means that in order to "complete" a reading of Alma's body castle, I had to turn away from reading the reinscription of the female pudendum with the observation that it disappears except in its negative form. This displaced part-object turns up again in the Garden of Adonis, to be discussed in chapter 5; in the meantime let it be noted that having reached the end of canto 9 we find not the phallic completion of the symbolic pattern we were following, but its calculated displacement into the following canto. There Spenser undertakes the daunting task of assimilating chronicle history to his "pleasing analysis" of the Tudor dynasty and its translation of Christian empire. In the process, he also begins the recuperation of feminine fertility that is fully developed only in Book III.

THE ORIGIN OF HISTORY

Spenser frames his redaction of chronicle materials in much the same way as he has framed the temperate body. The broad paradigm within which he grasps and presents British history is that of an ascent from "ground . . . vnto the highest skies" (st. 1.3–5) or "from earth . . . to heauens hight" (st. 2.4–5). These terms carry a whole complex of associations, linking matter, death, lust, blindness, fantasy, and fertility on the one hand, against spirit, life, love, vision, reason, and formative power on the other. Underlying this vertical paradigm in the chronicles is the specular relation between poet and monarch. In order to launch the dialectical ascent which both desire, Spenser must ostensibly repress one-half of that specular relation: the self-constitutive role of judgment in framing the present moment, or here, the constitutive force of the poet's representation of monarchy. The image of an ascent from the ground to the sky, for example, occurs twice in the first two stanzas of canto 10, first as a task confronting the poet and then as an achievement of the Tudor lineage. The difference in verb tenses—Elizabeth's ancestry *doth* ascend; how *may* my verse do likewise?—clearly suggests that the poet's "haughtie enterprise" is simply to "equall" in his own vein the accomplishments of the British rulers, giving them their literary due. Yet we learn in stanza 4 that the deeds of these celebrated ancestors were "enrold" in the heavens by "Immortall fame" (line 8), which is to say by written praise. The poet who undertakes to "blazon farre away" the name of his "soueraine Queene" (st. 3.9) participates in the action of immortal fame and so augments the means "By which all earthly Princes she doth farre surmount" (st. 1.9) And if this surmounting renders the Tudor ancestry "Argument worthy of *Maeonian* quill, / Or rather worthy of great *Phoebus* rote," then by reflex it also ennobles the latter day Homer or Apollo who dares to "equall" his argument in a speculation whereby each serves the other's ascent into the immortality of fame.

Spenser's praise of Elizabeth appears in this light as an expression of poetic rivalry and cultural ambition. The first three stanzas of canto 10 translate *Orlando Furioso* iii.1–3, diverging only in stanza 2, where Ariosto's barely concessive "s'in me no erra / quel profetice lume che m'inspiri" (if the prophetic light that inspires me does not err) gives way to a typically more emphatic Spenserian topos of inadequacy:[21]

[21] Cain, *Praise in "The Faerie Queene,"* p. 116.

A labour huge, exceeding farre my might:
How shall fraile pen, with feare disparaged,
Conceiue such soueraine glory, and great bountihed?

(II.X. 2.7–9)

The exaggerated humility of this passage is a paradoxical expression of Spenser's professed desire to overgo Ariosto, for the poet's self-effacement magnifies his subject, and this magnificence reverts upon the poet insofar as the subject is *his*. The subtext of artistic rivalry that generates such claims for the Tudor descent may be glimpsed indirectly in the structure of stanza 1, for Elizabeth overgoes the House of Este just in the alexandrine—the ninth line by which the Spenserian stanza "surmounts" Ariosto's *ottava rima*.[22]

The chronicle proper, which begins in stanza 5, reflects both the vertical paradigm of an ascent from earth to sky and the circularity out of which that ascent must rise. Spenser traces Britain's path to glory from "antique times," which he describes entirely in terms of what the land was *not*:

The land, which warlike Britons now possesse,
And therein haue their mightie empire raysd,
In antique times was saluage wildernesse,
Vnpeopled, vnmanurd, vnprou'd, vnpraysd,
Ne was it Island then, ne was it paysd
Amid the *Ocean* waues, ne was it sought
Of marchants farre, for profits therein praysd,
But was all desolate, and of some thought
By sea to haue bene from the *Celticke* mayn-land brought.

(II.X. 5)

Stanza 6 begins "Ne did it then deserue a name to haue"—and although the stanza goes on to describe the land's acquisition of the name "Albion," the building momentum of the negative clauses unmistakably comes to rest in the opening line, as

[22] Cf. Cain's discussion of the proem to Book 1 (*Praise in "The Faerie Queene,"* pp. 37–44).

193

though earning and then "blazoning" an imperial name were the crowning moments in that long labor through which "warlike Britons . . . haue their mightie empire raysd." They may be, for the phrase "Ne did it then deserue a name to haue" not only strikes a tonic chord against the acceleration of "ne" clauses in stanza five, it also deliberately echoes the repeated phrase on which Spenser turns from stanza 3 into stanza 4: "Thy name, O soueraine Queene, to blazon farre away. / Thy name O soueraine Queene, thy realme and race." A similar pattern is reflected in line 4 of stanza 5, where the sequence "Vnpeopled, vnmanurd, vnprou'd" is capped by the final term "vnpraysd," once again suggesting discreetly that the elevation of empire is perfected only by poetic praise.

Stanzas 7 through 9 turn to a more substantive description of the land, but the terms of the description—which stress earthly origins, disordered fantasy, and bestiality—are still emphatically privative. The land was possessed by a savage nation of "hideous Giants" (st. 7.2), associated through popular etymology with the earth (*geos*). They are also associated with the Titans who assaulted heaven. Since Spenser has just evoked Phoebus Apollo's song about the "triumphes of Phlegraean Ioue" as a model—preferable to Homeric epic—for his own celebration of *Briton moniments* (st. 3.1–5), this negative rendition of British prehistory appears as a playing out of the honorific parallels linking Elizabeth's ancestry to Ioue and Spenser to Phoebus Apollo. Stanza 8 treats the dubious origins of the monster race, which seems to be derived in one way or another from the evil effects of fantasy—though it remains unclear whether the fault lies with the "vaine illusion" that led Diocletian's daughters to couple with devils, or the "monstrous error" that leads modern historians to repeat such superstitious fables (lines 7, 3). It hardly matters, of course: the real point of the stanza is elegantly sketched in the phrase "monstrous error," which conflates the bestiality of the giants with that of the fantasy ungoverned by reason, while implicitly likening "assotted" historians to Diocletian's fantasy-ridden daughters.[23] When we learn in stanza 9 that the Giants'

> owne mother loathed their beastlinesse,
> And gan abhorre her broods vnkindly crime,
> All were they borne of her owne natiue slime,
>
> (II.x.9.3–5)

the equation is complete: monstrosity = chthonic origins = ungoverned fantasy = feminine weakness = bestiality, the whole complex of values attached to the terms "earth" and "ground."

The land figures in this imagery as an implicit Errour, slimy origin of unnatural offspring. It is contrasted with the masculine Sun, which appears in typical fashion at the beginning of stanza 2 as the heavenly origin of "life and light" (line 2). These contrasting images of origin are related to one another through a series of passages that begins with the sun in stanza 2, continues through the land as lamenting maternal figure in stanza 9, and concludes with Arthur's apostrophe to the motherland in stanza 69. Stanza 2 stresses the origin of "all that liues" in life and light *borrowed* from the sun, and declares that although Elizabeth's lineage may derive from the earth it seeks a truer origin in heaven (lines 1–5). Stanza 9 refigures the land's "natiue slime" as a source of "beastlinesse" and "vnkindly crime." The brood turned against its own mother recalls Errour's den in I.i; the symbolism of that episode involves a ghastly parody of the communion,[24] and at III.ix.49 we learn that the unnatural crime this mother "gan abhorre" was in fact cannibalism: the ancient Giants "fed on liuing flesh, and drunke mens vitall blood" (line 9). In stanza 69 Arthur,

---

[23] Cf. Gross, *Spenserian Poetics*, pp. 93–98.

[24] For an extended discussion of the scene in Errour's den, see "The Nausea of Fertility," in chapter 5 of this text.

having perused "The royall Ofspring of his natiue land," cries
out

> Deare countrey, O how dearely deare
> Ought thy remembraunce, and perpetuall band
> Be to thy foster Childe, that from thy hand
> Did commun breath and nouriture receaue?
> How brutish is it not to vnderstand,
> How much to her we owe, that all vs gaue,
> That gaue vnto vs all, what euer good we haue.
>
> (II.X.69.2–9)

This passage balances piety for the nurturing motherland (in
contrast to the brutishness of Giants and traitors) against the
qualification "foster Childe," a reminder of that other origin,
the phallic source of "what euer good" we derive more imme-
diately from the earth.

The analogy between Brutus and "Phlegraean Ioue" aligns
Spenser himself with the formative influence of the sun. If the
tale of Diocletian's daughters and their demonogamy serves as
an image of chthonic female origin both for nations and for
historical knowledge—a sort of Spenserian "Thus they relate,
erring"—then the stories of Brutus and Arthur should serve as
antithetical figures of proper derivation, both for a race of he-
roes and for knowledge of its paternity:

> Thy name O soueraine Queene, thy realme and race
> From this remowmed Prince deriued arre,
> Who mightily vpheld that royall mace,
> Which now thou bear'st, to thee descended farre
> From mightie kings and conquerors in warre.
>
> (II.X.4.1–5)

> They held this land, and with their filthinesse
> Polluted this same gentle soyle long time:
> ....
> Vntill that *Brutus* anciently deriu'd
> From royall stocke of old *Assaracs* line,

Driuen by fatall error, here arriu'd,
And them of their vniust possession depriu'd.

(II.x.9. 1–2, 6–9)

The most advanced historiography of the time (represented by
Polydore Virgil) was openly skeptical of both these myths. In
his *History of the Reign of King Henry VII*, Bacon remarks off-
handedly that the name Arthur was chosen for Henry's first
son "according to the name of that ancient worthy King of the
Britons, in whose acts there is truth enough to make him fa-
mous, besides that which is fabulous."[25] In *A View of the Pres-
ent State of Ireland* Spenser practiced a historiography that was
modern for its time, and there is one manuscript passage in
which he expresses skepticism about "our vayne Englyshe-
men" and their "tale of Brutus."[26] Yet in demonstrating his
sophistication as humanist historiographer, Spenser also ex-
plains the value of such "vayne" patriotic devices: they serve
to elevate "a barbarous and salvage nation" in relative dignity.
Such are the means by which *any* earthly prince "surmounts"
all others—and within his own realm what prince does not?
Camden rejected the Brutus myth in his *Britannia*, but "felt
moved to accept it" in his poem *De Connubio Tamae et Isis*.[27]
Gorden Braden observes that "the College of Antiquaries, of
which Camden was the most famous member, understood its
own task more as the completion of a national self-image than
as disinterested and indiscriminate research; and even Cam-
den's own scholarly judgment was at times warped by the pres-
sures involved." The pressures involved, as Braden notes,

---

[25] Cited by Sidney Anglo, "The *British History* in Early Tudor Propa-
ganda," *Bulletin of the John Rylands Library*, 44 (1961): 29. The citation is
to *The Works of Francis Bacon*, ed. James Spedding (London, 1858), pp.
43–44.

[26] See *A View*, p. 27

[27] Gorden Braden, "riverrun: An Epic Catalogue in *The Faerie Queene*,"
ELR 5 (1975): 29. Other citations from Braden in this paragraph are to the
same page.

came down to the emotional and political need for an image of common origin. As Ben Jonson puts it in a passage cited by Braden: "Rather then the Citie should want a Founder, we choose to follow the receiued storie of *Brute*, whether fabulous, or true, and not altogether vnwarranted in Poetrie: since it is a fauor of Antiquitie to few Cities to let them know their first Authors."

Not knowing our first authors, we author them ourselves. Yet if desire, rather than truth, is the unacknowledged origin of the "solar" line and its conquest over the sons of earth, then "our vayne Englyshemen" in "their great lightnes" are not so utterly different from Diocletian's daughters and the assotted historians who fable about them. The difference is the *aim* of their desires, not the origin, for Spenser adopts the originary fable best suited to his own desire, at once literary and political, to taste "some relish of that heauenly lay" sung by Apollo (st. 3.6). The self-authorizing character of this mixed desire reflects the circularity out of which judgment constitutes the present as its sphere of concern: much as the transtemporal vantage point in canto 9 rises on the back of an infinite regress it cannot acknowledge, the dialectical elevation of British history from earth to the heaven's height requires a legitimating image of paternal origin, however arbitrary. In supplying this image the poet may refine the raw materials of popular tradition, but he cannot secure a truth independent of either the fantasy or his own desire. Even if the poet's need for an originary fable comes to him as a cultural and political "given," his redaction of chronicle materials is a conversion of this mandate that both reaffirms and, prospectively, reconstitutes the politico-cultural order from which the mandate arises. The poet and the nation incorporate mirror one another; each borrows desire from the other, as living things are said to borrow light from the sun, and each returns that desire to the other in displaced form, reinscribed in the image of an origin and a promised end that abide forever "aboue the Northerne starre" (st. 4.7).

HOW TO READ HISTORY PRUDENTLY

Most commentary on the *Briton moniments* tries to find some ordering principle underlying its apparent chaos. Building on the work of Carrie Harper, Berger notes the significance of the interregna, which divide the primitive dynasty of Brute from the "age of law" ushered in by Donwallo, and the pre-Christian era of both dynasties from a post-Lucian era of divine law (*Allegorical Temper*, p. 94). He nevertheless concludes that "There is a muddiness, a residue of meaninglessness, in the historical facts which disappoints the reader seeking allegorical clarity or instruction" (p. 93); in this reading the dialectical elevation of matter into form remains frustratingly incomplete. Building on this argument in his turn, Mills demonstrates several related points: that the chronicle materials are numerologically ordered according to the same ratios as the temperate body in ix.22; that Spenser's departures from Geoffrey of Monmouth tend "to clear away ambiguity . . . and heighten the utility of the example in terms of its application to virtue or vice"; and that the "meaningless residue" Berger found can be assimilated to a meaningful providential scheme by means of an interpretive notion common to Elizabethan historiography, namely that God's "punishments were often deferred to generations yet unborn."[28]

[28] Jerry Leath Mills, "Spenser and the Numbers of History: A Note on the British and Elfin Chronicles in the *Faerie Queene*," *PQ* 55 (1976): 281–87 (hereafter cited parenthetically as "Numbers"); "Prudence, History, and the Prince in *The Faerie Queene*, Book II," *HLQ* 41 (1978): 83–101 (hereafter cited parenthetically as "Prudence"); and "Spenser, Lodowick Bryskett, and the Mortalist Controversy: *The Faerie Queene*, II.ix.22," *PQ* 53 (1973): 173–86 (hereafter cited parenthetically as "Controversy"). More recently Joan Warchol Rossi, "*Britons moniments*: Spenser's Definition of

These arguments suggest that, if Spenser does not explicitly complete the dialectical elevation of British history into British glory, he nevertheless structures the chronicle so as to *antici-pate* its sublation without remainder in the act of reading—Arthur's reading, and ours insofar as we allow the text to identify us with Arthur. The point of view from which this reading takes place is the transtemporal perspective allegorically represented in the turret of Alma's castle. As Mills observes, "the three counselors stand not only for sensitive functions but also for *memoria*, *intelligentia*, and *providentia*, the three parts of the rational virtue of Prudence" ("Controversy," p. 180). The tendency among sixteenth-century manuals of instruction was "to equate all the practical uses of history with prudence itself" (Mills, "Prudence," p. 89), and the practical use of *Briton moniments* is to instruct its reader in the virtue of prudence. In his treatment of the history Spenser therefore implants certain patterns that invite the reader to exercise the synthetic faculty of the middle chamber as it coordinates the subordinate functions of *memoria* and *providentia*:

> What converts imperfect into perfect history is of course the interpretive power of the historiographer, who finds causal relationships and "compounds" these raw materials into coherent form. Spenser, I believe, has a similar procedure in mind: the perfecting of the British history is up to Arthur, and to the reader. His emphasis is not on history per se but on the process of prudential reasoning in which the prince is being trained. The superficial moral confusion of the his-

---

Temperance in History," *ELR* 15 (1985): 42–58, argues that the British and Fairy histories both reflect the general allegory of Temperance in Book II. Rossi's emphasis on temperance as an essentially violent virtue offers a salutary corrective to the usual emphasis on mixture and balance, but there is too much evidence in support of the latter view for it to be simply abandoned. The appearance of contradiction between these two notions of the virtue is merely superficial, for Temperance as harmonious synthesis is (like all syntheses) dialectically dependent on potentially violent exclusions.

tory is a challenge to Arthur's prudence, and he must find
in it patterns to inform the conduct of his present affairs.
("Prudence," p. 90)

Thus "imperfect" rulers such as Locrine (st. 17) or Madan
(st. 21) are assimilated to perfection through an act of judg-
ment that apprehends them as moral essences—negative ex-
emplars whose past errors will be redeemed in a future shaped
by the actions judgment dictates in the present. In that future,
the earthly "body" of history is gathered into its risen and per-
fected form much as the numerical symbolism of ix.22 gathers
the vegetable and sensitive souls into the rational (Mills,
"Controversy," pp. 183–85): hence the chronicles are organ-
ized around multiples of 7 and 9, the respective numbers of
body and mind that structure the temperate body at ix.22.

The perfected form into which British history is prospec-
tively or prophetically gathered is a vision of the "body poli-
tic," the corporate sovereignty of England as personified in the
monarch. Berger remarks that the emphasis of the chronicle
falls "on the kingship itself; the narrative limits itself to the
name of the ruler, the quality of his rule (the grievous errors
or great virtues), and its mode of termination. The result of
this method is that no one ruler is seen to be the hero. The hero
is Britain itself insofar as it triumphs through divine assistance
over the evils of physical and moral nature, and insofar as it is
ordered to its proper end" (*Allegorical Temper*, pp. 103–4).
Later, commenting on the contrast between the British and
Fairy histories, he observes that "the idea of the two persons of
the queen . . . underlies the two worlds juxtaposed in Canto
x" (p. 114). Taken together, these remarks suggest that the
difference *between* British and Fairy history—the difference
between an uninstructive succession of random triumphs or
failures and an ethical-political paradigm of the ideal body pol-
itic—is the same as the difference at work *within* the text of
British history. From this point of view, the relation between

Briton moniments and the *Antiquitie of Faerie lond* is more complex than simple juxtaposition or contrast between ideal and actual, since both are structured with reference to the ideal body of the sovereignty.

Spenser stresses from the beginning that while his chronicle may list monarchs, it is really a history of the monarchy:

> Thy name O soueraine Queene, thy realme and race,
> From this remowmed Prince deriued arre,
> Who mightily vpheld that royall mace,
> Which now thou bear'st, to thee descended farre
> From mightie kings and conquerours in warre. . . .
>
> (II.x.4.1–5)

He reinforces the point at each of the interregna, which are characterized implicitly as sunderings of a bodily wholeness:

> The noble braunch from th'antique stocke was torne
> Through discord, and the royall throne forlorne:
> Thenceforth this Realme was into factions rent. . . .
>
> (II.x.36.4–6)
>
> . . . great trouble in the kingdome grew,
> That did her selfe in sundry parts diuide,
> And with her powre her owne selfe ouerthrew. . . .
>
> (IIx.54.2–4)

Here as elsewhere in the chronicle, Spenser presents the details of his story in privative terms, as the absence or, in these passages, the *sparagmos* of that ideal body the history so imperfectly imitates. This is necessary because in and of itself the body politic is "utterly void" of defect, and strictly speaking ought not to *have* any "history" at all. The chronicle of its uneven fortunes is therefore in an important sense a history of that dangerous supplement the body natural, which is extrinsic and subordinate to the body politic, yet essential to its perpetuation. The function of prudential judgment in reducing this succession of accidents to essential form is precisely to reassimilate agents and events, through a dialectical canceling-and-preserving, to the sacred body they have torn and scattered.

Discerning the numerological form into which the chronicles are cast is one way of reassimilating them into this sacred body: as Mills has shown, both Alma's castle and the chronicles are structured according to multiples of 7 and 9. Recognizing a providential pattern in the chronicles involves a similar perception, for the notion of deferred retribution depended for its justification on the notion of families and states as corporate wholes. Mills quotes a passage from Justus Lipsius that makes this point explicitly:

> Know this, that God joyneth together those thinges which we through frailty or ignorance do put a sunder: And that hee beholdeth families, townes, kingdomes, not as things confuse or distinguished, but as one body and intire nature. . . . And there is good reason it should be so. For there is a certen bonde of lawes, and communion of rights that knitteth together those great bodies, which causeth a participation of rewards and punishments to bee betwixt those that have lived in divers ages. Therefore, were the Scipioes good men in times past? Their posteritye shall speede the better for it before the heavenly judge. . . . Because in al external punishments God doth not onely beholde the time present, but also hath respect to time paste; And so by pondering of both these together, he poyseth evenly the ballaunce of justice. ("Prudence," p. 94)

We can grasp the course of providence only by reading dynasties as the "heavenly judge" reads them, gathered into corporate unities that transcend temporal difference.

Stationed at the crisis point in this dialectical movement, Arthur is invested with the function of converting its negative moment. As a figure of divine grace he shadows the functions of Christ throughout *The Faerie Queene*, and Spenser invokes this analogy once again in stanzas 49–50 of the chronicle, as

Berger remarks. Stanza 50 mentions the birth of the savior during Cymbeline's reign:

> Next him *Tenantius* raigned, then *Kimbeline*,
> What time th'eternall Lord in fleshly slime
> Enwombed was, from wretched *Adams* line
> To purge away the guilt of sinfull crime. . . .
>
> (II.x.50.1–4)

In purging mankind's universal genealogy, Christ establishes a doctrinal paradigm for the imperial ascent from "natiue slime" to heavenly glory that "old Assaracs line" (st. 9.5–7) will seek to perfect through Arthur and again through Elizabeth. This must explain Spenser's odd remark in stanza 49 that Androgeus' betrayal subjected England to "ambitious Rome . . . / Till Arthur all that reckoning defrayd" (lines 7–8). The remark is odd because Arthur, unlike Redcrosse and Britomart, supposedly never receives such direct knowledge of his destiny. Perhaps we are meant to understand the lines as an interpolation for our benefit by the narrator, not part of the text read by Arthur, but it seems likely in any event that Spenser is drawn from his usual practice at this point because the analogy between Christ and Arthur is so crucial.

Mills's numerology locates Arthur at the "middle climacteric" of British history ("Numbers," p. 283). When the chronicle resumes in III.iii as Merlin's prophecy, it will continue through eighty-one total stanzas, completing the third climacteric, before culminating in the advent of the Tudors. This advent is introduced in stanza 48 by the line, "Tho when the terme is full accomplishid" (line 1). What is completed, or "full accomplishid," by the visionary turn from the second through the third climacteric is precisely that descent of the royal mace which Spenser evokes at the beginning of the chronicle, quoted above; and there too he stresses Arthur's pivotal role in the descent from "mightie kings and conquerors in warre" (II.x.4.5) to "a royall virgin" under whose reign "sacred Peace shall louingly perswade / The warlike minds, to learne her goodly lore" (III.iii.49.6, 2–3). Meanwhile, the *Antiquitie of Faerie lond* takes up seven nine-line stanzas, "ending with the reign of Gloriana and producing of course a total of sixty-three lines," so that "the number symbolism [of Fairy history] would seem to be identical with that of the Castle of Alma itself" (Mills, "Numbers," pp. 283, 285). The last generations of Fairy monarchy are also identical with the historical advent that will complete the British chronicles, a convergence Spenser signals through the transparent historical allegory that equates Elficleos with Henry VII, Elferon and Oberon with Arthur Tudor and Henry VIII, and Tanaquill with Elizabeth (II.x.75–6).

The crisis point Arthur occupies is an image of the historical present into which past and future are gathered in the act of judgment. We saw in chapter 3 how Spenser's doubling and dividing of historical materials complicates this image of present time, since the historical present of Spenser's writing is displaced by the narrative present of his fable, which then prophesies the age of Elizabeth as time's virtual culmination in a millennial kingdom. The trace of this displacement may be read in the striking aposiopesis of stanza 68, where the moment *in which* Arthur reads emerges from *what* he reads with disruptive force:

> After him *Vther*, which *Pendragon* hight,
> Succeeding There abruptly it did end,
> Without full point, or other Cesure right. . . .
>
> (II.x.68.1–3)

Hamilton notes that "abruptly" was "a new word in 1590, from Lat. *abruptus*, broken off": with characteristic subtlety, Spenser uses a neologism to mark the rupture through which the future emerges from the past. "Cesure," or caesura (Latin *caedere*, to cut) probably glances at *Caesar*, since the history does eventually reach its "full point" or "terme" in the sacred empress Elizabeth. "Succeeding" is obviously ironic in that nothing comes after it: here is the most radical imperfection yet in the chronicles. If Arthur "perfects" this imperfect history by responding to it properly (st. 69) and by mightily upholding the royal mace in his turn (st. 4), then his conversion of the past into the future will be in effect a conversion of successiveness into success.

Arthur's timely healing of "so vntimely breach" (st. 68.6) will perfect British history in the sense of completing it, and in so doing will make *Briton moniments* more like the *Antiquitie of Faerie lond*, which Guyon "all this while . . . did read, / Ne yet has ended" (st. 70.1–2). Guyon's reading obviously contrasts with Arthur's, since it continues uninterrupted in the narrative, yet the phrase "ne yet has ended" may secondarily imply that he is still reading in 1590—like Caesar's sword, "yet to be seene this day" (st. 49.5). It echoes the phrase with which Merlin's prophecy breaks off in III.iii, just after the events of 1588: "But yet the end is not" (st. 50.1). There is something peculiarly timeless about Guyon's reading of Fairy history, despite the fact that he breaks for "supper" at the end of canto 10, just as there is something peculiarly timeless about the elfin chronicles themselves, despite their temporal organization: here succession *is* success, generations of "right" Caesars proceeding without breach or fall. As I remarked earlier, such an ahistorical "history" is the only kind the sovereignty proper should have.

Spenser indicates the fictiveness of the Fairy genealogy in various ways. It derives from a classical fable of second creation, interpreted in the late middle ages as an allegory of how urban civilization began.[29] From this origin Elf wanders into

[29] Roche, *Kindly Flame*, pp. 34–36.

the Gardens of Adonis, where he finds a "goodly creature" of supernatural appearance, takes her to wife as "Fay," and begets the Elfin line (st. 71), which then proceeds without Fall or Original Sin to the reigns of Oberon and Tanaquill. The transparent historical allegory in which this descent eventuates is one way Spenser identifies the destined form of the British chronicle with the splendid simplicity of Fairy genealogy: the two converge in the House of Tudor, foreshadowing Arthur's union with Gloriana. Yet in the midst of this convergence occurs one of the most conspicuous signs of the Fairy genealogy's fictiveness: for Oberon, says Spenser, "dying left the fairest *Tanaquill*, / Him to succeede therein, by his last will" (st. 76.4–5). In other words, the troubled reigns of Edward VI and Mary I simply disappear from the history of sixteenth-century England, insofar as that history is "assimilated" to the ideal body of the sovereignty. "Pleasing analysis" indeed: the body politic passes from Henry VIII into Elizabeth without pause, delivering "this howre" (st. 76.6) without breach or failure out of the past.

Briton moniments ends, says Spenser, "As if the rest some wicked hand did rend," and the *Antiquitie* ends as though some well-intentioned hand had carefully suppressed untimely breaches in the Tudor line. Both hands belong to Spenser, and the image they return to Elizabeth has been displaced and perfected by his intervention. Her title to the throne, though not in question, was a subject of continual debate because it was intimately connected with the tangled issues of the "succession question" that troubled her reign for decades. Given the persistence and prominence of her subjects' concern over this issue, Spenser's tendency to avoid it in *The Faerie Queene* is striking. Equally striking, however, is the emphasis placed on the *general* problem of succession in the chronicles: the whole account is organized around crises in the dynastic succession. In this context what looks like a complimentary, or at worst innocuous, reference to the will of Henry VIII carries an uncertain charge. J. J. Scarisbrick refers to the argument against the sufficiency of the will as "a plausible, but later, invention by parties interested in asserting the claims of Mary Queen of Scots to the throne of England."[30]

We might assume, then, that Spenser's affirmation of the will here is of a piece with his treatment of Mary in Book v. On the other hand the will was not really important to Elizabeth's title,[31] and in fact gained most of its notoriety from the role it played in the succession controversy. For example, Mary's leading apologist in England used Henry's will as an argument for settling the succession—preliminary, of course, to arguing that it should be settled on Mary. God, he argued, has given every creature "a speciall gifte and grace . . . to continewe, to renewe, and to preserve eche of hys owne kind," but man is the only creature able to do this through wit and reason, by anticipating future peril and providing against it.[32] Since civil dissension would be likely if the queen were to die with the succession unresolved, prudence demands that she address the question—and at this point Henry's will is cited as an exemplary precedent (Leslie, *Defense*, sig. G4ᵛ). Thus Spenser's reference to the will may well be an ostensible compliment that functions as a subtle hint to the queen; given her notorious reluctance to have the subject discussed, this seems quite possible. The immediate context supports such a reading, for stanza 75 celebrates the good fortune by which a potential breach in the Elfin line was "Doubly supplide" by Oberon (lines 6–9), who also ensured that Tanaquill would succeed

[30] J. J. Scarisbrick, *Henry VIII* (Berkeley: Univ. of California Press, 1968), p. 493.

[31] Mortimer Levine, *The Early Elizabethan Succession Question: 1558–1568* (Stanford: Stanford Univ. Press, 1966), p. 161.

[32] Bishop John Leslie, *Defense of the Honour of . . . Mary Queen of Scotland*, SCT 15505 (1569), sig. G2ᵛ, the beginning of the second book (hereafter cited parenthetically as Leslie, *Defense*).

him (st. 76.4–5). The next line reads, "Fairer and nobler liueth none *this howre*" (emphasis added), and the alexandrine concludes: "Long mayst thou Glorian liue, in glory and great powre." The ostensible compliments veil a discreet reminder of the queen's mortality, and of the need to preserve dynastic continuity: for as Merlin will cry out in Book III, despite the proto-millennial glory of Elizabeth's reign, "yet the end is not."

THE FEMININE SUPPLEMENT

Once founded, the race of Fairy quickly produces "puissaunt kings, which all the world warrayd, / And to them selues all Nations did subdew" (st. 72.2–3). After these conquerors comes the builder Elfinan, "who layd / Cleopolis foundation first of all," followed by the consolidator Elfiline, who "enclosd it with a golden wall" (lines 7–9). The functions of conquest and construction are carried on by Elfinell in his defeat of the "Gobbelines," by Elfant in his raising of Panthea, and by Elfar, "who two brethren gyants kild" (st. 73.1–6). Next comes Elfinor, who builds by magic art:

> Then *Elfinor*, who was in Magick skild;
> He built by art vpon the glassy See
> A bridge of bras, whose sound heauens thunder
> seem'd to bee.   (II.x.73.7–9)

The emphasis on his "art" suggests Elfinor as a culture bringer. This completes the specific record of early Elfin rulers; stanza 74 declares that the next seven hundred princes were all brave examples "both of martiall, / And ciuill rule to kings and states imperiall" (lines 8–9). One reason the intervening regimes are not "much materiall" (st. 74.6) may be that the paradigm for martial and civil rule is completed in the first list of seven, so that the next seven hundred simply dilate the pattern. That pattern, if I have described it correctly, is a cumulative progression from conquest through construction and consolidation to the miracles of art and white magic.

The British chronicles are never so paradigmatic, needless to say. But there are moments when they rise to a kind of imperfect mimesis of this pattern. The second Brutus, for instance, arrives in stanza 23 to renew Britain's lapsed conquest of France, and is honored with an additional stanza celebrating his victories in the field: "Let *Scaldis* tell, and let tell *Hania*, and let the marsh of *Estham bruges* tell" (st. 24.1–2). His son King Leill enjoys an era of peace won by Brutus's "labour long," and proceeds to build cities: he "built *Cairleill*, and built *Cairleon* strong" (st. 25.1–3). Huddibras, the next to reign, "did not his realme encrease, / But taught the land from wearie warres to cease" (lines 4–5). He is a consolidator,

> Whose footsteps *Bladud* following, in arts
> Exceld at *Athens* all the learned preace,
> From whence he brought them to these saluage parts,
> And with sweet science mollifide their stubborne harts.
>
> (II.x.25.6–9)

After the consolidator, the culture bearer (an early exponent of Renaissance humanism) employs classical learning to achieve exactly that mollification of the savage which was conventionally attributed to poetry as the nurse of civilization. Puttenham, for instance, assures us that

> The profession and vse of Poesie is most ancient from the beginning, and not, as manie erroniously suppose, after, but before, any ciuil society was among men. For it is written that Poesie was th'originall cause and occasion of their first assemblies. . . . Whereupon it is fayned that *Amphion* and *Orpheus*, two Poets of the first ages, one of them, to wit *Amphion*, builded vp cities, and reared walles with the stones that came in heapes to the sound of his harpe, *figuring thereby the mollifying of hard and stonie hearts by his sweete and*

eloquent perswasion. And *Orpheus* assembled the wilde beasts to come in heards to harken to his musicke . . . implying thereby, how by his discreete and wholsome lessons vttered in harmonie and with melodious instruments he brought the rude and sauage people to a more ciuill and orderly life, nothing, as it seemeth, more preuailing or fit to redresse and edifie the cruell and sturdie courage of man then it.[33]

Like Elfinor, who used his magic art to raise a bridge of brass, Bladud next constructs the "boyling Bathes at Cairbadon" (st. 26.2). He dies, like Icarus, when he tries to ascend into heaven on merely mechanical wings—which makes him a culture bearer *manqué*, resolved into a negative type of the poet whose visionary art elevates man spiritually and not bodily into heaven.

After the interregnum in which Brutus's line terminates, Donwallo arises to reunite the fragmented kingdom. Combining politic wisdom with military valor, he brings England, Scotland, and Wales back under a single government:

> Then made he sacred lawes, which some men say
> Were vnto him reueald in vision,
> By which he freed the Traueilers high way,
> The Churches part, and Ploughmans portion,
> Restraining stealth, and strong extortion;
> The gracious *Numa* of great *Britanie*:
> For till his dayes, the chiefe dominion
> By strength was wielded without pollicie;
> Therefore he first wore crowne of gold for dignitie.
>
> (IIX.39)

Combining the roles of conqueror, consolidator, and culture bringer, Donwallo civilizes power, refounding the monarchy on a basis of law. He is called "the gracious Numa of great

---

[33] George Puttenham, *The Arte of English Poesie* (1589), excerpted in *Elizabethan Critical Essays*, ed. G. Gregory Smith (Oxford: Clarendon, 1904), 2: 6–7, emphasis added.

Britainie" because some say that his "sacred lawes . . . Were vnto him reueal'd in vision," just as Numa "feigned that he devised them [the laws] by the instruction of the goddesse or nymph Aegeria."[34] It might be arbitrary to read Donwallo as a figure of poetic inspiration just on the basis of his reputed visions, but the connection is reinforced three stanzas later when his descendant Guithiline marries "Dame Mertia,"

> A woman worthy of immortall prayse,
> Which for this Realme found many goodly layes,
> And wholesome Statutes to her husband brought;
> Her many deemd to haue beene of the Fayes,
> As was *Aegerie*, that *Numa* tought;
> Those yet of her be *Mertian* lawes both nam'd
>   and thought.   (II.x.42.4–9)

Culture bearer and lawgiver, Mertia resumes the functions of Donwallo, whose sons and grandson distinguished themselves exclusively as conquerors. The reference to Numa links the pair, but is here expanded to include Aegerie explicitly, as Spenser identifies inspiration with Fairy instruction. Once again the culture bringer *cum* lawgiver is discreetly linked with the figure of the poet.

Spenser himself is, after all, the creative source from which Fairy instruction proceeds. Quickened with Promethean fire, Elf wanders into "the gardins of Adonis" to locate the prototype of Aegerie and Mertia:

> A goodly creature, whom he deemd in mind
> To be no earthly wight, but either Spright,
> Or Angell, th'authour of all woman kind;
> Therefore a *Fay* he her according hight,
> Of whom all *Faeryes* spring, and fetch their
>   lignage right.   (II.x.71.5–9)

[34] Thomas Cooper, *Thesaurus Linguae Romanae et Britannaicae*, 1565, cited in Hamilton's gloss to stanza 39.

Mills concludes that the fertility of the Elfin line reflects the values of "nature, fecundity, life" associated with the Garden of Adonis.[35] In the ideological formation that underwrites Spenser's symbolism, these values are associated with the body natural, which in turn is generically female. The subordination and exclusion of the female—which we have seen played out in the architecture of Alma's castle and in the monstrous chthonic origins of Britain's race of giants—must therefore be dialectically balanced by a reappropriation of feminine procreativity, that "dangerous supplement" without which the masculine value complex of culture, form, and spirit cannot extend itself in history.

I commented earlier that the phallic completion of the temperate body is displaced into canto 10 and our reading of the two histories. There we find the closure of the ideal body once again displaced, this time into a prophetic future. In the meantime, the need to reappropriate "feminine" values in the service of empire emerges as an undertheme. It is interesting, in this context, that when the knights' digestion of the chronicles is interrupted by a call to supper, the phallic completion of history's body is once again displaced, not simply to the ensuing canto but into Book III. There an earlier beginning is remembered and a later end prophesied. The end is still "not yet," but the double displacement of imperial history into cantos 3 and 9 does serve to encompass the Garden of Adonis in its numerical midst. By this structural device Spenser regathers feminine procreativity into the phallic quest for unbroken dynastic continuity.

This reappropriated femininity already appears in canto 10 of Book II as a twofold figure for the vital source of dynastic unity and continuity. First is the fertility that enables generations of Elfin queens to serve the reproduction of patriarchy,

[35] Mills, "Prudence," 99–100, quoting C. S. Lewis.

traced back to the Garden as a trope of fecundity; this fertility is dialectically opposed to the degenerative progeny of earth's "natiue slime" by its more perfect subordination to the masculine origin. But as *Briton moniments* shows, mere bodily continuity is not enough; the mind too must become a symbolic womb, must bring forth fruit and multiply, for the empire to reproduce itself as a structure of value. I will argue in the next chapter that the Garden of Adonis presents an allegory of this function as well; for the moment, let us simply observe that if the Garden is a seminary of cultural forms as well as living species, then its *femina loci* Fay, "of whom all Faeryes spring, and fetch their lignage right," implies a witty derivation of the ideal kingdom from the poetic imagination.[36] This covert genealogy extends through the figures of Mertia and Aegerie, who bore their royal husbands laws as well as sons, and therefore suggest the assimilation of creative imagination by judgment in a subordinate or wifely role. This is the role that Spenser himself would play for Elizabeth: the prominence of the inspired magician, culture bearer, or lawgiver in both sets of chronicles, taken together with Spenser's references to Fairy inspiration, traces the glory of the realm back through the monarch to her humanist counselor-poet, who embodies the trope of Fairy instruction for Elizabethan England. In this way Spenser once again inscribes himself at the effaced origin of that "ciuill gouernaunce" which consolidates the body of empire—"Now one, which earst were many, made through variaunce" (st. 38.9).

[36] In deriving the Fairy race from the poet's "erected wit," this notion would explain the absence of any fall or original sin in Fairy history.

For by a male animal we mean that which generates in another, and by a female that which generates in itself; wherefore men apply these terms to the macrocosm also. . . .—*Aristotle*

The female is the victim of the species. —*Beauvoir*

5. The Wide Womb of the World

istoricism affirms that human existence is historical, not a phenomenon of nature. Yet human beings are also living organisms, whose apprehension of themselves and their world is mediated by the body as biological substratum of all consciousness, perception, and existence in general. There is no way to grasp human existence in a purely natural or purely cultural moment; instead we tend to grasp nature in terms of culture, culture in terms of nature, constructing each as an allegory of the other. Attempts to understand the phenomenon of gender in human beings proceed along both sides of the unstable boundary between nature and culture, and are therefore especially prone to allegory.

Beauvoir's essay on "The Data of Biology" in *The Second Sex* is a case in point. Committed to an existential phenomenology whose basic assumption is the radical autonomy of the individual human subject, and whose basic themes are authenticity, alienation, and self-transcendence, Beauvoir cannot avoid construing the "data" of biology as an allegory of feminine existential alienation. Concerned to refute the notion that "biology is destiny," she acknowledges certain "facts" about women's bodies in comparison with men's, only to assert that "in themselves they have no significance."[1] The relative muscular weakness of the female body, for instance, acquires sig-

[1] Simone de Beauvoir, *The Second Sex*, trans. H. M. Parshley (1952; New York: Vintage, 1974), p. 38 (hereafter cited parenthetically as Beauvoir, *Second Sex*).

nificance only with reference to "the ends man proposes, the instruments he has available, and the laws he establishes" (*Second Sex*, p. 38). Yet Beauvoir's own exposition of the biological "data" is saturated from the beginning by the values of existential phenomenology; she grasps the existence of the female organism in terms of a pathos proper to the feminine subject, seeing the individual organism as oppressed by the demands of the species. Hence some of the more curious moments in her account, like the explanation of morning sickness during pregnancy as signalizing "the revolt of the organism against the species" (p. 33). Hence also the ominous tone pervading what are ostensibly factual descriptions of the anatomy and mating behavior of the male animal: "In impregnation he very often shows more initiative than the female, seeking her out, making the approach, palpating, seizing and forcing connection upon her. Sometimes he has to do battle with other males. Accordingly the organs of locomotion, touch, and prehension are frequently more highly evolved in the male" (pp. 21–22).

The political allegory underlying this account of nature reflects the ethical centrality of the individual subject for existentialism, which values the social collective by how well it serves individual freedom and autonomy. "Species" in this allegory is the biological collective, which acts like a totalitarian state when it commandeers the female organism. The male appears as implicitly threatening because he is the agent through which the species commandeers the female body: "Even when she is willing, or provocative, it is unquestionably the male who *takes* the female—she is *taken*" (p. 23). In the shape of the male individual, the species "invades her individuality and introduces an alien element through penetration and internal fertilization" (p. 24).

My point is not that Beauvoir falsifies biology, but that her influential contribution to gender theory illustrates what one might call "inescapable allegory": the impossibility of grasping nature or culture without making them allegories of each other. Spenser's allegory of feminine nature in *The Faerie Queene* is similar to Beauvoir's in conceiving "species" as a covertly political category, but opposed in explicitly privileging the masculine over the feminine and the collectivity over the individual. In his ethical concern for tempering masculine aggressiveness, and in his sympathetic exploration of feminine sexual ambivalence, Spenser may well approach the ethical concerns of feminism as nearly as is possible for a male writer in a nondemocratic, patriarchal tradition and social order. His exploration of gender in Book III of *The Faerie Queene* sets out to redeem the impulse to mastery latent in the opposition of active to passive, or of penetration to wounding. But it does so incompletely. Male desire seeks restlessly to cross the threshold of the feminine "Other"; like allegory itself, it mingles the impulse to seek out what is mysterious with a need to domesticate it, to make otherness a medium through which sameness reconstitutes itself.

To see Book III as Spenser's Legend of the Feminine is to see only one side of this desire; it is to miss a principal function of such gender symbolism, through which patriarchal culture woos feminine allegiance.[2] The recovery of sameness, imagined as a compensation for human loss and a defense against

---

[2] In *Milton's Spenser* (hereafter cited parenthetically), Quilligan approaches the gender symbolism of Books III and IV by way of a salutary emphasis on the historical construction of an ideology of womanhood (pp. 176–79). But the readings that follow are diametrically opposed to my emphasis on the subordination of the feminine in Spenser's allegory. When a critic as talented as Quilligan frames a reading of Book III by asserting that Spenser's "genius is to call each gender to experience the heroism of the other" (p. 181), and that the Garden of Adonis offers both "a vision of male sexuality brought safely and creatively under the control of an awesome female power" and "a look at female power from a peculiarly female perspective" (pp. 196–97), I think we see compelling evidence of the literary canon's continuing power to co-opt representations of the feminine on behalf of a patriarchal ideology.

the knowledge of death, is a fantasy to which human desire
always returns. When virtually all forms of representation in
a culture conspire to allegorize the same as masculine, women
are constructed as subjects who can scarcely distinguish their
desire for the one from their ambivalence toward the other. If
Spenser explores the regions and values of "the feminine" for
his own culture with unusual sympathy, then, he does so
within the limitations of an allegory that assimilates the femi-
nine to the masculine in a subordinate role. Those limitations
are especially evident in the dialectical splitting of femininity
that results, for Spenser's most positive images of the feminine
are organized by a scheme that apprehends femininity apart
from the masculine origin as an object of nausea.

THE THRESHOLD OF METAPHOR

Amoretti 67 sketches the larger movement informing Book
III:

> Lyke as a huntsman after weary chace,
> Seeing the game from him escapt away,
>   sits downe to rest him in some shady place,
>   with panting hounds beguiled of their pray:
> So after long pursuit and vaine assay,
>   when I all weary had the chace forsooke,
>   the gentle deare returnd the selfe-same way,
>   thinking to quench her thirst at the next brooke.
> There she beholding me with mylder looke,
>   sought not to fly, but fearelesse still did bide:
>   till I in hand her yet halfe trembling tooke,
>   and with her owne goodwill hir fyrmely tyde.
> Strange thing me seemd to see a beast so wyld,
>   so goodly wonne with her owne will beguyld.

As if consciously revising Wyatt's "Whoso list to hunt," this
sonnet transvalues the sexual game of conquest and surrender.

When the deer in Spenser's poem turns back, she does so in part because the speaker himself is no longer a "hunter," having assumed a feminine passivity. This leads to a series of asymmetrical reversals: the male surrenders his will to mastery, and the female surrenders her freedom; he possesses her by yielding the initiative, and she is bound with her own goodwill. These reversals in their turn center on a moment of strangeness and wonder that does not just reverse roles, but unsettles the very difference between conquest and surrender. This moment is evoked in line 11, "till I in hand her yet halfe trembling tooke"—in which the central action of the poem, the taking possession, occurs. But within the "I took" this line opens an interval for the phrase "in hand her yet halfe trembling," as though Spenser had slowed the action to explore the emotional resonance of mutual surrender from within the moment itself. This impression is intensified by the alliteration that binds the first and last words of the line "fyrmely" across the (literally) breath-taking suspirants that delay the verb, and across the halting stresses of "yet halfe trembling." That phrase itself, as the rhythm falters, seems to modify "her" at first, but slides with the alliteration to modify "tooke," so that the blending of fear and desire into a single quiver does not just happen to one or the other, but leaps the gap between them with syntactic precision. And yet the best this line can do is delay the unambiguous closure of "I took." The next line seems flat by comparison, poising "her owne goodwill" against "fyrmely tyde," which chimes with the alliteration of "till" and "tooke" but replaces the tremors of line 11 with masculine firmness.

In a sense this sonnet is about crossing thresholds: the threshold between courtship and betrothal, between resistance and surrender, between surrender and conquest, between the male animal and the female in Aristotle's definition. But the liminal moment with its threatened loss of distinction is "fyrmely" contained by the quiet reassertion of masculine authority in the active voice, as the speaker muses on what he has "wonne." Book III follows a similar pattern when heroic initiative passes to the female quester Britomart, who will return it to Arthegall in Book V once he learns the difference between finesse and emasculation. Britomart is then "fyrmely tyde" with her own goodwill to a submissive role, and vacates the poem.

Book III also resembles *Amoretti* 67 in elaborating the Garden of Adonis as a threshold scene. Many of the Garden passage's notorious difficulties can be traced to an affinity with the sonnet's eleventh line, for the Garden "exists" not only as a projection of the female anatomy but also as the imaginative expansion of a threshold between states of being. It is consequently a shifting ground, where dualities like form and substance or nature and culture risk their distinctness by exchanging properties, and where mythic lovers rediscover one another translated beyond the destinies classical culture imagined for them. In this sense the Garden is all threshold, truly "the Figure of Transport," as Puttenham labels metaphor; it is an effort to conceive conception, to represent the "scene" of carrying over (*meta pherein*). And yet, while the passage itself crossbreeds natural philosophy with metaphysics and hexameral commentary with mythography, forms in the Garden are ranked by species: the female earth mediates God's seminal Word back to him in recognizable copies of divine ideas.[3] The masculine journey into otherness thus resolves itself like a sound Aristotelian metaphor, planted squarely on the four corners of a proportional analogy. In the macrocosm as in the

---

[3] Compare Douglas, *Purity and Danger: An Analysis of the Concepts of Purity and Taboo*, 2d ed. (London: Routledge, 1969, pp. 41–56, on dietary laws in the Hebrew scriptures. "Unclean" foods, she argues, are those that transgress the categories of creation in Genesis: "Those species are unclean which are imperfect members of their class, or whose class itself confounds the general scheme of the world" (p. 55).

microcosm, the first term seeks, and finds, its own reflection in the difference of the second.

This basic need to recover otherness in the form of the same leads to a dialectical splitting of the feminine. Procreativity is an orderly reproduction of divine ideas or it is a monstrous force; maternity re-presents the paternal origin or degenerates toward chaos. In this sense desire for the return of the same poses in its most radical form the problem of successiveness. The wheel of generation turns and life repeats the Logos *without* evolution because nature makes good corporeal metaphors, carrying type forms on a bridge of resemblance across the engulfing death. Essentially the same terms apply if we speak of succession as a dynastic problem: the body politic is male, by Aristotle's definition, since it achieves perpetuity only in and through the fecundity of the body natural. Finally, we may say that the problem of successiveness is resolved at the narrative level in much the same way as it is resolved in natural and dynastic terms. In Book III, the basic contrast we have often observed between chance and providence works itself out in a marriage of entrelacement with allegory, which tends to unify episodes at a fairly high level of abstraction. Thus characters, events, and images that seem discontinuous at the literal narrative level are dialectically gathered into a network of analogies. This gathering is a retractation of the poem's narrative body into its allegorical unity—for if plot, as Aristotle said, is the soul of tragedy, the soul of allegory is a concordance of its themes.[4]

We have seen that the first two books of the poem emphasize the motives of ascent, Book I through its eschatology and Book II through the architectural metaphor that "erects" the turret of

---

[4] Compare Chapman on Homer's *Odyssey*: "If the Bodie (being the letter, or historie) seemes fictive and beyond Possibilitie to bring into Act, the sence then and Allegorie (which is the Soule) is to be sought" (*Chapman's Homer*, ed. Allardyce Nicoll [Princeton: Princeton Univ. Press, 1976], 2: 5).

the brain. Book III reverses this emphasis, borrowing the structures of Neoplatonic symbology to focus on the erotic motives of the spirit's descent and unfolding in the forms of natural being. While Books I and II focus on the harmonious reduction of many into one (Una, wholeness, the frame of temperance, the glorified body of history), Book III repeatedly focuses on the multiplication of one into many. At the same time, the protagonist, ideal "person," and audience of Book III all become feminine for the first time in the poem (Quilligan, *Milton's Spenser*, pp. 185–96). Britomart's quest emerges as a counterpart to Arthur's, but the appearance of symmetry is once again deceptive insofar as Britomart pursues an explicitly corporeal union with Arthegall, whereas Arthur (although the "story" pretends not to know this) seeks a purely symbolic union with Gloriana. This shift in symbolic focus should not be taken as evidence of Spenser's protofeminism, then, because it seems more likely to be dictated by quite traditional patterns of association linking descent and material embodiment with the feminine reproductive function: the book of form's descent into matter and multiplicity must also, for Spenser, comprise a legend of good womanhood.[5]

We have seen that Arthur's quest for Gloriana leads through a metaphorically feminine phase in which the hero gives birth to virtuous actions, converting desire for the body into desire for glory. In Book III it is as if the poem itself must pass through a feminine phase at its midsection: even the arabesquing of the narrative is implicitly feminine, like the interlaced branches shading Venus's arbor in the Garden (vi.44). As in the architecture of Alma's castle, however, the risen hermaphroditic form toward which Book III tends is a reinscrip-

---

[5] Pamela Joseph Benson, "Rule Virginia: Protestant Theories of Female Regiment in *The Faerie Queene*," *ELR* 15 (1985): 277–92, argues persuasively that Book III, while more moderate than Book V, still adheres to a traditionalist view of women.

tion of the masculine, which has been sublimated into the universal form of the divine circle. Thus our Tiresias-like sojourn in the domain of sexual otherness and the matrix of natural formation is apprehended from the start in terms of a symbolism of conversion and reascent, just as in Alma's house we descend into a physical allegory, but one which is already an allegory of "digestion," or the conversion of matter back into spirit. In Book III we descend into gestation and parturition, allegories not of sublimation but of embodiment; yet here too the perspective that always gathers experience back into the closure of the divine circle will be found to preinform the symbolism of descent, guaranteeing in advance that this phase of being will be grasped in terms of its relation to the phases of conversion and reascent. We progress through the divine threefold rhythm of being with a comic or providential assurance that nothing of value will finally be lost.

The most comprehensive image of this cycle in Book III is the Garden of Adonis, but the surrounding narrative is also filled with images of descent into multiplicity. There is Venus, descending from her celestial house to the mutable realm in which she appears divided, the Venus of the Garden and that of the tapestries. There is Cupid, who also descends and divides, appearing as an author of strife in the tapestries and the reports Venus hears, but as Psyche's long-sought lover in the Garden. There is the fable of Chrysogonee, in which the formative influence of the sun descends into softened matter to generate twins—and there is a second set of twins, the grossly misformed Argante and Olliphant. There is Florimell, who enters in canto 1 as a comet, comes to earth in canto 7 at the witch's hut—where she is doubled—and ends up under the ocean as the prisoner of Proteus.[6] There is also the contrast between Proteus himself, the prophet of mutability who plays "with

[6] Compare III.i.16.5–9; vii.4.1, 10.4–8, 13.3; viii.41.8–9.

double senses" (iv.28.8) and Merlin, who discerns "the streight course of heauenly destiny, / Led with eternall prouidence" (iii.24.3–4). These doubles are clearly distributed into positive and negative registers, however: they are preunderstood in relation to a presumed whole, and are therefore apprehended from the start in terms of their exclusion from or regathering into the divine circle, as it emerges from the zone of duplicity through which it passes at its lowest point and begins to close on its divine origin.

We will observe the workings of this dialectical pattern first on the level of narrative sequence and then in the Garden. As we approach the Garden passage and explore its structure in detail, we will pay special attention to the analogies that link the reproductive cycle in nature with two of the poet's chief concerns: problems of artistic representation and the problem of dynastic succession. Both of these enter into the problem of historical continuity, which Spenser addresses by offering his poetry as a symbolic womb for the reproduction of an imperial ideology.

BELPHOEBE'S VIRGINITY

The technique of romance entrelacement raises questions in Book III about narrative continuity. Through the first five cantos the narrative line follows Britomart, then Arthur, and finally Timias as he pursues the "foule foster" (i.18.9); from Timias we pass to Belphoebe, and then to the story of her birth, which leads us in turn to Amoret and thus to the Garden where she was raised. We seem to slide laterally into the Garden by a process of association; the transitions are metonymic in their appearance of arbitrariness, as though expressing Book III's pervasive concern with "succession" at the level of narrative structure. Often, however, they also hint at metaphoric continuities, as when Belphoebe enters Book III on the trail of a wild beast she has wounded, only to find that the "tract of bloud" leads to Timias instead. This substitution suspends both characters uneasily between contrasting points of reference, for it makes Belphoebe a Diana partly transformed into Venus even as it confuses Timias with the force that hurt him; he seems at once Venus's lover and Diana's prey. The sharp ambivalence of his relationship with Belphoebe can almost be "read out" into these contrasting but superimposed mythic scenarios: Timias in effect *becomes* the slain beast, and *makes* Belphoebe a castrating Diana, insofar as his love cannot transcend carnal desire; while in a compensatory countermovement Belphoebe becomes Venus, and makes Timias a languishing Adonis, insofar as her pity for him takes on erotic power.[7]

The same tension we see embodied in the mythic structure of the episode also works to unsettle the literal and figurative levels of the action.[8] In itself this is an important distinction: Marinell nearly dies in canto 4 because his mother has misconstrued the "deadly wound" prophesied by Proteus as "hartwounding loue" when in fact it is a physical gash or puncture (iv.28.1–4). The crisis in canto 5 once again turns on the difference between physical and emotional wounding. At first Spenser gives elaborate stress to the physical nature of the wound and its treatment:

> The flesh therewith she suppled and did steepe,
> T'abate all spasme, and soke the swelling bruze,
> And after hauing searcht the intuse deepe,
> She with her scarfe did bind the wound from cold
> to keepe.   (III.v.33.6–9)

---

[7] Barkan, *Nature's Work of Art*, p. 241, notes that Belphoebe herself is "wounded" at v.30.9.

[8] DeNeef, *Spenser and the Motives of Metaphor*, pp. 163–65, discusses the contrast between literal and metaphoric wounding in the Timias episode.

But as Belphoebe heals the physical wound, she inflicts its emotional counterpart. Spenser describes this process in terms that recall the anatomy of temperance:

> She his hurt thigh to him recur'd againe,
> But hurt his hart, the which before was sound,
> Through an vnwary dart, which did rebound
> From her faire eyes and gracious countenaunce.

(III.v.42.3–6)

The framing of temperance in Book II displaced eroticism upward from the loins to the heart, where Cupid was admitted *without* his deadly arrows. The castration implicit in this body symbolism remains implicit in Book II, perhaps because Alma "had not yet felt Cupides wanton rage" (II.ix.18.2). But Timias, struck full force with passionate love, bears the silent erasure of sex as a deadly wound, one whose elevation from the loins to the heart only compounds his anguish. He is left to despair "without aleggeaunce," or relief (st. 42.9)—and the characteristic pun in "a*leg*geaunce" plays wittily on the body values informing the imagery, since relief to a leg is all poor Timias gets.

If his substitution for the wounded beast suspends Timias between alternative identifications, something comparable emerges from the substitution of heart for thigh. Metaphorically wounded, Timias languishes between cures: desire for a carnal remedy pulls him toward identification with the beast and with the fosters who initially hurt his thigh, whereas if he could be satisfied with the sublime cure of Belphoebe's chaste regard—if he could perfect the upward conversion of desire—Timias would recuperate from his heart wound like a saved Adonis.

He would also be gathered upward in the scheme of Spenser's allegory, assimilated from the body of death into that of life. What renders this episode problematic is Spenser's emphasis in Book III on the congruence of natural and cultural forms of perpetuity; here they are made discontinuous by Belphoebe's semidivinity, an expression of the sexual taboo surrounding Elizabeth. Since a major theme of Book III is the importance of natural love to the perpetuity of empire, it is not at all clear that Spenser sympathizes fully with Elizabeth-Belphoebe in her withholding of "that *soueraigne* salue." The language designating her virginity slides between literal and figurative status like the squire's wound, and this may reflect a comparable ambivalence in the poet.

Stanza 50 extends the metaphoric play on wounding and healing that runs through the episode: Belphoebe treats her patient with rare and costly cordials,

> But that sweet Cordiall, which can restore
> A loue-sick hart, she did to him enuy;
> To him, and to all th'vnworthy world forlore
> She did enuy that soueraigne salue, in secret store.
>
> (III.v.6–9)

But stanza 51 promptly shifts metaphors:

> That dainty Rose, the daugher of her Morne,
> More deare then life she tendered, whose flowre
> The girlond of her honour did adorne.   (III.v.51.1–3)

The words "more deare then life" are doubly charged by the context, where Timias's life in particular and the reproductive function in general make up the price of Belphoebe's "tendered" honor. The dainty rose "suggests her virginity but is not equated with it," as Hamilton tactfully puts it; combined with the phrase "daughter of her Morne,"[9] it evokes an image of

---

[9] Nohrnberg, *Analogy*, p. 533 (hereafter cited parenthetically), reads the phrases "daughter of her Morne" and "of the wombe of Morning dew" (st. 3.1) as a rhetorical placing of Belphoebe's virginity "in the second generation. To maintain itself generically—or allegorically—Virginity must assume into itself its own succeeding issue."

227

nascent feminine sexuality like that we encounter in the Bower of Bliss: "Ah see the Virgin Rose, how sweetly shee / Doth first peepe forth with bashful modestee" (II.xii.74.4–5). The rose has associations (reflecting various degrees of euphemistic displacement) with the hymen, the breasts, and the cheeks, any of which may signify the emergence of an adolescent sexuality. In stanza 51, however, the image cannot be tied to this or that zone of the female anatomy. Instead the stanza enacts a bizarrely evocative transformation of the image, one that seems independent of, or at best obscurely related to, any particular referent it might have:

> Ne suffred she the Middayes scorching powre
> Ne the sharp Northerne wind thereon to showre,
> But lapped vp her silken leaues most chaire,
> When so the froward skye began to lowre:
> But soone as calmed was the Christall aire,
> She did it faire dispred, and let to florish faire.
>
> (III.v.51.4–9)

The image of concealment and display in this passage is broadly suggestive, and its resemblance to the image of Diana surprised at her bath does little to dispel the suggestions.[10] (Why else do commentators stress that the rose is *not* a genital image?) In this respect the blossom of Belphoebe's honor again resembles the virgin rose of the *carpe diem* song in Acrasia's Bower, that "Doth first peepe forth with bashfull modestee," and "fairer seemes, the lesse ye see her may; / Lo see soone after, how more bold and free / Her bared bosome she doth broad display" (II.xii.74.5–8). Everything in the Bower, from

---

[10] At st. 19.6–9 Spenser describes Diana's response when Venus intrudes on her bath: ". . . / Soone her garments loose / Vpgath'ring, in her bosome she comprized, / Well as she might, and to the Goddesse rose, / While all her Nymphes did like a girlond her enclose." Hamilton notes that "the governing image, taken from v.51, is of the rose of maidenhead whose leaves spread out at a time of safety."

the maidens in the pool to Acrasia herself languishing in post-coital repose, "fairer seems, the lesse ye see her may": alternations of concealment and display or invitation and delay are the essence of Acrasia's tantalizing art. The diction of stanza 51 imparts a far more delicate tone to this simile, yet its curious opacity as a metaphor combines with its sensuous particularity as an image to produce an uncannily similar aesthetic effect.

Stanza 52 transforms the simile once again, offering both an etiological fable and an anatomical locale for the rose:

> Eternall God in his almighty powre,
> To make ensample of his heauenly grace,
> In Paradize whilome did plant this flowre,
> Whence he it fetcht out of her natiue place,
> And did in stocke of earthly flesh enrace,
> That mortall men her glory should admire:
> In gentle Ladies brest, and bounteous race
> Of woman kind it fairest flowre doth spire,
> And beareth fruit of honour and all chast desire. (III.v.52)

The etiological fable (elaborated in the proem to Book VI) makes the flower into a moral idea, an example of heavenly grace. As such it is "natiue" to Paradise, or marked by its origin as intrinsically unfallen; God then translates it downward into "stocke of earthly flesh" specifically to excite admiration for the moral idea among men. Once planted in the flesh, however, the moral idea tends to slide into its opposite, a tendency reflected in the diction and imagery of the passage itself. The metaphor of plant and garden is potentially ambivalent from the first, since it makes an image of natural propagation signify a moral idea that, in the present context, denies propagation. This ambivalence emerges full force when the flower "doth spire, / And beareth fruit" in the hearts of women. The metaphor works only by refiguring the female half of the human species as a "bounteous race" or "kind" unto itself—a moral species that breeds asexually, through imitation of exemplary figures like Belphoebe.

The phrase "stocke of earthly flesh" also carries with it strong connotations that work against the unfallen and asexual meaning of the rose. Among other things a stock may be a tree stump, a line of descent, or a penis. In the first three books of *The Faerie Queene* Spenser uses the word "stocke" thirteen times in these and related senses, while it occurs only once in Books IV-VI. In Book I, for instance, it designates the withered tree of death outside the Cave of Despair. In Books II and III it refers four different times to the line of royal descent, a meaning that is crucial to the analogy between natural and imperial perpetuity—and that consequently has clear implications for any treatment (however obscure) of Elizabeth's virginity. Finally, in canto 8 of Book III it refers to the old fisherman's withered member, which "gan refresh" in the presence of Florimell (st. 25.3). In short, the word evokes precisely that range of difficulties the poet is ostensibly trying to finesse, and context (to paraphrase Hamlet) cannot so inoculate our old word "stocke" but it shall relish of these connotations.

Still, the rose "beareth fruit" in the female heart, not the womb—an upward displacement parallel to that of Timias's wound. But here the sublimation of membrane into moral idea is complete, at least in the action of the poem; the troublesome remainder, the awkward tension, persists not as a feature of Belphoebe's experience but as a series of improprieties in the poet's handling of diction and imagery. Stanza 53 completes the sublimation of flesh into glory (and the anatomical ascent from the loins through the heart to the head) as it urges adolescent female readers to add the rose to their garlands, and so "crowne your heades with heauenly coronall, / Such as the Angels weare before Gods tribunall" (lines 8–9).[11] This reference

---

[11] Hamilton notes an allusion to 1 Pet. 5:4, "And when the chief shepherd shal appeare, ye shal receiue an incorruptible crowne of glorie." Note that the image is implictly typological, associated with the second coming.

completes a cyclical pattern like the one we saw in Alma's house: the rose descends from heaven into "earthly flesh," but bypasses the womb in favor of the heart, from which it then reascends to the head, seen as a type of our eventual return to heaven.

The labor of conversion takes place at the low point on this circle, represented in the Garden and in the Temple of Venus as the "lap" of feminine nature.[12] Spenser approaches this point once again in stanza 54 when he urges "Faire ympes of beautie" to imitate Belphoebe as a paradigm:

> To youre faire selues a faire ensample frame,
> Of this faire virgin, this *Belphoebe* faire,
> To whom in perfect loue, and spotlesse fame
> Of chastitie, none liuing may compaire:
> Ne poysnous Enuy iustly can empaire
> The praise of her fresh flowring Maidenhead;
> For thy she standeth on the highest staire
> Of th'honorable stage of womanhead,
> That Ladies all may follow her ensample dead.   (III.v.54)

Like the Biblical phrase "daugher of her Morne," "fresh flowring Maidenhead" uses an image of natural reproduction to describe a condition specified by its exclusion of that function. This catachresis risks its carnal associations strikingly, for if "Maidenhead" rhymes with "womanhead," and thus appears to mean "maidenhood"—a safely abstract expression— nevertheless the floral image materializes the abstraction almost graphically, seeming to name the insistently unspoken

---

[12] Cf. IV.x.52.3. John Erskine Hankins notes Spenser's reference to "Venus lap" in HB. 62 and suggests that it may derive from Ficinian usage, where the genital nature of the World Soul figures as its "lap"; see *Source and Meaning in Spenser's Allegory: A Study of "The Faerie Queene"* (Oxford: Clarendon, 1971; reprint, 1973), pp. 257–59 and 285–86 (hereafter cited parenthetically as Hankins, *Source*).

referent of the rose just at the moment of confirming its "perfect" and "spotlesse" sublimation.[13]

The phrase "ensample dead" likewise cuts against the grain, for while it passes as a compression of "her example after she is dead," the reading "her dead example" is awkwardly plausible.[14] Canto three, stanza 29 offers a comparable locution:

> With thee yet shall he leaue for memory
> Of his late puissaunce, his Image dead,
> That liuing him in all actiuity
> To thee shall represent. . . .   (III.iii.29.1–4)

Here the phrase "Image dead" clearly means "his image when he is dead," and only that. It refers to Arthegall, who will leave a son behind when he dies. Spenser's language makes the child a "natural" signifier, in whom reproduction-as-representation ensures the return of the same. The immediately following lines stress the importance of this figure to dynastic continuity:

>   . . . He from the head
> Of his coosin *Constantius*, without dread,
> Shall take the crowne, that was his fathers right,
> And therewith crowne himselfe in th'others stead.
>   (III.iii.29.4–7)

Again substitution is figured as the return of the same—first in the natural body, then in the body politic, the second following from and depending on the first. Arthegall's "Image dead" is very much alive, unlike Elizabeth's "ensample dead," and the succession therefore proceeds through metaphor, or the return of the same, rather than catachresis, or the derangement of categories. The closing stanzas of canto 5 imply a compensatory succession for the moral ideal of virginity, which survives

---

[13] The *OED* recognizes no usages at all in which "maidenhead" refers to the vaginal membrane. Its earliest recorded usage of "hymen" with an anatomical reference is 1615.

[14] See Anderson, " 'In liuing colours and right hew,' " pp. 54–58.

its bearer as a paradigm inscribed in praise and therefore imitated by "Ladies all." Yet insofar as this language applies to Elizabeth, the unavoidable question of royal succession measures what is missing. Elizabeth's successors in virginity may aspire to rule through love or to heavenly coronation, but the rule and crown of empire will not be available to them, and therefore cannot be restored by "her ensample dead."

We have already seen how deeply implicit Spenser's criticism of Elizabeth remains; it tends to emerge, if at all, through equivocation. Here equivocation allows an implicit criticism to emerge from within what is ostensibly a language of praise. Belphoebe's chastity is balanced by her courtesy, so that "all did make in her a perfect complement" (v.55.9), "so great perfections in her [she] did compile" (vi.1.3). Like the garden image of stanza 52, this invocation of courtesy anticipates the analogy between Books III and VI, which function within the broad scheme of the poem as parallel phases of descent and embodiment. This emphasis on Belphoebe's courtesy is anticipated early in the episode, when her first response on discovering the wounded Timias—one of horror—gives way to "soft passion and vnwonted smart: / The point of pitty perced through her tender hart" (v.30.8–9). The result is expressed as a tempering of her haughtiness: "Meekely she bowed downe, to weete if life / Yet in his frosen members did remaine" (st. 31.1–2). This gesture recalls similar moments in the first two books, when Arthur descends into Orgoglio's dungeon or Guyon stoops to wash Ruddymane's hands. The image of piercing Belphoebe's heart suggests that this emotion is a substitute for erotic attachment, and may qualify our sense of her divine self-sufficiency. Thus when Timias asks "Angell, or Goddesse do I call thee right?" (st. 35.5), Belphoebe can decline the attribution of divinity so as to stress her participation in the mortal condition:

> We mortall wights, whose liues and fortunes bee
> To commun accidents still open layd,
> Are bound with commun bond of frailtee,
> To succour wretched wights, whom we captiued see.
>
> (III.v.36.6–9)

This is a deliberate echo of Arthur's response to Guyon at II.viii.56.1–6, and combines with the other references, forward to Book VI and backward to the first two books, to inscribe Belphoebe's courtesy in the network of analogies that links various images of divine love's descent into the world.

Yet in the immediate context of Book III, and more particularly of canto 5, the difference between pity and erotic attachment is more important than their similarity. Belphoebe's virginity fixes on the negative moment in the analogy between spiritual and corporeal forms of descent, excluding corporeal forms and restricting itself to spiritual ones, and it does this in the very legend that celebrates their congruity. The substitution of courtesy for procreative love in Belphoebe's character lets Spenser play both sides of this analogy: Belphoebe's haughtiness relents and she acknowledges her subjection to the common condition of mortality insofar as she is courteous; yet she refuses the common remedy for death and reasserts her superiority to other degrees of womanhood (st. 54.7–8) insofar as she remains a virgin. Thus at the end of the episode Spenser is able to convert Belphoebe's courtesy from a sign of her mortality back into a sign of her perfect self-possession, or from an expression of what she has in common with Timias to a justification of her absolute unavailability to him. Yet when we read this passage back against the historical figure of Elizabeth, the all-but-silenced context of royal succession and the body politic reintroduce—at a higher level, so to speak—the same tensions Spenser has tried to finesse within the episode. The "masculine" perseity of Elizabeth's *political* body depends on the "feminine" fertility of the natural body in which it breeds, while the virgin self-enclosure of that lesser body in turn calls the reproduction of the body politic into crisis. Thus if Belphoebe's self-sufficiency stands in plain contrast to Timias's anguished experience of insufficiency (his symbolic castration), there is nevertheless an odd sense in which Timias's plight shadows that of the body politic, potentially castrated by Elizabeth's refusal to be bred in. We glimpse this only through the equivocation of Spenser's language. But given the proximity of this episode to the garden of natural procreation, and given also the link Spenser establishes in Book II between the Garden and the stability of the Fairy dynasty, the equivocations are very hard to ignore.

THE CONCEPTION OF ALLEGORY

Between the Garden of Adonis passage in canto 6 and the episode of Timias and Belphoebe in canto 5, there intervenes the fable of Chrysogonee. One purpose of this fable is to mediate between the allegories of virginity and procreativity: where canto 5 projects the cultural "line of succession" available to virginity, canto 6 opens by looking back to its *natural* genealogy. As the episode unfolds, however, this genealogy turns out to lie on the threshold between nature and supernature—a parthenogenesis seen under the aspect of Immaculate Conception:

> Her berth was of the wombe of Morning dew,
> And her conception of the ioyous Prime,
> And all her whole creation did her shew
> Pure and vnspotted from all loathly crime,
> That is ingenerate in fleshly slime.   (III.vi.3.1–5)

This analogy is not without precedent. Commenting on Spenser's description of solar fertility in stanza 8, Hankins observes that "this same explanation was sometimes given for the conception of Christ in the womb of the Virgin Mary" (*Source*, p. 278 and n. 3); while in an essay on Renaissance notions of embryology, he cites Alanus de Insulis's assertion that "a worm is born from the earth without seed and without show; it is trodden on, despised, and considered vile. So Christ was born of the Virgin without masculine seed; he lived humbly among men; contemned and despised . . . he was put to death."[15]

Roche suggests that the two terms of this analogy, the natural and the religious, frame the "meaning" of the episode: "Between these two analogies—the one from the order of grace, the other from the order of nature—is the meaning of Spenser's myth, which should harmonize with both."[16] Citing stanza 52 from canto 5, with its etiological fable describing God's creation of virginity as a moral idea, Roche suggests that "the myth of Chrysogonee is the story of the incarnation of virtues already existent in Spenser's Platonic heaven" (*Kindy Flame*, p. 107). He concludes: "The Chrysogonee myth, then, is the act of embodiment of the Platonic Idea, which had already existed in Paradise" (p. 108). This interpretation retrospectively clarifies the tenor of Belphoebe's "rose," which must represent the Platonic Idea's equivalent to seminal reasons planted in the Garden of Adonis. This equivalent is the "interior forms" of natural species and moral ideas. Plato thought the soul must have fully beheld these forms in a preexistence it dimly remembers after its embodiment in the flesh.[17] Boethius's Philosophia explains the correspondence between such vestigial ideas in the mind and the forms of natural species: "When light strikes the eyes, or sound the ears, the aroused

[15] John Erskine Hankins, "Hamlet's 'God Kissing Carrion': A Theory of the Generation of Life," *PMLA* 64 (1949): 515.

[16] Roche, *Kindly Flame*, p. 108 (hereafter cited parenthetically).

[17] This speculation is broached in the *Phaedo* and the *Phaedrus*. In *The Works of Plato*, trans. Benjamin Jowett, sel. and ed. Irwin Edman (1928; New York: Random House, Modern Library College Edition, 1956), see pp. 129–36 and 290–91.

power of the mind calls into action the corresponding species which it holds within, joining them to the outward signs and mixing images with the forms it has hidden in itself."[18] This is Marvell's "mind, that ocean where each kind / Does straight its own resemblance find" ("The Garden," lines 43–44). If Roche is correct, and the Chrysogonee story amplifies the etiology of Belphoebe's rose, then the middle term between the analogies of nature and grace is that of "mind," or intellection, understood after the manner of Ficino and Plotinus as a mode of begetting. Ideas are retained ("implanted") as sparks or seeds in the memory; they are activated by sense perceptions, clarified by reason through dialectic, beheld in their simplicity by intellect, and embodied in sensuous forms by the imagination.

Understood in this way the story of Chrysogonee entails a genealogy of allegorical poesis. The story is linked to Belphoebe because the reproduction of a moral idea like virginity proceeds according to the methods by which a poet fashions gentlemen or noble persons; it is linked to the Garden of Adonis because the poet's mind was by convention a metaphysical womb where abstractions take on sensuous form. Thus both Amoret and Belphoebe are described as "ripening" to perfection (vi.3.9, 52.1), and the poet is unusually direct in referring to them as feminine paradigms. At the end of canto 5 he urges young female readers to frame themselves an example from Belphoebe's perfection, and at the end of canto 6 he says the same thing about Amoret:

> . . . when she to perfect ripeness grew,
> Of grace and beautie noble Paragone,
> [Venus] brought her forth into the worldes vew,
> To be th'ensample of true loue alone. . . .   (III.vi.52.1–4)

---

[18] Boethius, *Consolation*, p. 112.

The echo of stanza 52 from canto 5 is unmistakable. Amoret has been "trained vp in true feminitee" (st. 51.5) by Psyche, and insofar as her later adventures elaborate the Apuleian pattern of suffering through Love's apparent cruelty to a final reconciliation with him, Amoret is indeed drawn from a mythic type form.[19] One implication of her birth and nurturing in the Garden, then, may well be that the embodiment of natural species through seminal reasons offers a direct analogy to the work that reason, intellect, and imagination perform on the sparks, or "internal forms," of moral species. The difference is that natural species reproduce sexually, whereas the mind's begetting of images is purely contemplative; the Biblical archetype for generation is Genesis, "the mightie word, / Which first was spoken by th'Almightie Lord" (vi.34.4–5), but the Biblical archetype for contemplative begetting is the Immaculate Conception.

Spenser's earlier references to the idea of immaculate conception appear to support this reading. In the April eclogue of *The Shepheardes Calender*, Colin Clout sings in praise of the shepherd-queen "Elisa," said to be "Syrinx daughter without spotte" (line 50). This conceit turns the Ovidian tale of Pan and Syrinx into a fable about the immaculate conception of a pastoral mask for Elizabeth. Since the name "Syrinx" has migrated from the virginal nymph who bore it to the pastoral pipes she turned into, Spenser's reference makes "Elisa" the daughter of his voice, the purified or immaculate offspring of his own shaping faculty. In canto 6 of Book III Spenser is again tracing the genealogy of a female character who represents the queen. Like Syrinx, Belphoebe is a nymph of Diana's, yet one through whom the force of love expresses itself in sublimated form: thus both she and Elisa are associated with the disguised appearance of Venus in Book I of the *Aeneid*. Spenser adapts

[19] Cf. Judith C. Ramsay, "The Garden of Adonis and the Garden of Forms," *UTQ* 35 (1966): 204.

Aeneas's wondering recognition of his mother as the emblem, or tag line, for "Aprill": "O quam te memorem, virgo? O dea certe!" He introduces Belphoebe into *The Faerie Queene* in a striking burlesque of the Virgilian episode, complete with a comic echo of this tag line (II.iii.33), and he echoes it again when Timias wakes in Belphoebe's bower, wondering "Angell, or Goddesse do I call thee right?" In each case the Virgilian tag signals a blending of Venus with Diana (in the Timias episode, an imperfect blending). But it also signals a reference to Elizabeth, the political deity glimpsed through her allegorical rustication. Together with the motif of immaculate conception, this Virgilian subtext creates a remarkably self-conscious allegory of the poet as begetter of imperial icons.

Spenser's comprehensive treatment of Elizabeth's historical genealogy begins in canto 10 of Book II. There, as we have seen, the poet intimates his role as author of imperial glory by identifying himself with the formative influence of the sun in opposition to the monstrous chthonic parturition of history figured in the tale of Diocletian's daughters. The same motifs converge again in the figures of Belphoebe and Chrysogonee, except that here the political dimensions of the symbolism are not emphasized, since Elizabeth's virginity was awkward as a political topic. The linking of virginity and married love as twin sisters also serves to shift emphasis toward private or personal virtues, even though the centrality of Britomart's quest and historical destiny means that such shifts in emphasis can never be more than provisional inflections of the broad analogies that unify the poem; they are strictly "local" phenomena. In addition to shifting emphasis away from the imperial theme, the Chrysogonee myth brings the motif of immaculate conception into new prominence, and this, together with the analogy from nature sustained through most of the canto,[20]

[20] Hankins, *Source*, pp. 228–86, offers a sustained commentary on the physical allegory of the Garden.

tends to focus the allegory less on the political object of poetic imitation than on the internal dynamic of poesis itself.

The episodes do not, however, draw attention to the poet. Belphoebe's virgin succession is defined by the absence of mortal fathers, and so is the analogy that links parthenogenesis with immaculate conception. The Chrysogonee story equates this absence with the bypassing of sexual pleasure in conception and of labor pains in parturition: "Vnwares she them conceiu'd, vnwares she bore"—and in case we may have missed the point: "She bore withouten paine, that she conceiued / Withouten pleasure: ne her need implore / *Lucinaes* aide" (st. 27.1–4). Together with the pronounced emphasis in stanza 3 on virgin birth as a bypassing of original sin ("all loathly crime, / That is ingenerate in fleshly slime"), this linking of sexual pleasure with labor pains suggests a reading of Chrysogonee as "gold-birth," or unfallen begetting: Hankins cites Aquinas to the effect that, "since Christ was not born from coition of his mother with an earthly father, there was no lustful pleasure involved in his conception and no pain for his mother at his birth" (*Source*, p. 137 and n. 4). This goldbirth does not, however, introduce an allegory of radically feminine creativity. As in the architecture of Alma's house, the literal exclusion of the inseminating penis makes possible a symbolic reappropriation of feminine procreativity, for the "mother" from which Belphoebe and Amoret allegorically proceed is the male poet's female brain. As I suggested at the end of chapter 4, this aspect of the allegory may also have its equivalent in Spenser's handling of the chronicles, where the figures of Mertia, Aegerie, and Fay implicitly trace the ideal imperial commonwealth back to the garden of poetic forms. In this respect Spenser's allegory comes very close to Sidney's emphasis in the *Defense* on poetry as a golden world, and on the poet as one who works *substantially* in that he "bringeth forth" fully imagined paradigms of the "perfection" he knows through his "erected wit." The figurative language running through this passage from the *Defense* in effect makes the poet's mind, together with that of the right reader, into an allegorical womb, a cultural Garden of Adonis where moral species may be conserved and reembodied in particular substances—"making many Cyruses," as Sidney puts it.

THE NAUSEA OF FERTILITY

By now it should be evident that the process of association through which we seem to slide laterally into the Garden passage is deceptive. We saw in Merlin's account of Britomart's son (III.iii.29) that both the natural and political bodies are conserved through the power of likeness to refigure substitution as a return of the same. In considering the episodes of Belphoebe and Chrysogonee, we see substitution repeatedly converted in this way at the level of plot. We see Timias substituted for the boar, and later Adonis for Timias, with the boar safely contained. We see Belphoebe's "rose" and its Platonic offspring substituted for the child she will not bear, and then her own immaculate conception substituted for the etiological fable of the rose. We see Diana substituted for Venus in the Timias episode and its Virgilian prototype; Venus's descent from her "house of forms" substituted for the sun's "impression" of generative power on Chrysogonee; then Amoret, or wedded love, substituted for the love bandit Cupid that Venus seeks; and so on, as characters, events, and images that seem discontinuous at the literal or narrative level are dialectically gathered into a network of analogies.

This process of substitution-and-translation is the basic content of the Garden as a poetic conceit. In the Garden of Adonis Spenser casts *natura naturans* in the image I have called an ideological solidarity, a conventional network of analogies whose elements—God, nature, idealized imperial monarchy, and al-

241

legorical art—all mutually signify one another. Nature's reasons are copies of ideas in the Divine Mind; the "internal forms" of human reason are also copies of these ideas, and if neither memory nor procreation copies perfectly, nevertheless the dialectical interplay between such inner and outer forms enables the mind to approach the divine ideas through its "erected wit." Just as the theory of anamnesis underwrites the possibility of true knowledge by regulating the production of mental representations, so the theory of seminal reasons preinscribes the truth of nature by regulating her production of substantial forms, limiting their variability within the domain of resemblance and so ensuring that nature will remain an adequate reflection of her Author's intentions. Such is the model for Sidney's theory of reading in the *Defense*, which explains its resemblance to the Garden: the poet embodies his foreconceit in a fiction from which the reader then infers the foreconceit, closing on the fiction's origin in the mind of the poet like a philosopher deducing the forms of ideas in the Divine Mind.[21]

[21] DeNeef, *Spenser and the Motives of Metaphor*, pp. 3–14, proposes this model of reading as a paradigm for interpreting Spenser. DeNeef's commentary is better than his theory, however, which offers no way to account for the openness he attributes in practice to the uses of metaphor. In "Spenser's Gardens of Adonis: Force and Form in the Renaissance Imagination," *UTQ* 30 (1961): 128–49, Harry Berger, Jr., goes to the other extreme. He reads the garden passage in terms of a concept of period style: "a style which seems the natural outcome of an intellectual climate in which the visible forms of the real are no longer felt as external or given, but are created and stabilized through the experience of the individual soul and the creative effort of the individual imagination" (p. 130). The romantic concept of creative imagination on which this definition relies is distinctly anachronistic when applied to Spenser. More seriously, the definition turns on a needlessly reductive dichotomy: in the diluted Neoplatonism popular among English poets of the Renaissance, forms would be understood as given, but given to contemplation (not "external"); and they would be understood as stabilized through the experience of each (generic) human soul through a dialectical interplay between reason and sense experience. It would be more accurate, I

This closing of the interpretive circle is based on a doctrine of resemblance: should mimesis go astray in either phase of the cycle, the mind cannot close on its origin in God. Thus Nature always works, as Diogenes Laertius has it, by "effecting results homogeneous with their sources" (Nohrnberg, *Analogy*, p. 538). Any failure to close this divine circle in nature is either miracle or monstrosity, the ambiguous category of the prodigious—what we might call nature's catachreses. Such a theory finds that Nature and Aristotle are the same because it assumes nature to be objectively structured by the ratios that govern the exchange of names within a closed system. And this, as Pico della Mirandola explains in the second proem to *Heptaplus*, is precisely the enabling assumption of the science, or "natural magic," of hermeneutics.[22]

The hexameral tradition, which evidently supplied Spenser's chief sources for the Garden of Adonis passage, is particularly interesting in its strategy for recuperating prodigies back into the structure of the divine foreconceit. Spenser notes that among the infinite shapes bred in the Garden are "vncouth formes, which none yet euer knew" (st. 35.2). These are explained with reference to the tradition of a "double creation": first God made "form, matter, and the seminal reasons of all future beings"; then He caused natural forms to spring forth from these reasons, inaugurating nature's reproductive cycle (Hankins, *Source*, p. 280; Nohrnberg, *Analogy* pp. 540–42). The first creation establishes the divine foreconceit of the second, so the appearance of forms in nature that do *not* correspond to a known kind must somehow be brought within the

---

think, to see the Garden as conveying the thematic structure DeNeef assumes by way of the style Berger describes.

[22] Pico Della Mirandola, *On the Dignity of Man, On Being and the One, Heptaplus*, trans. Charles Glenn Wallis, Paul J. W. Miller, and Douglas Charmichael (Indianapolis: Bobbs-Merrill, 1965), pp. 78–79. For the reference to "natural magic" see *On the Dignity of Man*, pp. 26–29.

limits of that first creation. Augustine supposes that among the first causes of things are some which God has "reserved to himself, [and] which appear in such mysteries as the creation of Eve and the bringing of salvation out of sin" (Nohrnberg, *Analogy*, p. 542). In this way nature as a rhetoric of God's thought recovers its catachreses by positing for each of them a previously unactualized divine original. Since the prodigious thing in question is the only evidence of its cause, it functions in the argument as a Derridean supplement, playing origin to its own origin.

In effect the theory of double creation leads to a doubling of femininity against itself. While the intellectual subtleties of theology brought various prodigious creations mentioned in the Bible back under the rule of divine causality, Renaissance embryology attributed monstrous births to an excess or defect in the *materia* supplied from the womb, or sometimes to the corrupting influence of fantasy in the mother.[23] A comparable pattern is observed by Jonathan Goldberg in Jacobean state portraits, which array the patriarchal family as a kind of political icon. Two reciprocal but imbalanced displacements characterize this ideological formation: on the one hand, "the natural event of procreation becomes an extension of male prerogative and male power," just as nature's procreativity is understood ultimately as an extension, through mimesis, of God's prerogative and power; and on the other hand, representations of infant mortality refigure the mother's body as "the

[23] See, e.g., Ambroise Paré, *On Monsters and Marvels*, trans. Janet L. Pallister (Chicago: Univ. of Chicago Press, 1982), pp. 38–42 (hereafter cited parenthetically as Paré, *Monsters*); and see below for further discussion of monstrous embryology in connection with Errour's den. La Primaudaye, *Second Part of the French Academie*, inviting his readers to consider "a marvailous providence of God, in the similitude that is between the creature engendering, and that which proceedeth from it," actually suggests that the degree of divergence from perfect similitude in generation is proportional to the strength of imagination in the progenitor. Plants reproduce themselves most perfectly, he writes, and beasts are second, while mankind copies itself least reliably "because our mindes are more floting and unstable" (p. 388).

body of death."[24] Yet another version of this pattern may be seen in the intellectual traditions Nohrnberg has documented, for the hexameral "primavera of the world" has its materialistic, Lucretian counterpart:

> Hence, doubtless, Earth prodigious forms at first
> Gendered, of face and members most grotesque:
> Monsters half-man, half-woman, not from each
> Distant, yet neither total; shapes unsound,
> Footless and handless, void of mouth or eye.[25]

This image of scrambled chthonic parturition is just what the Garden of Adonis, with its seminal reasons and type forms, its implicit theories of double creation and causes held in reserve, is designed to foreclose. The Garden, as a scene of Aristotelian metaphor, leads back to its tenor in the Divine Mind, but this image leads to the scene in Errour's den, with its concentration of "subterranean horror at the slime of origin" (Quilligan, *Milton's Spenser*, p. 82).

Let us consider the scene in Errour's den at greater length. We saw in chapter 4 that Spenser's image of the human frame at II.ix.22 refigures the contrast between form and substance partly as a contrast between the masculine—"immortall, perfect . . . set in heavens place"—and the "imperfect, mortal, foeminine" that stretches from the genitals to the ground. Since the difference between divine perfection and mortal imperfection is itself the deepest division within human nature, caused by and corresponding to Original Sin, this stanza participates in the tradition of those Church "Fathers" who traced the fall of man to woman.[26] Yet insofar as its "epithalamial" dimension stresses the unity of human nature—the single her-

---

[24] Goldberg, *James I* , pp. 97, 100.

[25] The lines from Lucretius are given in this translation by C. W. Lemmi, "Monster-Spawning Nile-Mud in Spenser," *MLN* 41 (1926): 235.

[26] Hamilton notes that the spelling "foeminine" at II.ix.22.4 "suggests that the feminine is 'foe to man.' "

maphroditic being into which man and woman are compounded by marriage—the stanza reassimilates the feminine back into the masculine in a subordinate role, once again dividing the feminine against itself.

A link to Book I is established in the immediately preceding stanza. There Spenser laments the mortality of Alma's house, a "worke divine" that is nevertheless destined to fall like the tower of Babel, evidently because it is constructed of similar material: "thing like to that Aegyptian slime, / Whereof king Nine whilome built Babell towre" (II.ix.21.5–6). This "Aegyptian slime" reappears just outside the Garden of Adonis as "mud, on which the Sunne hath shynd" (III.vi.8.9), to which Spenser compares Chrysogonee. Another version of this simile occurs in stanza 21 of the poem's opening canto:

> As when old father *Nilus* gins to swell
> With timely pride aboue the *Aegyptian* vale,
> His fattie waues do fertile slime outwell,
> And ouerflow each plaine and lowly dale:
> But when his later spring gins to auale,
> Huge heaps of mudd he leaues, wherein there breed
> Ten thousand kindes of creatures, partly male
> And partly female of his fruitfull seed;
> Such vgly monstrous shapes elsewhere may no man reed.
>
> (I.i.21)

Here the comparison refers to Errour's vomit, a sickening macédoine of half-digested literature and eyeless creeping amphibians:

> Therewith she spewd out of her filthy maw
> A floud of poyson horrible and blacke,
> Full of great lumpes of flesh and gobbets raw,
> Which stunck so vildly, that it forst him slacke
> His grasping hold, and from her turne him backe:
> Her vomit full of bookes and papers was,
> With loathly frogs and toades, which eyes did lacke,

And creeping sought way in the weedy gras:
Her filthy parbreake all the place defiled has.   (I.i.20)

The combination of texts with toads is not utterly without rationale, as Hamilton notes, since John says in Revelations that he saw unclean spirits "like frogges" come out of the mouths of the dragon, the beast, and the false prophet (16:13). Thus as the Geneva gloss implies, anyone who croaks (or otherwise publishes) the lies of the Antichrist contributes to the general nausea. And yet the passage also insists on the incongruity of the images; it would be wrong to "solve" their surrealistic disjunction too readily. Between them, stanzas 21 and 22 multiply unholy compounds that collectively travesty the unity and perfection of the risen body in which there is neither male nor female. Not only is the vomit itself a strange brew, the act of vomiting passes by way of similitude into a peculiarly unsavory image of generation. In stanza 22 this image will metamorphose yet again into a parturition that (as Hamilton notes) resembles defecation: "She poured forth out of her hellish sinke / Her fruitfull cursed spawne of serpents small" (lines 5–6). Meanwhile, Mother Errour has modulated into Father Nile, and back; the "frogs and toads" she coughs up are themselves of mixed (amphibious) nature; and the simile of stanza 21 has compared them to Nile's "vgly monstrous" brood, "partly male / And partly female"—an image, as the repeated word suggests, not of perfected form but of incomplete formation and dreadfully mixed anatomy.[27]

Of course we have already encountered such a horrific compound anatomy in our first glimpse of Errour herself:

. . . he saw the vgly monster plaine,
Halfe like a serpent horribly displaide,

[27] Lemmi, "Monster-Spawning" suggests that Spenser has "substituted his 'partly male and partly female' for the 'some perfect, some half-formed' " of the passage in Lucretius he is imitating (p. 238).

But th'other halfe did womans shape retaine,
Most lothsom, filthie, foule, and full of vile disdaine.

(I.i. 14.6–9)

This image draws on many sources, but prominent among them must be the book of Genesis, for the woman-serpent notoriously consolidates the two agencies by which man fell from grace in Eden. In order to redeem Eden, Redcrosse will have to sojourn with Duessa: to learn her difference from Una is in effect to separate the woman from the serpent, a necessary preliminary to slaying one and wedding the other. Since Una also represents the true Church and her betrothal to the knight prefigures the marriage of Christ to his risen congregation, Errour and Duessa both travesty that mystical body in their monstrosity.

In order to become an acceptable ecclesiastical symbol Una has to divest herself of bodily sexuality, and not until Book III will the poem turn back to recover this loss. The only gestation and parturition we encounter in the Legend of Holiness are spiritual processes. Nohrnberg includes among the "psychological archetypes" for Book I a series of parental figures: "the House of Holiness has this parental function," he observes, "and so does the rescue provided by Una and Arthur" (*Analogy*, p. 134). Redcrosse languishes in Orgoglio's dungeon for nine months (viii.38); when he is then given over in the House of Holiness to a Charissa "late in child-bed brought" (x.29.7–9), we are tempted to infer with Hamilton that Redcrosse "is the child to whom Charissa has given birth." The poles of maternal symbolism, Errour and Charissa, thus correspond to alternative communions, gathering their broods into the bodies of death and life at the respective "hospitals" of Pride and Holiness.[28] From the House of Pride we descend to Aesculapius's chamber in the classical underworld, where we encounter a

[28] Compare the parturition image at I.v.1, discussed under "The Catachrestic Body," in chapter 2 of this text.

physician who cannot heal himself and who is punished for transgressing the limits of mortal life; the art of medicine as he practices it becomes a demonic, literalizing parody of resurrection. In the House of Holiness we meet the team of metaphysicians who supervise the Redcrosse knight's retractation into glory, a rebirth into resurrected life.

We saw in chapter 2 what an extraordinary mortification of the flesh is involved in the spiritual "gestation" that brings the knight from Errour's den to Charissa's "fruitfull nest" (x.29.8). If the scene in Errour's den represents a symbolic antithesis to this rebirth in the spirit, then it should indeed suggest, as Maureen Quilligan puts it, "nauseated horror at the facts of monstrous female creation" (*Milton's Spenser*, p. 82). It may also suggest that the subterranean terrors of male Elizabethans were if anything more intensely gynophobic than our own. Renaissance medicine moved in a shadowy, mythic world that tended to overpower and reinterpret such empirical observation as there was,[29] and in the case of the female anatomy and the mechanics of pregnancy this was especially true. Maclean's survey of sixteenth-century medical texts on women indicates how thoroughly they were imbued with "the metaphorical association of woman with mother earth, nutrition, fruitfulness and the fluctuations of the moon, which is deeply embedded in the substratum of ancient medical thought, and sometimes explicit there. The implications of these metaphors—passivity, receptiveness, compassion, mutability—may account in part for the Renaissance view of female psychology."[30] Hankins notes specifically that conception was

[29] By the same token, the growth of empirical anatomy tended to undermine the traditional notion of the body as a moralized emblem of the soul. See the excellent commentary on the anatomical illustrations to Vesalius' *Fabrica* offered by Devon L. Hodges in the first chapter of *Renaissance Fictions of Anatomy* (Amherst: Univ. of Massachussetts Press, 1985).

[30] Ian MacLean, *The Renaissance Notion of Woman: A Study in the Fortunes of Scholasticism and Medical Science in European Intellectual Life* (Cambridge: Cambridge Univ. Press, 1980), p. 44.

thought to resemble spontaneous generation because "the menstrual flow of the mother combined with the seminal fluid of the father, and these must decay or coagulate or 'work' before new life could sprout from them in the form of an embryo."[31] The womb, in other words, is a place where life emerges out of rot.

In popular works we see the mainly positive connotations of "mother earth, nutrition, and fruitfulness" mingled with more or less explicit signals of disgust. La Primaudaye, for example, thinks amniotic fluid is the accumulated excrement of the foetus. He describes the breaking of the water during childbirth as follows: "The skinnes wherein both the Urine and the sweate are contained bursting asunder, whole streames gush out, which shew that the birth is at hand" (*Second Part French Academie*, p. 400). It also seems instructive that treatises on monsters, which "by the end of the sixteenth century . . . had become a veritable genre,"[32] were in fact largely composed of Ripleyesque anecdotes about birth defects, accompanied by crude drawings; even Ambroise Paré, a relatively undogmatic investigator with an empirical turn of mind, could not effectively separate the genres, and so treated medical questions about birth defects in a volume entitled *Des Monstres et prodiges* (Paris, 1573).

Hermaphrodites are on prominent display in many such volumes, including an anonymous English translation of Boaistuau.[33] Another important source for such volumes was Aristotle's *Problemata*, which supplied one of the commoner scientific explanations for hermaphrodism. The textual history of the *Problemata* remains tangled—so that the Loeb edition,

---

[31] Hankins, "Hamlet's 'God Kissing Carrion,' " 510.

[32] Janet L. Pallister, introduction to *On Monsters and Marvels*, by Ambroise Paré (Chicago: Univ. of Chicago Press, 1982), p. xxii.

[33] *Certaine Secrete Wonders of Nature* STC 10787 (London, 1569). Since Boaistuau was one of Paré's chief sources, the English volume contains material identical with sections of *Des Monstres*.

for instance, bears little resemblance to the anonymous and partly spurious English translation of 1597—but on sig. E8ʳ of the latter (Anonymous, *Problems of Aristotle*) we learn that nature always aims at perfection in the masculine and sometimes just falls short, an argument which effectively classes women and hermaphrodites together as variant birth defects. Paré offers a different explanation: both the masculine and the feminine seed, he thinks, are imbued with nature's "formative virtue, which always tries to make its likeness," and occasionally the result is, as it were, a draw (*Monsters and Marvels*, p. 26). The doctrine of feminine imperfection returns in altered guise, however, at the end of chapter 7, "Memorable Stories about Women who have Degenerated into Men," when Paré comes to explain why there are no memorable stories about men degenerating into women: "We therefore never find in any *true* story that any man ever became a woman, because Nature tends always toward what is most perfect and not, on the contrary, to perform in such a way that what is perfect should become imperfect" (p. 33, emphasis added).

The antifeminism that runs through these books and treatises, whether in its grosser or its more "scientific" forms, glimpses the medical facts of gynecology and obstetrics (when it glimpses them at all) through deep patterns of association that seem also to underlie the scene in Errour's den. This antifeminism provides an interesting context for rereading Spenser's description of Errour in stanza 14:

> . . . he saw the vgly monster plaine,
> Halfe like a serpent horribly displaide,
> But th'other halfe did womans shape retaine,
> Most lothsom, filthie, foule, and full of vile disdaine.
> (lines 6–9)

Perhaps the poet's conscious intention here is to balance line 7 against line 8 in a parallelism that recapitulates the fearful symmetry of the anatomy he is describing, and then to summarize the incoherent whole in the alexandrine. Yet both the sequence of reading and the closure of the couplet rhyme tend to attach the alexandrine immediately to line 8, in which case it balances "horribly displaide" (also a predicate) in an expansive paralleling that also matches "halfe like a serpent" with "th'other halfe did womans shape retaine." The principle objection to this reading would be that the horror reiterated in the epithets of the final line should attach itself primarily to snakiness, or to the unnatural mixing of forms, not to femininity. But as the episode develops its phantasmagoric nexus of theological error, imperfect formation, slimy fertility, prodigious birth, vomit, defecation, "deadly stinke," and hermaphrodism one begins increasingly to wonder whether the underlying scene of horror may not be that of the womb itself as it haunts the Renaissance male unconscious.[34] La Primaudaye comments aptly on the typological sublimation of such symbolism in Book 1 when he refers to mortal nativity as "image and similitude" of "that birth whereby we are borne unto an immortal life" (*Second Part French Academie*, pp. 402–3); what we behold in Errour's den is the residue voided in that sublimation.

[34] And not only that of the Renaissance male. Existential phenomenology may express the "negative moment" of subjective transcendence—the subject's disgust with the *en soi*—in an imagistic complex strikingly similar to the one I am tracing in Spenser's text. Compare Beauvoir: "This quivering jelly which is elaborated in the womb . . . evokes too clearly the soft viscosity of carrion for [man] not to turn shuddering away. Wherever life is in the making—germination, fermentation—it arouses disgust because it is made only in being destroyed; the slimy embryo begins the cycle that is completed in the putrefaction of death. Because he is horrified by needlessness and death, man feels horror at having been engendered; he would fain deny his animal ties." (*Second Sex* 164; quoted by Dorothy Kaufmann McCall, "Simone de Beauvoir, *The Second Sex*, and Jean-Paul Sartre," *Signs* 5 [1979]: 215). On Sartre's influence in connection with mysogynistic imagery in Beauvoir, see McCall; also Margery Collins and Christine Pierce, "Holes and Slime: Sexism in Sartre's Psychoanalysis," in *Women and Philosophy: Toward a Theory of Liberation*, ed. Carol C. Gould and Marx W. Wartofsky (New York: Putnam, 1976), pp. 112–27.

Another significant element in this pattern is the association of monstrosity and physical filth with the fantasy. The conventional wisdom of ancient medicine, retailed with full belief by Renaissance writers, held that monstrous births could reflect the influence of the mother's imagination on the formation of the foetus, at the moment of conception or during the first weeks of pregnancy (see, e.g., Paré, *Monsters and Marvels*, chap. 9). Errour too is linked with the corrupting influence of the carnal imagination: her words, for example, are altogether grossly made flesh, and her offspring destroy themselves by drinking her blood in a grisly, literalizing parody of communion. Here again she is the negative form of what Redcrosse encounters in the House of Holiness; as we have seen, he is assimilated to the Protestant communion by learning to read scripture in the spirit. When Fidelia opens the knight's "dull eyes, that light mote in them shine" (x.18.9), she is cleansing him of the blindness with which he so confidently waded into Errour's den, declaring that "Vertue giues her selfe light" (i.12.9); the same blindness is represented by Errour's "frogs and toades, which eyes did lacke."

We know that Spenser's poetics involves a visionary phase corresponding to the ascent of Mount Contemplation. The poet signals this correspondence explicitly by comparing the mountain to Parnassus as well as Sinai and the Mount of Olives (I.x.53–54), but it is implicit everywhere in the analogical system that organizes the poem. This ascent into vision alternates with a descending movement that reembodies visionary forms in heroic deeds and poetic fictions. Thus Redcrosse passes from the still-expectant Fidessa and Speranza to the wedded and fruitful Charissa, who leads him in turn to the visionary ascent into contemplation, from which he must then descend once more to do battle with the dragon. Since the immaculate conception is a recurrent figure in Spenser for this generative power of the poetic imagination, Errour figures as

253

the antithetical form not only of Protestant communion in the spirit, but specifically of the poet's form-giving creativity. Redcrosse's encounter with her, then, is perhaps the poem's most fully developed image of the negative moment in its dialectical assimilation of fertility to an essentially patriarchal symbolic order.

THE ALLEGORY OF POESIS

The patriarchy appropriates fertility through an upward displacement of the womb that both resembles and complements the reinscription of the phallus we observed in Alma's dwelling. The "phallic" mental function is judgment as it gathers memory and fantasy under its supervision; the "uterine" function is fantasy as it serves the higher offices of judgment and intellection. Nohrnberg observes that Ficino, whose discussion of seminal reasons clearly influenced the Garden of Adonis passage, "attributes analogous generative powers to the imagination," and he traces this analogy to the *Enneads* of Plotinus:

> Begetting originates in contemplation and ends in the production of a new form, that is, a new object of contemplation. In general, all things as they are images of their generating principles produce forms and objects of contemplation. . . . Moreover, animals generate due to the activity within them of seminal reasons. Generation is a contemplation. It results from the longing of pregnancy to produce a multiplicity of forms and objects of contemplation, to fill everything with reason, and never to cease from contemplation. Begetting means to produce some form; and this means to spread contemplation everywhere. All the faults met with in begotten things or in actions are due to the fact that one did stray from the object of one's contemplation. The poor workman resembles the producer of bad

forms. Also lovers must be counted among those who contemplate and pursue forms.[35]

Despite all its talk of begetting, this passage is closer to Book VI than to Book III because Plotinus weights the analogy by assimilating generation to contemplation, whereas Spenser's emphasis in Book III falls less on the pleasure of contemplating forms than on the pleasure of embodying them. The analogy of contemplation is nevertheless implicit throughout Book III, preinforming the allegory of natural begetting like a divine foreconceit.

Consider the figure of Genius, whose dual function of embodiment and disembodiment is duplicated in reverse by the meditative and imaginative phases of poetic creation. The *puer senex* motif, which Nohrnberg finds "slightly dissociated" in the compound figure of Genius and his flock of babes clamoring for life, appears similarly dissociated in the allegory of poetic intentionality that we observed in the turret of Alma's house. In the allegory of imagination, judgment, and memory this motif is distributed among three terms: Phantastes, "A man of yeares yet fresh" (II.ix.52.3); Eumnestes, "an old old man" (55.5); and the unnamed figure in the middle chamber, "a man of ripe and perfect age" (54.2) identified with the poet. (The motif recurs in the chamber of memory, where "a little boy" [58.4], Anamnestes, attends on Eumnestes.) Since judgment gathers the functions of memory and imagination under his supervision, he is a compound figure like Genius, responsible for a whole range of mental activities that have their Gar-

---

[35] The translation is that of Joseph Katz, *The Philosophy of Plotinus* (New York: Appleton-Century-Crofts, 1950); quoted by Nohrnberg, *Analogy*, p. 658. Compare the following passage from Ficino's commentary on Plotinus, cited and translated by Hankins, *Source*, p. 248: "Also the genital nature and imagination, the companion of nature, so from potentiality into act bring forth in themselves seeds of things and motions to be generated, that a most orderly and perpetual succession is made and at last there is a return to the same or similar [forms] in certain courses of time."

den equivalents, including the separation and rejoining of forms and their sensuous images and the capacity to stock each.

Book III's emphasis on embodiment makes the parallel with Phantastes explicit. His chamber is covered with "infinite shapes of thinges dispersed thin," including "Some daily seene, and knowen by their names" and others "such as in the world were neuer yit, / Ne can deuized be of mortall wit" (II.ix.50.3–6). The Garden likewise breeds "infinite shapes of creatures," including "vncouth formes, which none yet euer knew" (III.vi.35.1–2). The prevenient judgment of God, however, has always already ordered the Garden through the double creation, so where Phantastes' stock appears in sheer paratactic form (II.ix.50.8–9), the Garden's forms are "ranckt in comely rew" (III.vi.35.4); to elicit a comparable order from Phantastes' inventory requires the operations of the middle chamber.

Disengaged from its dialectical subordination to judgment, the fantasy might produce almost anything. Horace describes this danger in the well-known opening passage of his *Ars Poetica*:

> If a painter chose to set a human head on the neck and shoulders of a horse, to gather limbs from every animal and clothe them with feathers from every kind of bird, and make what at the top was a beautiful woman have ugly ending in a black fish's tail—when you were admitted to view his picture, should you refrain from laughing, my good friends? Believe me, Pisos, a book will be the very likeness of such a picture in which, like a sick man's dreams, the images shall be impossible, in the sense that no two parts correspond to any one whole.[36]

The artist too must order his images "according to their kindes" (III.vi.30.6). The centaur, the mermaid, the beast

[36] 1903 translation by E. C. Wickham, rpt. in *Critical Theory Since Plato*, ed. Hazard Adams (New York: Harcourt, 1971), p. 68.

whose anatomy contains all shapes—these reflect an aesthetic equivalent to the monstrous Lucretian parturition that underlies the scene in Errour's den. The poet must assimilate the female workings of his brain to judgment's ratios, making his book "one whole," or he is liable to produce no more than "a sick man's dreams."

This pattern divides masculinity against itself just as it does femininity. In Alma's house we saw how the erasure of the penis contributes to erecting the privilege of the phallus, in accordance with the Lacanian dictum that the phallus does its work only when veiled; thus the male organ is refigured in the divine circle. A similar erasure of the penis and male sperm form the basis of the Chrysogonee myth, through which the male poet, like the patriarch in des Granges' portrait *The Family of Sir Richard Saltonstall*, "absorbs female creativity."[37] Such retractations of male sexuality follow out a paradigm established in Plato's *Timaeus*, where the demiurge is said to have

> made the world one whole, having every part entire, and being therefore perfect and not liable to old age and disease. And he gave to the world the figure which was suitable and also natural. Now to the animal which was to comprehend all animals, that figure was suitable which comprehends within itself all figures. Wherefore he made the world in the form of a globe, round as from a lathe, having its extremes in every direction equidistant from the center, the most perfect and most like itself of all figures; for he considered that the like is infinitely fairer than the unlike. This he finished off, making the surface smooth all around for many reasons: in the first place, because the living being had no need of eyes when there was nothing remaining outside him to be seen, nor of ears when there was nothing to be heard;

[37] Goldberg, *James I*, pp. 98, 104.

and there was no surrounding atmosphere to be breathed.
. . .[38]

And so it goes: the cosmos is an organism reformed "by way
of retractation," eyeless, earless, and noseless—not to mention,
as the passage continues, mouthless, anusless, limbless, and
sexless, "for there was nothing beside him" (and certainly no
one next to him). The figure is constructed according to a doc-
trine of likenesses,[39] for the cosmos answers to the nature of its
divine creator. This doctrine interlocks with that of perfect
self-sufficiency: the divine creator is self-identical, so the cos-
mos must be a sphere, "most like itself of all figures"; he is
self-sufficient, too—so the cosmos must be a sphere, needing
none of the apertures and appendages that mark the organism's
dependency on an ecosystem. Finally, the doctrines of likeness
and self-sufficiency interlock with that of assimilation: "The
animal which was to comprehend all animals" assumes "that
figure . . . which comprehends within itself all figures."
Hence the comprehensively castrated animal, "round *as from
a lathe*," is also the plenum of animal forms. It is able to be
this at once despite and by virtue of its shorn appendages, as
the body's members become "members" in the category of ge-
ometrical forms.

Such is the globe, "immortal, perfect, masculine," from
which the "imperfect, mortall, foeminine" body represents a
falling away, and back into which that body is re-membered

---

[38] Plato, *Timaeus*, trans. Benjamin Jowett (Indianapolis: Bobbs-Merrill,
1949), pp. 15– 16. Plato's animal corresponds to what Deleuze and Guattari
call "the body without organs." They reject Freud's model of primal repres-
sion as an endogenic defense against hyperstimulation of the organism,
seeing it instead as an effect of the social or political "body without organs"
in its refusal of desiring machines and their linkages (*Anti-Oedipus*, pp. 8–
9, 11, 120–21). "Social repression" is then grafted onto the effects of primal
repression during the transformation of the narcissistic ego by the ego ideal
(see "Arthur's Dream," in chapter 3 of this text).
[39] Barkan, *Nature's Work of Art*, pp. 9–14.

by dialectic. Plato's cosmic animal comes to Spenser as the Neoplatonic World Soul, which may be feminine—like "Venus selfe" in *Colin Clovts come home againe*, a nominally feminine Goddess who "doth solely couples seeme" (line 801). But the World Soul corresponds by resemblance to a nominally *masculine* supratemporal deity in whose sole being all dualities, including that of gender, are resolved.

I suggested in chapter 2 that the masculine-hermaphroditic "universal" of *The Faerie Queene* may be a catachresis, although it would be described in more orthodox terms as synecdoche. Lila Geller has argued for the special importance to Book III of a triadic paradigm derived from Neoplatonic readings of the Three Graces, and her argument demonstrates that the paradigm itself is a perfect synecdoche:

> Much as Venus is the unity that unfolds into the Three Graces, Britomart in her function as the primary Chastity figure of Book III is also the unified embodiment of the related virtues of Beauty, Chastity, and Love as they are figured in the characters Florimell, Belphoebe, and Amoret. Unlike a simple fractioning of an entity into component parts, in the unfolding process each unfolded aspect of the unity contains the whole, so that no matter how we continue unfolding, and even though each unfolded virtue stresses one particular aspect of the whole, we can never break the complex entity into simple components. Though Britomart is Chastity, whole and complex, we can see her unity unfolded into Florimell, who is Beauty, modified by Chastity and Love; into Belphoebe, who is Chastity, tempered with Beauty and Love; into Amoret, who is Love, but a Love sustained by Beauty and Chastity. The reappearance of Chastity in the unfolded position as well as in the infolded one is typical of Ficino's pattern, illustrative of the principle that the whole is contained in the part.[40]

[40] Lila Geller, "Venus and the Three Graces: A Neoplatonic Paradigm for Book III of *The Faerie Queene*," *JEGP* 75 (1976): 60.

The value of this paradigm is to "reveal a logic of juxtaposition of incidents in the book and a distinction between bewilderingly similar characters" (p. 61); in other words, it regathers the "many" of character and incident back into the "One" of poetic foreconceit. Thus Ficino's pattern illustrates the principle that multiple aspects of the narrative are preunderstood in terms of their relations to a presumed whole, and are therefore apprehended from the start as unfolded and inherently re-infoldable.

As we have seen before, the eternal self-sufficiency of this pattern depends on a self-authorizing circularity in the mode of representation that sustains it. This circularity or specularity lies at the heart of any signifying structure, and may be projected upward as a divine mystery or downward as an image of chaos. Thus the mystical fusion of opposites in the One finds its counterpart in the confusion of Errour's brood, based on a myth of chthonic genesis: the uncanny relation between these supposed opposites may be glimpsed in the Lucretian reference to shapes "footless and handless, void of mouth or eye," which sounds oddly like a description of Plato's cosmic animal. Horace's reference to the "impossible" image of "limbs from every animal" clothed with "feathers from every kind of bird" also suggests a literalizing or carnal parody of "the animal which was to comprehend all animals." The interlacing of sexualities in nature's lap stands midway between such extremes, and is represented in the Garden by the couples inside the mons: Venus and Adonis, Psyche and Cupid. As we cross the threshold between nature and culture, these figures are doubled: Cupid becomes himself and another, and so does Venus, while the Venus-Adonis pair splits between Acrasia's watch over Verdant and Gloriana's visit to Arthur. At this level, however, the doubles are not mystically or monstrously confused, but distributed dialectically, so that only one figure from each pair really corresponds to nature. *Her* eros is simple love of the divine ideas and a desire to copy them: it is mimesis. But human eros divides between the metaphoric, or properly mimetic, and the catachrestic, or abusive, which receives its apotheosis in the figure of Busirane. Metaphoric eros tends toward reassimilation into the "one whole" of divine mystery, while catachrestic eros tends toward carnal (or idolatrous) imagination, undisguised aggressive mastery, and chaos.

Spenser's allegory suggests the uncanny relation between divinity and chaos (perhaps inadvertently) when it tells us that the goldbirth of paradigmatic forms is itself derived from an earlier birth. Amphisa, or "both equally." Amphisa's name suggests that Chrysogonee, too, may have a twin, although this prior sisterhood appears nowhere in the story. We have met Chrysogonee's sister, though: she is Errour. Her specular doubling of Chrysogonee, deeply implicit in the patterns of Spenser's imagery, reappears in the incestuous twins, Argante and Olliphant. Parallel to Belphoebe and Amoret, they are the antithetical twins of twins. Their copulation *in utero* travesties the coupling of genders in the Garden and in God, much as Errour and her brood travesty the communion symbolism of Charissa and her babies.

THE DOUBLE THRESHOLD

This minuet of repressed and explicit twinnings may provide the best approach to Spenser's Garden of Adonis. Barely half a canto long, the Garden passage contains more interpretive cruxes than any comparable section of the poem. Where is the garden located? Is it a "place" at all? Are its two walls concentric, or do they stand at opposite ends of the garden? Are the "naked babes" attending Genius rational human souls, or merely the forms of bodies? Why does Spenser call them babies if they don't have bodies yet? Is the ever-replenished "stocke" of stanza 36 that of forms or that of matter? Why does Spenser reverse his customary association of matter with death and form with permanence? Is "wicked Time" inside the Garden or outside it? Does Venus represent form and Adonis matter, or vice-versa? Long work it were here to recount the endless progeny of alternative readings these twenty-four stanzas have spawned. They almost seem to be deliberately cast in the stylistic image of Amphisa: Puttenham's "Amphibologia, or the Ambiguous," which begets hermeneutic twins by way of intellection.

Another pattern of doubling characterizes the Garden more explicitly: "There is continuall spring, and haruest there / Continuall, both meeting at one time" (st. 42.1–2). These lines contrast the endless summer of Acrasia's Bower with a stranger kind of duration, "one time" at once punctual and continuous, as though each moment contained all others within itself. Seedtime and ripeness coincide here the way birth and decay were thought to coincide in the womb; indeed, looking back at Time "with his scyth addrest" (st. 39.3) from the vantage of stanza 42, we cannot be sure whether he is an image of birth or death: if he harvests ripe forms inside the Garden, it may be to send them into the world, so that their death "here" is a birth "there"; whereas if he harvests moribund creatures in the world, it must be to return their forms for rejuvenation "from old to new," so that their death "there" equals replanting into a backward running time "here." Nohrnberg aptly remarks "the symbolic reversibility of the garden-world into a world-garden," and goes on to map the convergence of birth and death that results from this radical telescoping of the distinction between "inside" and "outside" (*Analogy*, pp. 530–32).

Just as we cross its textual threshold, Spenser remarks that he does not know *where* the Garden lies, but does know—"by tryall"—how pleasant it is:

Whether in *Paphos*, or *Cytheron* hill,
Or it in *Gnidus* be, I wote not well;
But well I wote by tryall, that this same
All other pleasant places doth excell. . . .

(III.vi.29.4–7)

These lines may remind us of the proem to Book II, where Spenser teases our wish for a cartography of Fairyland. Here his playful confession of ignorance as to the Garden's "literal" location sets up an even more playful assertion of familiarity with its qualities. Is the poet modestly disclaiming virginity? Since the fable of Chrysogonee and the Garden itself both sustain a detailed and elaborate physical allegory, the answer would appear to be yes. But since the fable of Chrysogonee and the Garden itself both make intellection analogous to natural begetting, we may also take the hint that Spenser has visited Nature's lap in a more visionary mode: insofar as the Garden is everywhere, one need only grasp the metaphor to have been there. "The garden," as Nohrnberg observes, "is to be met with in a lying-in hospital, or a kindergarten, or a nursery, or even in a supermarket," as well as in "the salvage yard" (*Analogy*, pp. 530–31). Because it is based on a metaphor, this list of places that "are" the Garden is open-ended: it can include the sexual organs, a compost heap, a zoo, a yeast culture, a cemetery, an incinerator, a botanical textbook, a chrysalis, a museum of natural history—anything that can be grasped in terms of the organic cycle or its taxonomies. The Garden's physical allegory might seem to locate it in the middle of the body, but its conceptual boundaries are established and re-established through acts of comparison.

In this respect stanza 29 resembles the "threshold" stanzas in Spenser's allegory of the temperate body: II.ix.33 and 44. We saw in chapter 4 that these stanzas mark the boundaries between discontinuous allegorical "frames" and figure forth the dynamics of retractation, through which we ascend from

263

the loins to the head. Of course the question that oriented our discussion of Alma's house—why are the genitals omitted?—received only half an answer as we traced the refiguration of the phallus in the divine circle of the (masculine) head. The topography of the Garden shows us the mons veneris and womb, while its physical allegory represents the menses and semen in slightly more veiled form. The penis and testicles are the most thoroughly veiled—conspicuously excluded from the fable of Chrysogonee, and appearing in the Garden, if at all, only as possible occult readings of Adonis and Genius, respectively. They appear more prominently in displaced form as the phallic circle, which gathers nature's fecundity back into the Logos. In broadly structural terms what this means is that while Alma's house presents an allegory of retractation or sublimation, like the *Fowre Hymnes*, the Garden presents an allegory of reversion, like the endings to the earthly hymns: its concern is with "All, that to come into the world desire" (st. 32.2). Here, though, reversion is contained as one movement within the wheel of generation: the masculine genitals are displaced from the physical allegory precisely so they can serve this larger structural function of regathering nature's brood into the taxonomy of God's word, and so re-marking the difference between the Garden and Errour's den.

The structural difference between the allegories of sublimation and descent means that stanza 29 marks the boundary of the Garden not by figuring forth the movement of retractation as a dynamics of reframing, but by figuring forth the movement of reversion as a scattering of the frame among disparate perspectives. Ascent in Alma's house was based on "avoidance," or exclusion by turning aside; descent in the Garden is based on multiplication and coupling, or inclusion by "meeting at one time." Ascent in Alma's House meant insisting on distinctions of place: the heart, *not* the loins, and the head, *not* the body. Descent in the Garden means confounding dis-

tinctions of place, including the fundamental distinction be-
tween inside and outside, which was critical to Alma's embat-
tled fortress. Life in the temperate body depended on
repulsing the world's onslaughts; life in the Garden *and* outside
it depends on crossing and recrossing the membrane that sep-
arates it from world.

Stanza 31, which locates the Garden "in fruitfull soyle of
old," also dis-locates it through a barrage of doublings:

> It sited was in fruitfull soyle of old,
> And girt in with two walles on either side;
> The one of yron, the other of bright gold,
> That none might thorough break, nor ouer-stride:
> And double gates it had, which opened wide,
> By which both in and out men moten pas;
> Th'one faire and fresh, the other old and dride:
> Old *Genius* the porter of them was,
> Old *Genius*, the which a double nature has.   (III.vi.31)

In nine lines we encounter a remarkable number of pairs: two
walls, two sides, two materials, two modes of intrusion pre-
vented, two gates, two directions of passage, two mortal con-
ditions, and a porter with two natures whose name is repeated.
There are also at least two ways of construing most of the syn-
tax. The walls, as we noted earlier, may be at opposite ends of
the Garden, or both on each end, one inside the other. The
gates may be "double" because there are two, or because there
are four, a pair on each end—depending on whether the walls
are opposed or concentric—or because each one is hinged on
either side, like saloon doors. "Men" pass in and out, but do
they enter "fresh" and leave "old," or leave "old" and enter
"fresh"? Do they pass in and out of both gates, or in one and
out the other?

Some of these questions are answered in stanza 32, which
explains the "double nature" of Genius in terms of his paired
functions: "He letteth in, he letteth out to wend, / All that to

come into the world desire" (lines 1– 2). The letting out means that he "sendeth forth to liue in mortall state" whatever is destined for life, while the letting in means that he receives decayed forms "by the hinder gate." And yet this seeming clarity only displaces the confusion, for if Genius is the single porter of nature's double gates, where is *he*—at opposite ends of the Garden? We can make sense of the lines only by thinking of the Garden as something like a single threshold that has been doubled to create an imaginary space or interval, within which two perspectives—the boundary seen from one side and from the other—are superimposed. For instance, the House of Pride's "privy postern" and the "backgate" of Alma's house are passages of excretion seen from one point of view; the "hinder gate" of the Garden is the same passageway seen as a port of entry rather than exit. We glimpse the conjunction of these opposed perspectives when Guyon and the Palmer "engraue" the corpses of Mortdant and Amavia by opening "the great earthes wombe . . . to the sky" (II.i.60.1–2), but the decorum of the scene remains that of a Roman funeral: "So shedding many teares, they closd the earth agayne" (st. 61.9). The Garden, however, couples these perspectives fully. If the House of Holiness focuses on the low point in the divine circle as a place of conversion, or spiritual rebirth, the Garden focuses on the same point in nature's wheel of generation as a place of natural rebirth, which entails a literal death of the body and not just a symbolic death of the body ego. The Garden, in this sense, is by definition the place where death and birth coincide, or where the way out becomes the way in. "So like a wheele around they runne from old to new," reversing the natural course of life from new to old.

Genius participates in this doubleness as a Janus figure or, together with his flock of babes, "a slightly dissociated *puer senex*, like the old man and babe shown . . . [in] the typical

266

first of January cartoon" (Nohrnberg, *Analogy*, pp. 529, 532).
As one who clothes the "naked babes" of the Garden with mat-
ter, he is related to the medieval genii of allegories like Ber-
nardus Silvestris's *Cosmographia*. These figures seem to repre-
sent the mimetic impulse itself. The Genius of the firmament
in Bernardus occupies the periphery of the created cosmos,
where he introduces Nature to Urania and continues to mediate
between their realms by "ceaselessly . . . inscribing forms
upon all created things and thereby ensuring that they will con-
form to the influence of the heavens."[41] At the central point of
the microcosm are placed two other genii, twin brothers who
"fight unconquered against death with their life-giving weap-
ons. . . . Blood sent forth from the seat of the brain flows down
to the loins, bearing the image . . . of ancestors" (*Cosmogra-
phia*, p. 126). In between are other genii, distributed through
the heavenly spheres, who perform the admonitory functions
Spenser assigns to "Agdistes" at II.xii.47–48. The Genius of
the Garden, if indeed he is Agdistes, would seem to combine
the functions Bernardus distributes into many places and fig-
ures, in keeping with the Garden's tendency to superimpose
places and perspectives.

But Spenser's Genius not only supervises the union of form
with matter; as porter of the "hinder gate" he must also preside
over the separation of form from matter in death. In this re-
spect Genius is indeed his own double, an inside-out image of
"wicked Time." Here again we may think of the New Year's
day cartoon to which Nohrnberg refers, where the old man
typically carries an hourglass *and a scythe*. We may also com-
pare one of Bernardus's genii, "the Usiarch of Saturn, an old
man everywhere condemned. . . . Whenever his most fertile

[41] *The "Cosmographia" of Bernardus Silvestris*, trans. Winthrop Wetherbee
(New York: Columbia Univ. Press, 1973), p. 44 (hereafter cited paren-
thetically as Silvestris, *Cosmographia*).

wife had borne him sons, he had cut them off at the first bud-
ding of life. . . . Nature was horrified by the old man's cru-
elty. . . . [W]henever there was no one whom he might de-
vour, he would mow down with a blow of his sickle whatever
was beautiful, whatever was flourishing" (*Cosmographia*, pp.
99–100). This link between Time and Genius offers another
way of understanding why Time is both inside and outside the
Garden: like Genius, he is a liminal figure, and Spenser lets us
see him from both sides of the double threshold that is death-
and-birth. We see him as the grim reaper whose work Venus
laments, but Time is a harvest genius, and no sooner have we
passed from the spectacle of his havoc (st. 39–40) to a celebra-
tion of natural pleasure (st. 41–42) than we meet him again in
the lines I quoted earlier: "There is continuall spring, and har-
uest there / Continuall, both meeting at one time" (42.1–2).
But harvest in stanza 42 has become an image of plenitude, of
trees "Which seeme to labour vnder their fruits lode" (line 6).
Meanwhile the opening lines of the stanza restate the double
nature of Genius, even echoing faintly the recursive cadence of
"He letteth in, he letteth out to wend." We meet a final trans-
formation of Time into his opposite in stanza 46, where we
learn that Venus resorts to the Garden to "reape sweet pleasure"
of Adonis—a phrase that collapses harvest into planting, or
death into conception, strikingly. The boar may be impris-
oned, but if the "rocky Caue, which is they say, / Hewen
vnderneath that Mount" corresponds in the anamorphic topog-
raphy of the scene to a womb, then in an important sense the
boar is inside Venus herself as she "takes her fill" of sweetness
from Adonis.

The intricacies of the passage have led some commentators
to postulate more than one garden—Berger finds three, Ram-
say two. In this respect the Garden might once again be com-
pared to Alma's house, which Spenser clearly divides between
kitchen, parlor, and turret. In the one we move upward to the

body's crown, in the other down to its "middest";[42] in the one
we pursue refigurations of the phallus, in the other images of
mons and womb. Our tour of Alma's house begins with a me-
chanical allegory of the vegetable soul's functions, and our tour
of the Garden begins with a schematic description of the veg-
etable soul's embodiment. In Alma's house we then progress to
the "modest" courtship of the parlor, while in the Garden we
progress to a paradise where "Franckly each paramour his le-
man knowes" (st. 41.7). In Alma's house we arrive lastly at
the seat of the rational soul, where past and future are coupled
by judgment in a middle space; while in the Garden we arrive
at the abode of Psyche "in the middest" of the sexual paradise,
where reaping and sowing are coupled by Venus in her enjoy-
ment of Adonis. But underlying all these similarities is the
fundamental difference mentioned earlier: the anatomical
zones of the body are sharply distinct in Alma's house, but the
phases of the Garden are really not separate places. As Tonkin[43]
and MacCaffrey have argued, the spatial and sequential terms
of the description are deceptive: "In fact," remarks Mac-
Caffrey, "stanzas 30 through 40 need to be imaginatively su-
perimposed, since they are simultaneous aspects of a single
though complex idea" (*Spenser's Allegory*, p. 265). I would re-
formulate this observation slightly, extending it beyond stanza
40 to the end of the account in stanza 52, and insisting that the
conceit itself is not single but double.

This means that the transitional stanzas in the Garden pas-
sage should function differently from those in the account of
Alma's house. We have seen that stanza 29 marks one of the
Garden's boundaries, but does so paradoxically, by unhinging

[42] In *Spenser's Allegory* MacCaffrey notes that as we approach the center of
the Garden "Spenser contrives to minimize the sensation of moving *up*. . . .
the spectator has the sense of an approach from below to within" (p. 261).

[43] Humphrey Tonkin, "Spenser's Garden of Adonis and Britomart's
Quest," *PMLA* 88 (1973): 409.

the closure of its allegorical "frame." Berger and Ramsay, who agree on little else, both see stanza 41 as marking the boundary of a "second garden":[44]

> But were it not, that *Time* their troubler is,
> All that in this delightfull Gardin growes,
> Should happie be, and haue immortall blis:
> For here all plentie, and all pleasure flowes. . . .
>
> (III.vi.41.1–4)

A closer look at stanzas 37–42, however, suggests that the whole passage repeatedly reframes the garden, as if turning it inside out and back. Stanza 37 leads us out of the Garden and into the world:

> All things from [Chaos] doe their first being fetch,
> And borrow matter, whereof they are made,
> Which when as forme and feature it does ketch,
> Becomes a bodie, and doth then inuade
> The state of life, out of the griesly shade.   (III.vi.37.1–5)

Note in particular that this transition is described from the perspective of matter, the "it" of line 3. Stanza 36 has already moved us from a focus on the forms that "daily forth are sent / Into the world, it to replenish more" (lines 1–2) to a focus on the "euerlasting store" of matter, which replenishes the "stocke" that in turn replenishes the world. When stanza 37 comes to speak of death, it maintains the same perspective:

> That substance is eterne, and bideth so,
> Ne when the life decayes, and forme does fade,
> Doth it consume, and into nothing go,
> But chaunged is, and often altred to and fro.
>
> (III.vi.37.6–9)

---

[44] Berger, "Spenser's Gardens of Adonis," p. 140; Ramsay, "Garden of Adonis," p. 201.

These lines have been interpreted as saying that matter does not return into the *nihil* out of which God created it, but passes into other forms. Such a reading is possible because the antecedent of "it" in line 8 can be either "substance," or "forme," or indeed "the life" in which they combine. The beginning of stanza 38 dispels this ambiguity, however, and makes "it" refer specifically to form:

> The substance is not chaunged, nor altered,
> But th'only forme and outward fashion;
> For euery substance is conditioned
> To change her hew, and sundry formes to don,
> Meet for her temper and complexion.   (III.vi.38.1–5)

In retrospect, then, the closing lines of stanza 37 say that substance is eternal and stays that way, whereas form, though not eternal like matter, is altered rather than annihilated by death. These stanzas therefore describe the forms' recycling through the Garden of Adonis—but they describe it from matter's point of view.

The close of stanza 38 shifts this point of view as it comes back to the subject of death:

> For formes are variable and decay,
> By course of kind, and by occasion;
> And that faire flowre of beautie fades away,
> As doth the lilly fresh before the sunny ray.
>
> (III.vi.38.6–9)

Two transitions occur in these four lines. First we move from the perspective of matter to that of form, and then from generic form to the particular creature, from "that faire flowre of beautie" to "the lilly fresh." The close of stanza 38 thus prepares for the image of "wicked Time" by leading us imaginatively into the world "outside" the Garden.

Stanzas 39 and 40 maintain the elegiac tone proper to this point of view even as they run through three different "phases" of the cycle. Time is an enemy to all that "springs" in the Garden (st. 39.2); he mows and crushes the "goodly things," including "both leaues and buds" (lines 4, 8). Any attempt to translate this metaphoric language must recognize that time cannot be isolated either inside or outside the Garden. "Buds" are baby flowers, and might be thought of as inside the Garden, or newly arrived from it into the world. But Time itself is the force that moves things out of the garden and into the world, as well as back again; he is present in all places, or phases, of the cycle. The perspective of stanzas 39 and 40 shows us Time as death, the Genius of the hinder gate—whether his work is performed *in utero* or after birth, whether it is viewed in prospect (from within the Garden looking forward), immediately, or in retrospect (from within the Garden looking backward).

The problematic of allegorical "framing" informs these stanzas far more intricately than it does the transitional stanzas in our tour of the temperate body. We are asked to follow rapid shifts in perspective that move, so to speak, along two different axes—for the perspective shifts between that of matter and that of form, as well as shifting from point to point in the cycle of natural life. When stanza 41 moves us back into the liminal space of the Garden, shifting focus from the swath of Time's scythe to the abundance of growth and pleasure found "here," it is sustaining a pattern of shifts and inversions that prevent *any* metaphoric or conceptual boundary from establishing itself. The opening lines of stanza 42, in which spring and harvest expand together into continuous copresence as they contract together into "one time," define the doubleness and elasticity of this compound liminal space-time about as succinctly as one could wish.

PRECOCIOUS MOURNING

In its own way this compounding of perspectives in descent is just as iconoclastic as the self-canceling movement of retractation. Both phases depend on what I called in chapter 4 the antirepresentational energy of writing, which makes the "space" of allegorical representation continually self-effacing, like Freud's "mystic writing pad" or the arras in Alma's parlor: as Roche observes, most of the apparent confusions, contradictions, and paradoxes in Spenser's account of the Garden arise when we try to *visualize* the conceit, which is relatively "easie to be thought" (II.ix.33.9; cf. *Kindly Flame*, pp. 118–22). In this sense the representational dynamics of the Garden are directly contrary to the visually imposing tapestries through which we approach Malecasta and Busirane, just as the arras in Alma's heart contrasts with the stunningly wrought ivory gate to Acrasia's Bower, and with art's *trompe l'oeil* impersonation of nature inside the Bower.

The analogy between Books III and VI supports a reading of natural begetting in the Garden as an allegory of poesis: the proem to Book VI approaches the scene of poetic creation on Mount Acidale by way of a garden metaphor, while the proem to Book III approaches the scene of natural procreation by exploring mimesis as a problem of artistic representation.[45] A comparable analogy sets the Garden against the Bower of Bliss, for the Bower shows us human art disguising itself as nature while the Garden shows us nature revealing itself as divine art. What this means of course is that the true and false paradises are twinned at the deepest level. Of the Bower Spenser says, "The art, which all that wrought, appeared in no place" (II.xii.58.9). Exactly the opposite is true—the art that wrought the Bower appears-and-disappears in *every* place, peeping coyly out from each cluster of grapes or wanton ivy vine like "Cissy and Flossie" in the fountain pool. Art is far more deeply repressed in the Garden of Adonis, where it appears as the form of God played out in the rhythms of nature. Only in the Garden do we meet a bower "not by art, / But of

---

[45] For a discussion of the proem to Book III see "Gloriana's 'Pourtraict,' " in chapter 3 of this text.

the trees owne inclination made" (st. 44.2–3)—a phrase in which human artifice effaces itself completely. In the Bower of Bliss Spenser intends us to see a systematic and manipulative reinscription of "nature" that stage-manages arousal within a theater of narcissism, and so threatens to reabsorb a potentially cultural and political energy back into hedonism. The ideological force of Spenser's own inscription of nature emerges through this portrayal of sensuality: it is a threatening otherness, a predatory and oblivious force[46] whose *erasure* of the insignia on "Verdant's" shield is carefully poised against the striking emergence of a dynastic subtext in the greening of Adonis, "by succession made perpetual." Between them these passages sketch the course of Arthur's quest, which emerges from his adolescent confusion of self with nature—his nap on "the *verdant* gras" (I.ix.13.3, emphasis added)—and proceeds toward his imperial transfiguration.

As an allegory of natural reproduction, the Garden of Adonis "means" something that overlaps with the organic dimension of human experience even as it corresponds by analogy with human experience in its aesthetic and political dimensions. This protohuman aspect of the Garden emerges more clearly as we approach its most anthropomorphic venue. The vegetal metaphor has tended to dominate Spenser's account from the beginning, although the passage slips into other figures of speech from time to time, as when "men" pass in and

---

[46] In the first volume of *The French Academie*, STC 15233 (London, 1586), La Primaudaye catalogues the unsavory consequences of "immoderate vse of the venereous act," which "spoileth beautie, defileth the body, drieth it vp, and causeth it to stink; maketh the face pale, wanne or yellow, weakneth the members and ioints, ingendreth Sciaticke gouts, collicke passions, griefes of the stomache, giddiness of the head, or dimnes of sight, the leprosie and pocks. It shortneth life, taketh away the understanding, darkneth the memorie, and as the Prophet Osey saith, taketh away the hart" (p. 238). See also Greenblatt, *Renaissance Self-Fashioning* (Chicago: Univ. of Chicago Press, 1980), pp. 170–78.

out (st. 31.6), or "babes" attend on Genius (st. 32.3). But humans and plants are more interestingly confused in stanzas 43–45. The unnamed "Mount" that sits "right in the middest" (st. 43.1) is an anamorphic pudendum: executed as a visual conceit, it would be almost pornographically explicit, a genital equivalent to the island heads and vegetable men we see in Renaissance experiments with illusionistic painting. Stanza 44, with its denial of "art," nevertheless half-animates the pubic foliage on the Mount: its trees copulate, "knitting their rancke braunches part to part" according to their "owne inclination" (lines 3–4). This image is supposed to contrast with the Bower of Bliss, where "braunches . . . broad dilate / Their clasping arms, in wanton wreathings intricate" (st. 53.8–9), grapes offer themselves or coyly retreat like the maidens in the fountain (st. 54–55), and ivy "low his lascivious armes adown did creepe" (st. 61.6). But the thematic contrast between art pretending to be nature and nature rising to artifice of its own inclination is less striking than the anamorphic style common to both passages, with its highly artificial, almost baroque decorum (and decor).

Human artifice enters explicitly in stanza 45, where the flowers on the Mount are identified as an anthology of metamorphoses: "And all about grew euery sort of flowre, / To which sad louers were transformd of yore" (lines 1–2). The fables that follow imply a metaphoric continuity within the logic of transformation: Hyacinth and Amaranth blossom red like the blood they replace, so that we seem to see the lovers' "wretched fate" re-presented in them; Narcissus "likes the watery shore," retaining its namesake's propensity. It is as if the elegiac impulse of poetic metamorphosis resembled the orderly workings of nature in "effecting results homogeneous with their sources." "Sweet Poets verse" resembles nature also in that it secures "endlesse date" for the individual only in generic form, as a "sort of flowre." With its fourth line cut short, its

explicit shift from Ovidian allusions to an immediately con-
temporary example,[47] and its alexandrine given over to the
eternizing power of verse, the stanza repeatedly implies poet-
ry's analogy to the Garden as a repairer of death and a nursery
of floral species.

In stanza 46 Adonis extends the slain-lover motif of the flo-
ral catalogue, but unlike the others he does not become a
flower. "*Lapped* in flowres and pretious spycery" (line 5, em-
phasis added), Adonis seems half like a penis sheathed in an
anamorphic vagina and half like a corpse laid out for burial.
In the embrace of Venus he hovers between those two condi-
tions, for if "he may not / For euer die, and euer buried bee"
(st. 47.1–2), he may not forever live, either, except through
the copulation that sustains the world. The allegorical tenor of
this mythic sex differs little from that of earlier stanzas—
Adonis's "by succession made perpetuall" restates "so like a
wheele around they runne from old to new" (st. 33.9), while
his mixed resemblance to corpse and copula restates the inter-
section of death with birth, like the bodies Guyon and his Pal-
mer "engraue" in the "great earthes wombe" (II.i.60.1–2) or
the "double nature" of Genius. Stylistically, though, the hu-
man element becomes increasingly prominent until it emerges
fully in the figures of Psyche and Amoret.

The appearance of Cupid, Psyche, and Amoret confirms our
meta pherein from nature into culture, as Amoret's "perfect
ripeness" indicates her readiness for bringing forth "into the
worldes vew" (st. 52.1–6). Amoret's later career implies that

---

[47] Hamilton notes that Amintas in l. 8 may be Sidney; he also cites Rin-
gler's argument for an allusion "to Thomas Watson's Latin *Amyntas* (1585),
or its English paraphrase by Abraham Fraunce (1587)." See Donald Che-
ney, *Spenser's Image of Nature: Wild Man and Shepherd in "The Faerie
Queene"* (New Haven: Yale Univ. Press, 1966), pp. 132–35. Compare also
Spenser's use of the neologism "abrupt" at II.x.68.2 to signal the advent of
a historical present tense.

the paradisal sexuality of the Garden reflects the imagined in-
nocence of erotic feeling in a state prior to the moral dialectic
that fashions human consciousness. At the same time, sexuality
in the Garden appears to reflect a condition *subsequent* to the
dialectic of erotic self-fashioning: Cupid resorts to his mother's
bower only after he has "Ransackt the world" (st. 49.6), and
we are told he is "*lately* reconcyld" with Psyche (st. 50.2, em-
phasis added). Thus as we rise to the threshold between nature
and culture, we move from the simple and unproblematic im-
mediacy of pleasure to a narrative in which pleasure is the
"late" fruit— both recent and delayed—of a bitter struggle (st.
50.9).

The parallel between Amoret and Psyche implies that hu-
man love follows a cycle analogous to the wheel of generation.
Just as the Garden represents a condition that both precedes
and follows life in the world, it represents a sexuality that both
precedes and follows the frustrations of adult erotic experience,
frustrations we view in prospect with Amoret and in retrospect
with Psyche. In the realm outside the Garden love is not the
unproblematic repletion suggested by a phrase like "takes her
fill" (st. 46.9); it is at best a painful wound, and the relation of
the sexes an experience of mutual aggression. Inside the Gar-
den two other conditions are superimposed: in terms of the two
"earthly" hymns, it is as though the soul's blissful preexistence
and its earthly delight in a lover's embrace—the beginning and
ending phases of its cycle—had been telescoped into a single
passage. What these conditions have in common is their inte-
gration of sexuality with the source of life, confirmed in the
Garden by the personification of "Pleasure" as a child but also
implicit in the phrase "of his sweetnesse takes her fill," where
orgasm and insemination cohabit like spring and harvest meet-
ing at one time.

The overwhelmingly maternal ambience of the scene sug-

277

gests that one name for the condition in which love is attached to the source of life might be "infancy." Charissa, whose breasts undoubtedly flow with "the syncere milke of the worde" (1 Pet. 2:2), represents the spiritual form of this condition; another form might be "wedded love," since marriage, like infancy, weds eroticism to the biological reproduction of life. The technical vocabulary of psychoanalysis offers a complementary allegory in the notion of *anaclisis*,[48] which is central to the theory of human instincts. Sexual pleasure, Freud thought, is at first a sort of bonus accompanying the satisfaction of organic needs, and is thus undifferentiated from such body functions as nourishment and elimination. The gradual process by which sexual gratification differentiates itself from the need for self-preservation and emerges as an independent function is what makes Duessa or Acrasia possible as an object of desire, and it is this process that Christian and Platonic erotics seek to reverse. "Anaclitic" attachments in later erotic experience are distinguished from narcissistic love by a dependency in which the body's needs give way before those of that second body, the ego, in its attachment to a spectral interior parent. We saw in chapter 3 that Gloriana comes to break the spell of Arthur's adolescent narcissism, attaching his libido to the mirage of an ego ideal which figures as a symbolic replacement for the maternal breast: it offers in a highly sublimated way to fulfill the fantasy of bodily completion. The Garden offers wedded love as a fantasy of more immediate reconciliation between the erotic instincts and those of self-preservation, and thus as a healing of the breach between culture and nature that defines the "human" condition.

The complex transformations of desire on which family and state depend originate in the incest taboo, which severs libido

---

[48] Freud develops the notion of "attachment" (*anaclisis* is not his term) in *Three Essays on the Theory of Sexuality* (1905). See the article on *anaclisis* in Laplanche and Pontalis, *The Language of Psychoanalysis*, pp. 29–32.

from its first, most literal attachment to place it under the authority of the social order. Nohrnberg and others have lately drawn attention to the prominence of incest symbolism throughout Book III: "The virtue of chastity could hardly exist without sexual consciousness; it might therefore be described as an elaboration of the conditions surrounding the emergence of sexual impulses, which are originally directed toward the parent of the opposite sex. 'Un-chastity,' so to speak, is incest, in its psychogenesis. Adult chastity is also sexual attachment to a parent of the opposite sex, but the potential parent of one's own children" (*Analogy*, p. 436). Adult chastity, then, begins in a willingness to accept a sexual substitute for the parent—or a yielding to the necessity of substitution—and ends in the psychic conversion of substitute into replacement, so far as the fantasy is concerned. Thus Britomart's passion for Arthegall is tinged at first with incestuous overtones, and continues to suggest an odd convertibility between the images of parent and child. When Redcrosse confirms her anaclitic fantasy of Arthegall as an ethical paragon, Spenser tells us in effect that Britomart's imagination has had a baby:

> The louing mother, that nine monethes did beare,
> In the deare closet of her painefull side,
> Her tender babe, it seeing safe appeare,
> Doth not so much reioyce, as she reioyced theare.
>
> (III.ii.11.6–9)

This image of delighted maternity conveys the decorum of Book III, which celebrates the pleasures of embodiment, and it confirms the analogy between nature and imagination (*naturae comes*, Ficino called it, "nature's companion"): both beget embodied forms. But the image also envisions Arthegall by way of a remarkable prolepsis, collapsing him into the son Britomart is destined to bear. The passage we have already examined, in which Merlin prophesies Arthegall's replacement by

279

"his ymage dead," makes the same substitution. In terms of psychogenesis it suggests an elegant symmetry between the sublimations that resolve childhood incest complexes and the work of mourning, as though learning to accept the parent of one's child in place of one's own parent were somehow already to have grieved.

This fusion of love with mourning relates Britomart to her counterpart Arthur. But the children that represent Gloriana to Arthur "liuing . . . in all actiuity" are his own virtuous exploits, begotten in his noble imagination as metaphors of the fairy queen, and his love is therefore imbued from the beginning with a sense of loss. Since patriarchy opposes incest by drawing "mature" human love out of a premature work of mourning, in which death has not yet emerged from other forms of absence as a distinct object of knowledge, the incest taboo might be thought of as the castrative gesture of political authority in *its* psychogenesis. Britomart's love is marked equally by traces of its incestuous origin and of its destined transformation in mourning: moving away from the womblike chaos of Errour's den toward the prospective closure of metaphor, human love moves away from incest and toward that work of mourning through which it learns to accept authorized psychic and imperial replacements for the figure of the parent.

The dialectical splitting that characterizes this progress might be mythologized as the division of an incestuous ur-couple. The separation between these primal partners would occur phylogenetically as a splitting within each, and the ur-couple would persist as a kind of repressed twinship within the "postincestuous" individual. This individual feels itself to be constituted *as* individual on the basis of some loss or lack, which it may project backwards in the manner of Aristophanes' fable in the *Symposium* or forward in the manner of Spenser's typological allegory. In this way the individual understands itself as fallen from a prior wholeness or destined for a future one—and having canceled incest as a literal desire preserves it through the work of mourning as the form of promised wholeness. In its telescoping of fragmented perspectives, the Garden of Adonis idealizes wedded love as a provisional form of that final collapse of polarities.

A work of language is the body of language crossed
by death in order to open this infinite space where
doubles reverberate.—*Michel Foucault*

Afterword

 he 1590 text of *The Faerie Queene* ends with the rap-
turous fusion of Scudamour and Amoret, who look
as if "growne together quite" (st. 46.5). Once again
Amoretti 67, with its exchange of active and passive
roles and its tremors of surrendered autonomy, offers an illu-
minating parallel. In stanza 44 Scudamour, not Amoret, is
compared to "a Deare, that greedily embayes / In the coole
soile, after long thirstinesse, / Which he in chace endured
hath, now nigh brethlesse" (lines 7–9). Florimell was earlier
compared to a fleeing hind (III.vii.1.1–4); transferring the im-
age to a male lover, Spenser implies the exchange of properties
foreshadowed in the union of wedded love. In 1596 the image
will appear once more, this time in Scudamour's account of
how he won Amoret:

> . . . I which all that while
> The pledge of faith, her hand engaged held,
> Like warie Hynd within the weedie soyle,
> For no intreatie would forgoe so glorious spoyle.
>
> (IV.x.55.6–9)

At first line 8 seems to modify "hand," but in reasserting the
grammatical subject the alexandrine draws "Hynd" toward ap-
position with "I." This time, however, the wavering syntax
suggests not so much a dissolution of boundaries as a mutual
uneasiness, and the simile retains a trace of oddness no matter
which way you read it. If Amoret's hand is the "warie Hynd"
taking cover, as Upton suggests,[1] it seems awkward that its
refuge should be the hunter's grasp; while if Scudamour is

[1] Cited in Hamilton's gloss on the passage.

282

clutching the hand as anxiously as the hind keeps to its cover, then the alexandrine's assertion of masculine conquest emerges still more awkwardly from motives of flight and concealment. Meanwhile their reunion has disappeared from the end of Book III, and Amoret has disappeared from the poem altogether—discovered in IV.x not with Arthur, where the narrative left her, but in Scudamour's nostalgic fantasy of romantic conquest. In the large-scale movement of narrative as in the slighter movements of the verse, the image of perfect unity is gone.

The divine hermaphrodite does reappear in the animate statue of Venus (x.41) that smiles approval as Scudamour seizes Amoret. It is Scudamour, though, who sees Venus smile, and it is Scudamour telling the story now. The suggestion of narcissism in this situation is hardly dispelled by Scudamour's description of the smile:

> And euermore vpon the Goddesse face
> Mine eye was fixt, for feare of her offence,
> Whom when I saw with amiable grace
> To laugh at me, and fauour my pretence,
> I was emboldned with more confidence. . . .
>
> (IV.x.56.1–5)

The lines resonate tellingly against Arthur's naive misprision of Nature just before he dreams of Gloriana: "The fields, the floods, the heauens with one consent / Did seeme to laugh on me, and fauour mine intent" (I.ix.12.8–9).[2]

Recent commentaries on the canceled ending to Book III have tended to emphasize elements of ironic qualification and distancing in that passage as well.[3] The tone of stanza 45, however, suggests intense, unqualified delight:

---

[2] See the discussion of this passage under "Arthur's Dream," in chapter 3 of this text.

[3] Cheney set the tone for later discussions of this passage in his influential "Spenser's Hermaphrodite and the 1590 *Faerie Queene*," *PMLA* 87 (1972): 192–200. See also Harry Berger, Jr., "Busirane and the War Between the

Lightly he clipt her twixt his armes twaine,
And streightly did embrace her body bright,
Her body, late the prison of sad paine,
Now the sweet lodge of loue and deare delight:
But she faire Lady ouercommen quight
Of huge affection, did in pleasure melt,
And in sweete rauishment pourd out her spright:
No word they spake, nor earthly thing they felt,
But like two senceles stocks in long embracement dwelt.

(III.xii.45)

Even as the lovers merge into one another it is Scudamour who
acts (lines 1–2), while Amoret is "ouercommen." But in mak-
ing such observations we take our distance on the passage as a
whole, for these details are not in the least ironic. The lovers
disappear almost like Madeline and Porphyro in "The Eve of
St. Agnes"—except that Scudamour and Amoret disappear out
of the storm, not into it, removed to the erotic paradise Spenser
describes in the Garden of Adonis and in the hymns to earthly
love and beauty. The alexandrine brings the scene back into
focus as it shifts from how the lovers *felt* to how they *looked*,
their bodies like "senceless stocks" in the souls' absence. The
following stanza pulls back further to frame the scene, re-
minding us that we are not there and interposing the slightly
decadent image of an ornate Roman bath:

Had ye them seene, ye would haue surely thought,
That they had beene that faire *Hermaphrodite*,
Which that rich *Romane* of white marble wrought,
And in his costly Bath causd to bee site:
So seemd those two, as growne together quite,
That *Britomart* halfe enuying their blesse,
Was much empassiond in her gentle sprite,

Sexes: An Intepretation of *The Faerie Queene* II.xi-xii," *ELR* I (1971): 118–
21; Goldberg, *Endlesse Worke*, pp. 1–3; and Gross, *Spenserian Poetics*, pp.
171–74.

And to her selfe oft wisht like happinesse,
In vaine she wisht, that fate n'ould let her yet possesse.

(III.xii.46)

With its emphasis on decor, the simile offers a distraction of
exactly the sort to which the lovers are momentarily immune,
and the fact that no one knows what "rich Romane" Spenser is
talking about only heightens the distraction. The point of this
slight discord emerges in the reference to Britomart as *"halfe
enuying their blesse"*: we share with her the perspective of the
still divided, who can respond only in a divided way to the
emblem of perfect union. If that response is half-envious it is
also full of yearning, and remains thoroughly mimetic. Brito-
mart is "much empassiond" by what she sees, and while her
sense of incompleteness may set her apart from the reunited
lovers, the object of her unsatisfied desire is still *"like* happi-
nesse."

In a carefully low-key gesture, the last stanza begins to turn
us back toward the unity from which we have retreated:

But now my teme begins to faint and fayle,
All woxen weary of their iournall toyle:
Therefore I will their sweatie yokes assoyle
At this same furrowes end, till a new day:
And ye faire Swayns, after your long turmoyle,
Now cease your worke, and at your pleasure play;
Now cease your worke; to morrow is an holy day.

(III.xii.47.3–9)

The Virgilian poet turning from *versus* to *versus* in his journal
labor turns at last from labor to rest, or at least respite, his
sweat-soaked oxen a yeomanly counterpart to the harried deer
of stanza 44. He addresses the "faire Swayns" Scudamour and
Amoret in genial tones, and seems to see their long suffering
as something like a week's hard work in the fields as he offers
them the Biblical day of rest. Both his turning to the sabbath

285

and their entry into love's paradise look forward, however, to a later turning when "all shall changed be" (*Mutability Cantos*, vii. 59.4). So just as *Fowre Hymnes* marks its retractation of human love with a palinode, these lines are canceled in later editions—despite the fact "that many copies thereof were formerly scattered abroad" (*Works*, p. 586).

The 1596 *Faerie Queene* ends with a dispirited surrender to the Blatant Beast, which rages unleashed through all the estates of the kingdom. But the *Mutability Cantos*, which revisits the natural cycle from Book III as well as the sacred heights of poetic inspiration from Book VI, seems also to offer a retractation of previous endings. The social and georgic terms of the earlier passages are transformed into their cosmic equivalents—hope for eternal bliss and dismay at the spectacle of Mutability—while the sequence is reversed, so that the ending of 1590 seems restored in a finer tone: at once more directly personal and more openly eschatological, as the narrator looks to last things without the mediation of Virgilian topoi.

The *Cantos* may remind us of Arthur's dream. It is the narrator himself, kindled with "desire / Of heauenly things" (vii. 2. 5–6), who plays the visionary. A veiled and mysterious goddess appears to him, briefly setting aside her veil and promising a full revelation to come; then she vanishes, leaving the speaker to meditate her sentence and to battle despair as he yearns for the promised vision. Nature delivers her verdict "with chearefull view" (vii. 57.8); but if the goddess smiles on us, and favors our intent, have we beheld a revelation or only reentered "the infinite space where doubles reverberate"? The speaker's response is divided between heaven and earth, for unlike Nature, who beholds the natural cycle from above, his body is "crossed by death"; he feels the "consuming sickle" (viii. 1.9) approach as it lays waste to another swath of vanities. He looks forward in prayer to eternity, when Nature's broken cycles will be "firmly stayd" (st. .3), but the divine circle into which "all things" will finally be gathered remains an object of desire, not of knowledge.

Meanwhile the "work of language," the comprehensive retraction that erects this divine Imaginary, with its infinite power to recuperate, from "the body of language crossed by death," also anticipates the erasure of everything that keeps the natural body alive. Like Plato's cosmic sphere, sans apertures, sans appendages, sans everything, the ultimate *corpus mysticum* presumes the obliteration of nature. Purified down to nothing at all, the body becomes a symbol of absolute plenitude. At the same time, however, and by the same gesture, it becomes "nought"—or as American English has it, zero.

287

Index

GENERAL TERMS

The index to Works and Passages Discussed will directly follow the General Terms.

Acrasia, 96–97, 114, 149, 172–73, 228–29, 260

Adonis (*see also* Garden of Adonis), 96–97, 262, 264, 276

allegory, 12–13, 50, 52–53, 55, 63–64, 77, 78 n, 81, 93, 99, 129–30, 136–39, 151–53, 175–77, 183–85, 190–91, 207, 215–18, 221, 223, 226, 235–41, 241–42, 254–61, 263–65, 272–73

Alma: her castle, 133, 168–91, 203, 223, 240, 246, 254–55, 257, 264–65, 268–70, 269, 273–74, 275; castle and "avoidance" of the flesh, 168–78, 181, 182–83; castle as allegory of digestion, 175–80, 223, 266; the turret as image of heaven, 183–88, 200, 255

Alpers, Paul, 12, 24 n.35, 29–30 n.2

Amoret, 72, 175, 237–38, 241, 259, 261, 276–77, 282–85; and Psyche, 276–78

Amphisa, 261, 262

Anaclisis, 278

Anderson, Judith, 25, 232 n.14

androgyny, hermaphrodism, 7–8, 27–28, 112–13, 115–16, 129–30, 168–69 n.8, 182–83, 222–23, 245–47, 250–52, 259, 283, 283–84 n.3

Anglo, Sidney, 197 n.25

Antiquitie of Faerie Lond, 201–202, 205, 206, 207

Archimago, 82, 83, 185

Argante, 261

Ariosto, Ladovico, 192–93

Aristotle, 54, 244; *Nichomachean Ethics*, 32; *Problemata*, 166, 250–51

Arthegall, 232–33; and Britomart, 279–80, 282–85

Arthur, 110, 157, 160, 174, 203, 204; and Alma's castle, 133, 168–69, 170–72; and Guyon, 142–43, 144–45, 147–48, 149, 156–57, 158–60, 206; and Ignaro, 83–84; and history, 204–206; and "Mirror stage," 136–42; and psychoanalysis, 131, 132–35, 136–42; and Redcrosse, 115, 131; as Christ, 85, 203–204; as "king," 72, 97–98, 112–13, 127, 128–29; his dream and vision of Gloriana, 27, 79, 96–97, 113, 119, 125–26, 127, 128, 129, 130–42, 145, 283, 286; his history, 27, 125–26, 140–42; his "pregnancy," 112–13, 129–30; his quest for Gloriana, 20, 27, 71, 73, 139–44, 158–59, 163, 222, 274; his role in *The Faerie Queene*, 97–98, 111–12; his union with Gloriana, 72, 113, 116, 138–39, 140–42, 207, 222; rescue of Redcrosse, 24–25, 83–84, 129–30

assimilation (*see also* Body functions, processes: digestion), 73–74, 73–74 n, 82 n, 88–89, 110–11, 115, 136–37, 177–78, 178–79 n.13, 191, 200–201, 203, 206–207, 214, 226–27, 245–46, 253, 258–59

authority, 4, 6–7, 9–11, 29–

289

WORKS AND PASSAGES DISCUSSED

Library of Congress Cataloging-in-Publication Data

Miller, David L., 1951–
The poem's two bodies : the poetics of the 1590
Faerie queene / David L. Miller.
    p.   cm.
Includes index.
ISBN 0–691–06744–9 (alk. paper)
1. Spenser, Edmund, 1552?–1599. Faerie queene. 1. Title.
PR2358.M48 1988
821'.3—dc19

David Lee Miller is Associate Professor of English
at the University of Alabama.